Approaches to
Behavior and Classroom
Management

Approaches to
Behavior and Classroom
Management

Integrating Discipline and Care

W. George Scarlett
Tufts University

Iris Chin Ponte
Tufts University

Jay P. Singh
The University of Oxford

Los Angeles • London • New Delhi • Singapore • Washington DC

For information:

SAGE Publications, Inc.
2455 Teller Road
Thousand Oaks, California 91320
E-mail: order@sagepub.com

SAGE Publications India Pvt. Ltd.
B 1/I 1 Mohan Cooperative
  Industrial Area
Mathura Road, New Delhi 110 044
India

SAGE Publications Ltd.
1 Oliver's Yard
55 City Road
London EC1Y 1SP
United Kingdom

SAGE Publications Asia-Pacific Pte. Ltd.
33 Pekin Street #02-01
Far East Square
Singapore 048763

Printed in the United States of America

Library of Congress Cataloging-in-Publication Data

Scarlett, W. George.
Approaches to behavior and classroom management: Integrating discipline and care/W. George Scarlett, Iris Chin Ponte, Jay P. Singh; with contributions by Laura Beals and Yibing Li.
     p. cm.
Includes bibliographical references and index.
ISBN 978-1-4129-3744-3 (pbk.)
   1. Classroom management. 2. Behavioral assessment. I. Ponte, Iris Chin.
II. Singh, Jay P. III. Title.

LB3013.S287 2009
371.102′4—dc22   2008025102

Printed on acid-free paper

08   09   10   11   12   10   9   8   7   6   5   4   3   2   1

Acquiring Editor:	Diane McDaniel
Editorial Assistant:	Leah Mori
Production Editor:	Sarah K. Quesenberry
Copy Editor:	Diana Breti
Proofreader:	Anne Rogers
Indexer:	Michael Ferreira
Typesetter:	C&M Digitals (P) Ltd.
Cover Designer:	Bryan Fishman
Marketing Manager:	Christy Guilbault

Brief Contents

Detailed Contents

Foreword

Every fact is already a theory

—Goethe

With this statement, Goethe captures the essence of this book: There is no educational method that does not presuppose an educational approach or theory. The authors, however, present this insight from a very postmodern viewpoint. Indeed, it is this postmodern perspective that makes this book so timely and unique. In order to fully appreciate the magnitude of the achievement, it is necessary to put it into a historical context.

THE BELIEFS OF MODERNITY

Modernity began with the Renaissance and the Enlightenment and ended roughly in the middle of the 20th century. It was characterized by belief in progress, universality, and regularity. These beliefs were implicit in modern philosophy, art, literature, and architecture and are best exemplified by modern science. Until the mid-20th century, science was grounded in the belief that the world would be made better through scientific progress—"better living through chemistry," as the motto of one chemical company put it. For Newton, the main progenitor of modernity, natural laws were discovered by observation and experiment, were universal, and were held across time and space. Finally, natural laws were regular and brooked no exceptions. As Einstein put it, "God doesn't play dice with the universe."

These modern beliefs were also held by the social sciences when they broke from philosophy toward the end of the 19th century. Because they were new, they felt the need to establish their own identity and did this by defining themselves in opposition to philosophy and one another. Psychology was the study of the individual, sociology the study of society, and anthropology the study of culture. Each established its own theories and methods and arrived at its own, purportedly universal, laws. In American psychology, learning theory dominated the literature in the first half of the 20th century, and the learning ability of rats was studied, in the belief that learning principles were universal and held for all species.

Even within psychology, however, there were different schools that proclaimed their own universal laws and principles. While learning theory was concerned with stimuli and response, the Gestalt psychologists were concerned with parts and wholes and the Freudians with the ego and the id. Moreover, each school elaborated not only its own methods of investigation but also its own methods of application. Learning theory gave rise to what has become known as behavior modification. Gestalt psychology gave rise to Gestalt and holistic methods. Clinicians followed a number of different approaches and methods, from psychoanalysis to nondirective therapy. Individual psychologists identified with one or another school and labeled themselves, for example, as "Behaviorists" or "Freudians." The tendency was to emphasize the differences (not to mention the superiority) rather than the similarities between the approaches.

THE BELIEFS OF POSTMODERNITY

The beliefs of modernity were revolutionary and arose in opposition to the belief that all knowledge and authority came from the philosophers (namely Aristotle), from the church, and from the nobility. In contrast, the beliefs of postmodernity are not a rejection of the modern beliefs but rather a correction or editing of them. It was ushered in, as is usually the case with social transformations, by the arts, such as Impressionism in the beginning of the 20th century. It soon permeated the other arts, literature, music, and architecture. Later, it was articulated and elaborated by writers such as Foucault (1980). What the postmodern workers asserted was that while progress, universality, and regularity certainly held for many aspects of the world, they did not account for all of them.

During the modern era, the engine of progress was thought to be human reason. With respect to progress, no one can deny the enormous intellectual strides that we have made in medicine and technology. At the same time, the atomic bomb, pollution of land and water, and global warming give evidence that we do not always act in rational ways. This was a major point of Freudian theory. Likewise, the belief in universality has to be edited. To be sure, there are universal laws in chemistry and physics, but this is hardly the case in the social sciences.

In psychology, while the principles of conditioning may hold for all species, many of the methods of problem solving, such as hypothesis testing, are unique to humans, as is language. In addition to universality, therefore, we now have also to accept particularity and the fact that there are domain-specific laws and principles. Finally, with respect to regularity, we now have to accept irregularity. We now recognize that there are chaotic phenomena, like the weather, that cannot be fully predicted.

In contrast to the modern era's treating reason as the model of human endeavor, postmodernists argue that language makes for a better model. Language progresses, but the progress is not always uniform nor is it always positive or beneficial (e.g., Spanglish). Likewise, while some facets of language are probably universal, such as Chomsky's (1957) language acquisition device, much of language is unique to particular geographic regions. Finally, language has elements that are both regular and irregular. In addition, language also encompasses the emotions. That is why many sciences are now talking about their theories as "narratives."

Postmodernity, then, does not reject the past but tries to take only what is good from the past and adapt it to the present. The result is what has come to be known as *pastiche,* a blending of modern and postmodern ideas, styles, materials, and methods. Postmodern architecture (when it is good) brings together some of the best elements from different eras, like atria and columns from ancient Greece and Rome, with contemporary materials and methods of construction. In the arts, we see real objects embedded within the classical framework of a painting, and in literature, we see mixed genres in the novel, such as Capote's *In Cold Blood* and the writings of Borges, who argues for dissolving the boundaries between poetry and fiction. In music, we see this same mixing and merging, for example, in the blending of styles from Africa, the Caribbean, and the United States. All are examples of postmodern pastiche.

A POSTMODERN BOOK

What has all of this to do with the present book? A great deal, actually. One of the features of modernity was exclusivity and territoriality within the arts and sciences. Each discipline protected its own turf, and practitioners did not venture beyond the boundaries. But the postmodern mentality recognizes that all boundaries are man-made and not given. Postmodern boundary breaking can be observed in all domains of contemporary life. When famed opera star Ezio Pinza performed on Broadway in *South Pacific,* he brought postmodernism to classical music. When Erik Erikson (1950) wrote *Childhood and Society,* he brought sociology, anthropology, and history into psychoanalysis.

In contemporary social science, we have combined disciplines such as neurochemistry, psycholinguistics, and behavioral pediatrics.

Postmodernity, unlike modernity, which strove for the simplicity of Occam's razor, recognizes the overwhelming complexity of the contemporary world. In the social sciences, we now appreciate that human behavior is simply too complex and too intricate to be explained by any extant theory or approach. Indeed, that is the insight that infuses *Approaches to Behavior and Classroom Management*.

The authors have brought together the major approaches to behavior and classroom management and their respective methodologies. They demonstrate, and indeed advocate, that the teacher must be familiar with all the approaches and methods. They also encourage the practitioner to mix and match approaches and methods as demanded by the classroom situation. It is a stark departure from the more narrow doctrinaire approaches that are still all too common in the literature on behavior and classroom management. One of the reasons I went through the historical introduction was to bring onto center stage the true novelty and innovativeness of the present text. This integrative approach recognizes the complexity and diversity of the classroom situation, and that is what sets it apart from so many other texts in the field.

In keeping with its postmodern perspective, the material is presented with a pastiche of modern and postmodern teaching aids. In addition to the traditional text and chapter summaries, there are cartoons, brief biographies of major figures in the field, as well as instructor and student CDs with PowerPoint presentations. I believe this book is a major advance in the field. Paulo Freire wrote that education can be either domesticating or liberating. I believe that this text will liberate students from the constraints of abiding by a particular approach and methodology. In so doing, it will best prepare them for the complexity and diversity of personality, society, and culture that teachers will encounter in today's schools and among today's students.

—David Elkind
Eliot-Pearson Department of Child Development
Tufts University

Preface

*It is not the will or desire of any one person which establishes
order but the moving spirit of the whole group*

—John Dewey (1963, p. 54)

This book provides a unique and better way to organize the field of behavior and classroom management. It does so by organizing the literature, issues, and main theorists around a central distinction and five core concepts. The central distinction is between methods and approaches. Methods are what we see educators doing to keep students safe, orderly, on task, learning, and developing for the long term. Approaches include methods and are, in part, defined by which methods are emphasized and which are not. However, approaches also include much that is hidden, such as cultural values, theories of change, and images of what are good students, good teachers, and good classrooms.

Approaches differ from one another in the meaning they give to the five core concepts framing our discussion. The five core concepts are relationship building, learning, development, organization, and accommodating diversity. Consult almost any text or listen to almost any thoughtful discussion of behavior and classroom management, and these five will eventually be discussed in some way (Evertson & Weinstein, 2006). That is, though educators disagree about what these five concepts mean, thoughtful educators everywhere generally agree that the concepts provide a foundation for any thoughtful, effective approach to behavior and classroom management. And so, by organizing the book around these five concepts, we provide an easy and better way for student readers and seasoned professionals alike to bring order to what has often been a confusing field. It also helps instructors organize courses to fully engage students and better ensure that students will develop a deep understanding of both approaches and methods.

Here, too, we provide clear explanations of why approaches matter and of how to put approaches into practice. Books on behavior and classroom management normally are written to be practical. As practical books, they provide methods to prevent and manage problem behaviors. However, rarely do such books explain the practical necessity of understanding and using different approaches. Nor do they provide student readers with the historical and cultural perspectives needed to properly understand and evaluate current approaches and current methods.

This book differs, then, by making approaches to behavior and classroom management the central focus. The main goal is to teach readers how to make use of a variety of approaches in order to make good decisions about problem behavior and to create positive classroom communities. This goal is ambitious. However, adopting it is essential if readers are to develop the kinds of generative and flexible minds they need in order to teach or help teachers in today's classrooms.

Today's classrooms often include children from a variety of backgrounds and with different needs that have to be met if children are to thrive. Today, diversity is the watchword. To carry out behavior and classroom management using one approach only is, then, to restrict options when the opposite is required. This is another reason why the focus is on approaches.

The other main focus is on showing care. Throughout this book, we demonstrate that though the word *management* applies, it need not endorse a business approach to educating children. On the contrary, the business of behavior and classroom management should always be about showing care, so when it comes to managing children's and adolescents' behavior, the great dilemma for all caregivers, educators included, is to find ways to integrate discipline and care to keep children and adolescents safe and under control while supporting their long-term development and capacity for self-control. This book explains *how* and not just why showing care is essential.

However, the book goes further by explaining how behavior and classroom management is essentially a moral endeavor. Educators must help students go beyond self-control to participate fully and positively in just, caring, and learning communities. To stop at self-control would be to opt for an individualism inconsistent with the values and ideals of virtually every society, but especially of our democratic society. Put another way, students must develop self-control, but they must also develop as good citizens who are motivated and skillful at contributing to the common good. Educators must be high-minded even as they attend to the mundane tasks of maintaining order and keeping children "on task." This is true regardless of approach and regardless of the particular characteristics of a group of children. Here, then, another main focus is on explaining how readers can create the supports needed for students to not only manage their own behavior but also to contribute positively to the classroom and school community.

Our text is written primarily for those preparing themselves for careers in teaching and related professions. As such, the text is written for a diverse group of students and for instructors teaching required courses in different licensing and degree programs. However, the book is also written for professionals in the field—especially for those who are finding that their usual approach is not working well with a number of students.

PEDAGOGICAL FEATURES

To make *Approaches to Behavior and Classroom Management* appeal to a wide audience, we have given it several features that make it easier for readers to learn and for instructors to teach.

Chapter Opening Scenarios

Each of the "approaches" chapters (Chapters 3 to 10) opens with a scenario that sets the context for the material that follows and enables readers to "see" and "hear" the phenomenon being discussed—the problem behavior, response to that behavior, or particular child or educator that illustrates something essential about the approach and central concept.

Chapter Overviews

Each chapter includes an overview that lays out the contents and organization of the material that follows. The overview provides readers with a framework to help them understand where each topic and issue fits in relation to the others. Most important, it gives readers a clear idea of the major organizing concepts (the "headlines") and the subtopics. In short, it helps readers to organize their thinking hierarchically.

Preview, Review, and Reflect

Throughout the text, Preview, Review, and Reflect boxes are provided that help the reader to (1) connect what is being discussed to what will be discussed in later chapters in more detail; (2) review and summarize what has just been discussed by repeating the highlights that need to be remembered in order to retrieve the details; and (3) take moments to reflect, apply what has been said to personal experience or personal reactions, and otherwise digest the material.

Chapter Summaries

The chapter summaries provide a brief summary of what has been discussed and also ensure that readers understand the main points and implications of the chapter and how the chapter fits within the book. Also, chapter summaries often introduce new ideas about what a chapter might imply for practice—ideas that motivate readers to continue to reflect.

Key Concepts

The list of key concepts underlines the fact that certain words or phrases, when used to explain a scholarly, technical approach, take on a different meaning than they might take on in ordinary conversation. A chapter's key concepts, then, alert readers to the fact that if they don't know the professional, scholarly meanings of these concepts, they need to turn back to where the concepts were defined so that they understand and can apply them.

Discussion Questions

The discussion questions function in the same way as the Reflect boxes. They help readers actively engage with the material by asking them to apply what has been learned to their experience and/or by asking for personal reactions to ideas, distinctions, or issues discussed in the chapter.

Throughout the text, the writing avoids unnecessary jargon and highlights what is most important. We have provided real-life teaching examples that show the meaning of key concepts and how readers can put approaches into practice. Additionally, tables have been included that clarify what is discussed in the text. Human interest stories and cartoons are interspersed that give meaning to concepts and points. Finally, we have included photographs of past and current leaders in the field.

However, the single most important pedagogical support and feature is, as we have said, the way the book is *organized*.

ORGANIZATION OF THE BOOK

This book is organized into five parts.

Part I deals with introductory matters. In Chapter 1, we focus on distinguishing approaches from methods and on showing how the two relate. In Chapter 2, we show how the history of behavior and classroom management in America has been a history of approaches and not just of methods. We also show how some of the major issues concerning behavior and classroom management have been around since early times, particularly the issue of how to integrate discipline with care.

Subsequent parts deal with specific approaches to behavior and classroom management, with each part discussing approaches that go together in some logical way, either by their being linked to some overarching concept, such as the concept of relationship building, or by their being linked to concepts that complement one another, such as the concepts of learning and development.

Part II focuses on those approaches that feature relationship building, either at the dyadic (e.g., teacher-child relationship) or community level. Here, we explain the different meanings of relationship building, but the main focus is on approaches that take relationship building as the starting point and linchpin for successful behavior and classroom management. In Chapter 3, we look at approaches that emphasize building positive teacher-student relationships in which students feel known, affirmed, but also challenged. In Chapter 4, we look at approaches that emphasize community building, especially democratic communities that are both just and caring.

Part III focuses on approaches that feature learning or development as their central themes or concepts. In this part, we explain how the two differ and complement one another. In Chapter 5, the emphasis is on teaching for learning, using a variety of teaching models or a systematic behavioral-learning approach. In Chapter 6, the emphasis is on teaching to support long-term development by supporting children's mastering developmental tasks and inner processes such as perspective taking.

Part IV focuses on approaches featuring organization. In Chapter 7, we look at approaches that focus on organizing classrooms into effective learning communities by organizing time, space, materials, and groups of students and educators. In Chapter 8, we look at approaches that focus on interventions to change dysfunctional interpersonal systems, using reframing and other methods developed by family systems theory.

Part V is about accommodating diversity. Chapter 9 discusses cultural diversity and cultural approaches, both to indicate how much culture figures into approaches and to help readers accommodate to differences based on culture. Chapter 10 discusses the medical model and organic approaches to disability, particularly disabilities defined by the psychiatric system for diagnosing disorders. Here, we show how the medical model and organic approaches both complement and conflict with educational approaches.

We conclude with a summary chapter on the great dilemma linking all approaches; namely, the dilemma of integrating discipline with care. In this concluding chapter, we draw upon what has been said in previous chapters to show that educators need their own distinct approach to discipline, even as they attend to what is true regardless of approach. What is most true regardless of approach is the need to show care.

One final note about the organization of this book and the way approaches are discussed. All of the approaches discussed in this book are discussed in their *developed form,* and almost all of the examples are examples in which approaches have been applied properly. However, in a great many classrooms and schools, approaches are often underdeveloped or misapplied, leaving some to question their validity or appropriateness. Recently, this has been especially true of behavioral-learning approaches because so many educators use reinforcements and negative consequences to modify behavior, but they do so unsystematically. Examples of underdeveloped and misapplied approaches can be found for all other approaches as well. In this book, we emphasize that, in the hands of professionals, almost any developed approach, including behavioral-learning approaches, can be thoughtfully applied to manage both behavior and classrooms effectively.

LEADERS IN THE FIELD

This book purposely subordinates explaining the work of individuals to explaining those broad and widespread approaches that have been developed over many years and by many individuals. However, the book takes care to discuss and explain the contributions of leaders in the field so that readers can gain an understanding of those who have had the greatest influence. To better understand the special contributions of leaders in the field, the table that follows lists those leaders most discussed and most referenced in the book, often in more than one chapter.

Theorist	Historical Context	Associated Theory	Main Tenets, Ideas, Goals, Foci	Pages
Cynthia Ballenger	Late 20th c.	Sociolinguistic theory	Attending to a culture's "language of control"	59
Diana Baumrind	Late 20th c.	Parenting (socialization) theory	Promoting authoritative control	8
Larry K. Brendtro	Mid-20th c.	Milieu therapy	Relationship building	53
Jere E. Brophy	Late 20th c.	Classroom management theory	Classroom organization	153
Ronald E. Butchart	Late 20th c.	Constructivist educational theory	Critical constructivism and democratic classrooms	28, 80
Lee and Marlene Canter	Late 20th c.	Behavioral learning theory	"Assertive" discipline	118, 182
Lisa Delpit	Late 20th c.	Sociocultural theory of learning	Culture and assumptions about authority	208
John Dewey	Early 20th c.	Progressive education; constructivist theory	The many loci of classroom control	31
Walter Doyle	Late 20th c.	Ecological theory	Maintaining "programs of action"	154
Edmund Emmer	Late 20th c.	Ecological theory	Organization of classrooms	163
Forrest Gathercoal	Late 20th c.	"Judicious discipline"	The U.S. constitution as a management guide	83
William Glasser	Late 20th c.	Counseling and industrial psychological theory	"Quality schools," "lead managing," and meeting students needs	43, 81
Thomas Gordon	Late 20th c.	Humanistic psychology; Rogerian theory	Relationship-sensitive methods of control	62

(Continued)

(Continued)

Theorist	Historical Context	Associated Theory	Main Tenets, Ideas, Goals, Foci	Pages
Lawrence Kohlberg	Late 20th c.	Cognitive developmental theory; constructivist education	Development as the aim of education/moral education	40, 77 101, 132
Alfie Kohn	Late 20th c.	Developmental constructivist theory	Development, not obedience, as the goal	126
Jacob Kounin	Mid-20th c.	Ecological (Gestalt-field) theory	Prevention of problem behavior	44, 154
Ivar Lovaas	Mid-20th c.	Behavioral-learning theory	Systematic management of stimuli and consequences	42
Alex Molnar and Barbara Lindquist	Late 20th c.	Interpersonal systems theory	Changing dysfunctional classroom interpersonal systems	178
George Noblit	Late 20th c.	Sociocultural theory of learning	Authority, culture, and caring	207
Nel Noddings	Late 20th c.	Care theory	"Caring for" as the basis for teaching	77, 86
Larry Nucci	Late 20th c.	Domain theory and moral character education	Domain concordant vs. domain discordant forms of teacher control	89
Dan Olweus	Late 20th c.	Ecological theory	School bullying	92
Gerald Patterson	Late 20th c.	Behavioral learning	Stimulus, reinforcement, and punishment "traps"	115
Fritz Redl	Mid-20th c.	"Mental hygiene"; psychodynamic	"Ego supports" for preventing and managing problem behavior	21, 36, 139
Michael Rutter	Late 20th c.	Clinical-developmental theory	Diagnoses and developmental pathways of syndromes	233

Theorist	Historical Context	Associated Theory	Main Tenets, Ideas, Goals, Foci	Pages
Seymour Sarason	Late 20th c.	Systems theory	Understanding and treating schoolwide systemic problems	94, 140, 193
Thomas Skrtic	Late 20th c.	Sociological theory	Types of multidisciplinary special education teams	172
Robert Slavin	Late 20th c.	Classroom management theory	School and classroom organization	167
Marilyn Watson	Late 20th c.	Social-developmental theory	Building caring classroom communities	61
Charles Wolfgang and Carl Glickman	Late 20th c.	"Eclectic"	Matching management style to group characteristics	9

ANCILLARY MATERIALS

In addition to the text, ancillary materials further support and enhance the learning goals of *Approaches to Behavior and Classroom Management: Integrating Discipline and Care*.

Instructors' Resource CD

This CD offers the instructor a variety of resources that supplement the book material, including PowerPoint lecture slides, test questions, and video clips (also found on the Student Resource CD). Additional resources include teaching tips, sample syllabi, and Web resources.

Student Resource CD

This CD is bound into students' textbooks and contains video clips that correlate with key concepts found in the text. Each clip includes a prevideo and postvideo question to stimulate class discussion and reflection.

Web-Based Student Study Site

www.sagepub.com/scarlettstudy

The Web-based student study site provides a variety of resources to enhance students' understanding of the book's content. The site includes comprehensive study materials such as practice tests, flashcards, and suggested readings. Other resources include "Learning From SAGE Journal Articles," and additional activities created by the authors.

Acknowledgments

This book was several years in the making, and a good many contributed. At the top of our list of contributors is Laura Beals, whose intelligence and creativity are found in all the many features that make this book more readable, and Yibing Li, whose steadfast and thoughtful work helped craft several chapters. David Murray contributed the cartoons, and we are grateful for his obvious talents and humor. Our thanks also go to our editor at SAGE Publications, Diane McDaniel, who managed always to combine being supportive and patient with setting high standards.

We thank those who reviewed previous drafts and provided helpful suggestions, including Agnes Nagy-Rado, the Catholic University of America; Alandra Weller-Clarke, Benedictine University; Bradley L. Sidle, Wright State University; Burga Jung, Wright State University; David A. Almeida, Bridgewater State College; Dawn Hunter, Chapman University; Debra S. Lierman, Seattle Pacific University; Gary D. Jacobs, Walsh University; Greg Ruediger, Troy University Dothan; Heljä Antola Crowe, Bradley University; Judy Carrington Shipley, Hardin-Simmons University; Kim Fries, University of New Hampshire; Kim M. Wieczorek, Nazareth College; Luis T. Conde, Barry University; Margaret E. Gray, Fontbonne University; Matthew F. Pinder, Kentucky Christian University; Pam Kidder-Ashley, Appalachian State University; Pamela M. Stanfield, Missouri Baptist University; Robert Wolffe, Bradley University; and Susan M. Schultz, St. John Fisher College.

We thank Jennifer Gauvin, the Center for Lifespan Development, Inc.; Lauren White, Harvey S. Williams Elementary School; Laura Rogers, Tufts University; Sandra Kleinman, Harvard University; Elizabeth Spatola, St. Joseph's Hospital, Nashua, N.H.; Betty Allen, Tufts University; Janet Zeller, Tufts University; and Heidi Given, Tufts University, for providing invaluable suggestions and examples for improving the book. Finally, we would like to thank the American Educational Research Association and the Department of Education's Institute for Education Sciences for funding Iris Ponte's research that contributed to discussions on culture found in Chapter 9.

—The Authors

PART I

Introduction

Most discussions of behavior and classroom management explain by focusing on **methods,** and when the word **approaches** is used, it usually refers to leaders in the field (e.g., the Canters' approach, Glasser's approach, Gathercoal's approach). As a result, readers get the impression that approaches are the same as groups of methods and that history is irrelevant. More important, the impression is that one can easily construct a super, all-encompassing approach simply by taking the best from what various leaders have to offer, like a good chef sampling from a spice rack.

This introductory section explains behavior and classroom management quite differently. Chapter 1 explains the book's main distinction between approaches and methods and shows why this distinction is so important and why almost any approach in its developed form can serve better than a superficial sampling of methods associated with different approaches. Furthermore, the chapter shows how the field is best organized in terms of a manageable set of core concepts, rather than in terms of a list of leaders. In short, Chapter 1 offers a framework and language for understanding the field of behavior and classroom management.

Chapter 2 shows why a historical perspective is essential for a full understanding of approaches to behavior and classroom management. While there is a lot that is "new under the sun," most of what passes as "new" has roots in the past. Furthermore, despite our wishing we know more today than our predecessors knew, the facts often show otherwise. The facts show that many of our predecessors had wisdom that can help us today. Chapter 2, then, is about the roots of, and wisdom of, today's approaches to behavior and classroom management.

Chapter 1

Introduction to Approaches and Methods

Why a book on approaches to behavior and classroom management? Why not a book on just behavior and classroom management, giving straight talk on how to get the job done with a set of methods—those specific strategies or techniques needed to keep children and adolescents on task, developing positively, and contributing to classrooms and schools so that classrooms and schools become good communities? The reason is simple. Whenever we ask what it means to "get the job done" or what it means to "develop positively" or what it means to "become a good community," we are confronted with a variety of answers revealing a variety of meanings and values and assumptions about what children and adolescents really need. In other words, whenever we get beyond the surface slogans and get to how slogans and terms are being used, we find behavior and classroom management inevitably is about approaches and not just methods.

Approaches, then, have to do with meanings, values, and assumptions, as well as with methods. Because meanings, values, and assumptions are difficult to detect, let alone understand, approaches remain somewhat hidden, which is probably the main reason books on behavior and classroom management do not generally feature approaches. However, even when approaches are featured, it often remains unclear why it is important to understand approaches. The impression given is that understanding methods is all that really matters. This is regrettable because approaches are what generate methods in the first place. How else can we explain why experienced teachers often respond to problem behavior so quickly and effectively and in novel ways? Consider the following example to understand what we mean:

When Jimmy jumped up during class meeting and started to dance, the observer visiting this second-grade classroom thought for sure the teacher would follow with a stern reprimand. But instead of a reprimand, the teacher turned to the rest of the children and said matter-of-factly, "Jimmy likes to dance." Jimmy stopped, looked pleased, and then sat down. Later, when the observer asked this teacher why she said what she said to Jimmy, she replied she had no idea. (Scarlett, 1998, p. 26)

The method used in this example is that of **reframing**. Reframing happens when a teacher redefines a problem behavior (e.g., disrupting meeting time) by giving the behavior a different and positive interpretation or "spin" (e.g., "Jimmy likes to dance"). We will have more to say about reframing in later chapters, especially in Chapter 8, where it becomes a featured method in classroom (interpersonal) **systems approaches**.

Here, the main point is that what appeared to the outsider to be a method was, for this teacher, simply a natural response, one that flowed naturally (and unconsciously) from her emphasis on building positive relationships with children and accommodating their developmental stage. Put another way, what she said to Jimmy was more an expression of her approach than it was the result of her having chosen a particular method. Therefore, to understand where the method came from, we have to understand this teacher's approach.

Understanding approaches is also necessary to ensure flexibility. When teachers teach as if they have no particular approach or with an all-encompassing, eclectic approach, they become rigid and dogmatic in situations calling for flexibility and creativity. Why, after all, should one change one's approach if there is only one right approach to take or if one's approach is all-encompassing and eclectic?

We see just how restricting this attitude can be when some teachers stick to one approach, to the detriment of those students from quite different backgrounds and cultures with different value systems and different assumptions about what children and adolescents need. We become truly eclectic not when we try to have one approach that fits all, but when we know when and how to switch to another approach when a child or group demands it—as was the case in the following example of a student teacher having to switch approaches and methods.[1]

When Tried and True Approaches and Methods Fail

One student teacher had an excellent reputation as a graduate teaching assistant in the university's laboratory school. There, she excelled in applying a constructivist approach to behavior and classroom management and using a nonauthoritarian approach and getting children to discuss and negotiate their conflicts. However, when she took a part-time job in a large, urban after-school program, her nonauthoritarian approach and guidance methods completely failed. The children ignored her and continued to misbehave. Eventually, she learned how to adapt by adopting a more authoritarian, but still caring, approach and by using methods designed to provide more direction and give her more control.

Defining Approaches

When speaking about their own approach to behavior and classroom management, wise educators everywhere are apt to speak about the need for building relationships, teaching students how to behave properly, **supporting development**, being organized, and **accommodating diversity**. That is, **relationship building, learning, development, organization,** and accommodating diversity are apt to be core concepts in almost any developed, effective approach to behavior and classroom management.

Meanings Given to Core Concepts

However, the meanings of relationship building, learning, development, organization, and accommodating diversity are apt to differ from one approach to another. For example, approaches that concentrate on having children behave in a certain way (raise hands at meeting time, follow the rule about no talking during study hall, etc.) are likely to use the term *development* to refer to the acquisition of "good" or appropriate behaviors. In contrast, approaches derived from a constructivist tradition, one that emphasizes finding ways to actively involve students in problem solving, are likely to use the term *development* to refer to mental processes and the acquisition of mental tools needed for a child to eventually become a responsible, caring adult. Adopting one meaning of development rather than another will, then, partially determine one's approach to behavior and classroom management.

Values and Value Hierarchies

Approaches are also defined by their values and value hierarchies, especially the values and value hierarchies expressed in what we say we want individuals (ourselves included) to become and whether we want individuals to stand out for their personal achievements, for their capacity to care for others, for their creativity, or whatever. In addition, they are defined by those values that express what we want *communities* to become, whether we want communities to emphasize productivity, caring, democratic ideals, or whatever. Of course, we want everything good for both individuals and communities, but in our actions and efforts we often place some values higher than others, and in so doing, we express something about the nature of our approach to behavior and classroom management.

Put another way, we need to look at the values and value hierarchies that help define an approach in the first place and that set the standards for evaluating what are or are not effective methods. For example, later on, in Chapter 9, we will find that some cultures place much more value on children and adolescents fitting in and getting along with the group, while other cultures place more value on children and adolescents standing out and achieving individually. These and other value differences influence how educators from different cultures manage behavior and classrooms.

Assumptions About Effective Behavior and Classroom Management

We also need to look at the assumptions about what is needed to manage behavior and classrooms effectively. That is, assumptions also define approaches. Some educators assume that strong discipline and limit setting are most effective. Others assume that positive reinforcement is essential. Still others assume that creating an engaging curriculum works best. There are, then, different assumptions about what is most needed to support effective behavior and classroom management.

In sum, because approaches are, to some extent, defined by the meanings given to core concepts, by values and value hierarchies, and by assumptions, approaches are hidden, compared to methods (see Figure 1.1). The hidden nature of approaches helps explain why approaches and methods are often conflated. However, despite their being hidden, approaches are essential to effective behavior and classroom management and to our understanding of effective behavior and classroom management.

Review

Approaches are defined by

(1) meanings given to core concepts,

(2) values and value hierarchies, and

(3) assumptions about what makes for effective behavior and classroom management.

PREVIEW

In the coming pages, you will be reading in detail about how approaches are categorized. As a preview, approaches are categorized by

(1) how much control a teacher has over students,

(2) which components are emphasized,

(3) theories of change, and

(4) culture.

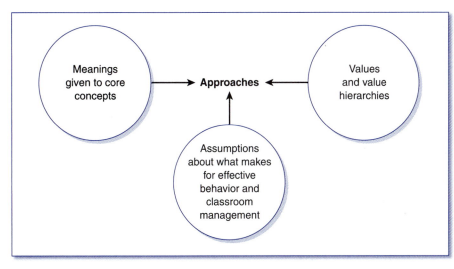

FIGURE 1.1   Approaches

Categorizing Approaches

Category 1: How Much and What Type of Control a Teacher Has Over Students

To better understand approaches, we can categorize them into logical groupings or types. Perhaps the most common way has been to type approaches according to how much direct control or power a teacher has over students. Diana Baumrind's (1970) types of authority, *authoritarian, authoritative,* and *permissive,* originally adopted to describe parenting styles, are widely used to type teaching approaches.

BAUMRIND'S STYLES OF CONTROL

Diana Baumrind

Authoritarian: The authoritarian teacher attempts to shape, control, and evaluate the behavior and attitudes of students in accordance with a set standard of conduct. The authoritarian teacher values respect for authority, respect for work, and respect for the preservation of order and traditional structure. In so valuing, the authoritarian teacher demands obedience and does not encourage verbal give and take.

Authoritative: Similar to the authoritarian teacher, the authoritative teacher also tries to control students and is firm when necessary, but the control is more through positive encouragement of students' autonomous and independent strivings and through actively listening to students and explaining the reasoning behind rules and demands. The authoritative teacher is, then, demanding but at the same time responsive to students.

Permissive: The permissive teacher generally does not try to directly control students or make high demands on students, but he or she does try to cultivate warm relationships.

In her studies of parenting styles, Baumrind (1970) found that authoritative parenting, which includes nurturance, communication, firm control, and maturity demands, best predicts children's well-being—at least in most Western cultures. Her findings are echoed by the research of other Western investigators (Barber, 2002).

Baumrind's (1970) categories are now widely used to describe and evaluate teacher-student relationships (Bear, 2004), so much so that many leading educators claim that authoritative teaching is the most effective. For example, Lilian Katz, a leader in early childhood education, has advised teachers to adopt an authoritative style of teaching—making it clear that what she means by authoritative is identical to what Baumrind meant (Katz, 1995).

Katz is not the only Western educator to favor authoritative teaching. For example, one study found that the strongest predictor of adolescents' academic achievement in math was an authoritative teaching style (Gregory & Weinstein, 2004). In another study, Hughes (2002) found that by extrapolating findings on Baumrind's (1970) parent-child relations to the classroom, teachers were able to develop better relationships with children so that children became less vulnerable to negative peer influence. Regardless of the study, the essential point derived from the Baumrind studies has been that educators need to be demanding but, at the same time, responsive to children.

Similar to Baumrind's ways of organizing styles, Wolfgang (2001) and Glickman and Tamashiro (1980) have organized teaching types along a control

A teacher's style of control can be either authoritarian, authoritative, or permissive.

continuum, with *relationship-listening* types, such as Gordon's (1974) "Teacher Effectiveness Training," at the least controlling end; *rules-consequences* types, such as the Canters' (Canter & Canter, 1976) "Assertive Discipline," at the most controlling end; and *confronting-contracting* types, such as Glasser's (1992) approach, in the middle (see Figure 1.2).

Using these categories to describe types of teacher control, several studies have demonstrated that teachers' type of control can be significantly influenced by training, gender, and context. In particular, being trained in alternative certification programs, being male, and teaching in a rural school all predict more direct, authoritarian control (Martin, Shoho, & Yin, 2003; Martin & Yin, 1997, 1999).

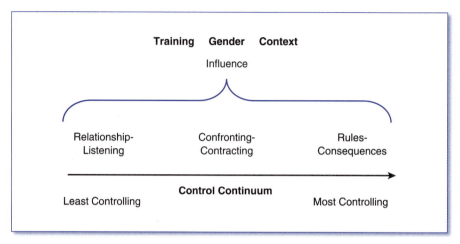

FIGURE 1.2   Control Continuum

Finally, with respect to types and degree of control, there are those who focus on a teacher's authority as being a construction rather than something inherent in the teaching role. As Pace and Hemmings (2006, p. 2) have emphasized, authority has different meanings depending on who you are talking to, so authority comes in multiple forms and types, each form or type deriving from (1) teachers' legitimacy, (2) students' consent, and (3) a moral order consisting of shared values and norms.

This *social constructivist* approach to authority has its roots in the ground-breaking work of sociologist Max Weber (1925/1964). Weber gave us three types of authority: traditional authority, charismatic authority, and legal-rational authority. *Traditional authority* is based on status; students grant a teacher authority based upon his or her status as a teacher. *Charismatic authority* is based on the exceptional qualities of an individual; students grant a teacher authority based upon his or her character, virtues, and ability to inspire. *Legal-rational authority* is based upon rules, regulations, and policy, which define an individual's "rights"; students grant a teacher authority based upon a school's bureaucracy, which has given the teacher certain rights that entail consequences should students not follow his or her lead.

As we shall see, students differ from one another according to which of these three types they best respond to. From this perspective, then, problems with authority are likely to be not so much problems in the teacher or in the students but in the match between teacher and students.

Category 2: Which Components Are Emphasized

Another way to organize approaches is to organize them according to which core concepts are emphasized or featured. We have already mentioned the five core concepts we take to be the basic components of any developed approach to behavior and classroom management: relationship building (which includes both dyadic relationships and communities), learning (teaching for learning), development (supporting long-term development), organization (attending to how the classroom or school is organized), and accommodating diversity (both cultural diversity and diversity based upon ability and learning differences; see Table 1.1). We chose these five because, together, they capture most of what the literature on behavior and classroom management is talking about. While virtually every educator endorses all five concepts, educators differ with regard to which components are emphasized.

Some educators emphasize relationship building. This is especially evident in traditional counseling approaches (Brendtro, 1969; Cutts & Moseley, 1941; Glasser, 1969; Gordon, 1974; Redl & Wineman, 1965) and in more recent approaches focusing on transforming classrooms into just and caring communities

PREVIEW

Relationship building will be discussed in more detail in Part II of this book.

TABLE 1.1   Categories of Approaches

Category of Approach (According to Emphasis)	General Examples of Approach	Specific Examples of Methods Following Naturally From an Approach
Relationship Building	Gordon's Teacher Effectiveness Training	"Active listening" to develop positive relationships
Teaching for Learning	Systematic behavioral-learning approaches	Modeling and then reinforcing civil behavior at meetings
Supporting Development	Kolberg's Approach for Stimulating Thinking About Justice and Caring	Holding a class discussion to have everyone figure out how to reduce teasing
Organization	Ecological approaches stemming from Kounin's pioneering work	Reorganizing desks and the classroom schedule to have better work groups and to better coordinate special education teams
Accommodating Diversity	Organic approaches rooted in the medical model	Providing medication to help children with serious attention problems

Review

The central components of behavior and classroom management are

(1) relationship building,

(2) teaching for learning,

(3) teaching to support development,

(4) organization, and

(5) accommodating diversity.

(Gathercoal, 1998; Kohn, 1996; Noddings, 2002; Watson & Battistich, 2006). The implicit assumption here is that positive relationships make children and adolescents want to participate and behave well.

Other educators emphasize learning. Included here are approaches that focus on ways to teach and reinforce alternative behaviors (i.e., alternatives to disruptive behavior) as well as approaches that teach and reinforce skills (e.g., the skill of participating positively in group discussions), the major premise being that children and adolescents often need to learn how to behave (Maag, 2004; Trieschman, Whittaker, & Brendtro, 1969; Walker, Shea, & Bauer, 2004).

Approaches that feature development are those that concentrate on supporting the long-term development of *inner resources* or *tools for thinking*—such as the capacity to symbolize (e.g., use words) and think deeply about issues pertaining to living in communities (Butchart, 1998a)—and on supporting major developmental tasks such as the task of "putting morality on the inside" by internalizing or "owning" rules (Kohlberg & Lickona, 1990). Developmental approaches also emphasize matching methods to level of maturity and supporting constructivist methods for behavior and classroom management (DeVries & Kohlberg, 1990). The major premise underlying approaches emphasizing development is that development is the ultimate "cure" for behavior problems (Scarlett, 1998).

Finally, approaches that feature organization are illustrated in classrooms where the focus is on such matters as seating arrangements, class routines, and ways of monitoring individuals and groups, as well as on the "built" environment (Moore, 1987; Weinstein & David, 1987). Organizational approaches are also especially attentive to the various ways of organizing students into different kinds of groups for different purposes (e.g., small groups for cooperative learning, large groups for discussing classroom rules) as well as organizing educators into different groups for different purposes (e.g., groups to teach in inclusive classrooms, groups to service a child with disabilities).

PREVIEW

Learning and development in relation to behavior and classroom management will be discussed in more detail in Part III of the book. Organization in relation to behavior and classroom management will be discussed in more detail in Part IV of the book.

Organization can also refer to the interpersonal systems in classrooms and schools that define teacher and student roles and patterns of interaction. Focus on systems leads to viewing problem behavior as a reflection of dysfunctional systems (Minuchin, 1974; Molnar & Lindquist, 1989; Sarason, 1982).

Category 3: Theories of Change

Still another way to categorize approaches is in terms of **theories of change.** In this book, we will discuss six theoretical traditions in particular: **behavioral-learning, psychodynamic, cognitive-constructivist, ecological, interpersonal (family) systems,** and **organic (biological) approaches.** We focus on these six because they have figured centrally in discussions of behavior and classroom management.

Because many educators have found discussions of theories to be largely irrelevant (no doubt a result of the way theories have been presented), we will here emphasize how each theory encourages an inquiry process. That is, we will emphasize how each helps educators pose and answer meaningful questions about a student, a group of students, or some classroom or school **system.** In so doing, we hope to show the truth in an oft-quoted statement by Kurt Lewin, the great Gestalt psychologist and forerunner of today's systems theorists, "There is nothing so practical as a good theory."

For example, using a behavioral-learning theory, an educator can inquire about what stimuli and reinforcements might explain why a child continues to misbehave. Using a cognitive-constructivist theory, an educator can inquire about whether a child's level of moral development helps explain the child's uncooperative behavior. The key to using a theory as a means to inquire is to observe closely in order to obtain the information needed to answer the question posed by the theory.

Category 4: Culture

A fourth way to categorize approaches is in terms of culture. **Culture** is a concept that is difficult to define but indispensable for understanding differences in the ways groups socialize their offspring and organize themselves into functioning communities. Strictly speaking, cultural approaches are different mixes of other ways mentioned for categorizing approaches. However, there are details in any cultural approach that are often missed when one describes using categories derived elsewhere—and the details matter. For example, many cultural approaches labeled authoritarian are, on close inspection, quite different from the approaches referred to when using Baumrind's categories, as we will discuss in Chapters 3 and 9.

Review

Approaches can be categorized according to

(1) how much and what kind of control a teacher has over students,

(2) which core components are emphasized,

(3) theories of change, and

(4) culture.

There are, then, a variety of ways to categorize or type approaches: by styles of control, by core concepts featured, by theories of change, and by culture. However one categorizes, what remains constant is the fact that approaches differ from methods. We need to make this clear by going on to discuss methods.

REFLECT

Now that you have read this discussion on approaches and before you read about methods, take a moment to reflect upon your own "natural approach." Think about the meanings, values, and assumptions that you bring into your work with children and adolescents. Doing so will enable you to choose from the wide array of methods of management available as well as enable you to realize your strengths and weaknesses.

METHODS

There are four points to be made about methods. First, any single method (e.g., time-out, having an adolescent provide a detailed story about what led up to a misbehavior) can fit comfortably within almost any approach, so wise educators make a point to collect a storehouse of methods—no need to rule out using a method because it fails to fit within an approach. Put another way, it is wrong to say "My approach is to use time-outs" or "I switched from a developmental to a behaviorist approach when I began to use time-outs."

Second, the meaning of any method depends on the educator's approach. For example, time-out may have one meaning within a behaviorist approach (as a way to stop misbehavior from being reinforced) but quite another meaning within a psychodynamic approach (as a way a child can regain composure and, when ready, reenter the group), and the differences in meaning matter.

Third, while a method can fit comfortably within almost any approach, approaches are defined, in part, by which methods are *featured*. One way to spot how an approach features certain methods is to organize methods into main types and ask which type is featured. Here, we organize methods into three main types.

Types of Methods

Type 1: Control Methods

One type functions primarily to gain direct and immediate control over children and adolescents. We will, then, refer to methods of this type as control methods. For children, control methods include invoking a classroom rule (e.g., "No running in the halls!"), using time-outs, providing rewards for good behavior, and implementing physical restraints. For adolescents, control methods include in-school suspensions and making the adolescent do extra work. Control methods may bring to mind only behaviorist approaches, but they figure in every approach because there are times when children and adolescents need to be directly controlled by teachers.

Type 2: Guidance Methods

Another type functions primarily to guide children and adolescents in order to support more mature behavior and long-term development. We will, then, refer to methods of this type as guidance methods. They include helping children and adolescents to think of alternative ways to negotiate conflict (e.g., "Can you think of something you might have done instead of grabbing John's marker?" "Can you think of some other way of being funny than by being funny at someone else's expense?"), holding class discussions about ways to improve the class, and directly suggesting trying out some more mature way of resolving a problem.

Type 3: Prevention Methods

A third type functions primarily to prevent problem behavior. We will, then, refer to methods of this type as prevention methods. Prevention methods for children include providing advance warnings that transitions are coming up (e.g., "Five minutes until clean up."), ensuring that every child has the materials needed to carry out some project, and being careful not to ask young children to sit still for longer than they are able. For adolescents, prevention methods include making the curriculum interesting and making students feel known and respected. One of the major findings from research on behavior and classroom management is that, regardless of approach, good teachers differ from others not so much by how they react to problem behavior as by how they prevent problem behavior (Kounin, 1970).

Table 1.2 lists the different types of methods, with a few examples.

TABLE 1.2   Categories of Methods

Type of Method	General Examples of Method	Specific Examples of Method
Control Methods	Directives (desists), rewards, time-outs	"No running in the halls!" (classroom rules)
Guidance Methods	Stimulating discussion, suggesting alternatives, negotiating conflict	"Can you think of something you might have done instead of grabbing John's marker?" (negotiating conflict)
Prevention Methods	Routines for transitions, organized lesson plans, organized schedules	"Five minutes until clean up." (warning of transitions)

Review

Methods are defined by

(1) actions that can be observed,

(2) their immediate goals of solving problems related to behavior and classroom management, and

(3) their meaning and purpose derived from approaches.

How Methods Relate to Approaches

One final point about methods and how methods relate to approaches: Professionals often differ from amateurs by their being *mindful* that their methods derive from their approaches. Being mindful, they can have more control over choosing the right methods because they can keep in mind the big picture (their values and goals as well as their theory and assumptions about change) while attending to details of the moment. They also can be in a better position to change approaches if the situation calls for change.

However, being mindful about one's approach does not mean introspecting and taking a long time to choose a method or alternative approach at those times when immediate action is needed. The cartoon below illustrates what we mean.

As with most skilled tasks, teaching requires quick thinking and action and not just being reflective.

Choosing Methods

Choosing methods takes more than being mindful of one's approach. There are other considerations as well, such as who is the child or group and what are the circumstances. This is a different way of talking about choosing methods. The usual talk implies that there is one method for every problem behavior. We hear this in questions such as "What should one do about hitting?" and "What should one do about swearing?"

However, choosing methods is almost never about matching methods to behaviors. Rather, it is about matching methods to children or adolescents and to circumstances. Furthermore, choosing methods is not about choosing the single, right method so much as it is about choosing a variety of methods for attacking problems at different points of entry. Finally, choosing methods is about managing dilemmas. We need, then, to make clear what we mean by matching methods to children or adolescents and to circumstances, by points of entry, and by managing dilemmas.

Matching Methods to Children or Adolescents and to Circumstances

To understand what is meant by matching methods to children or adolescents and to circumstances, consider the following example of children in different classrooms refusing to clean up.

> In the first classroom, the teacher had announced suddenly, "Time to clean up!" A child in the block corner looked startled and then refused to clean up. In the second classroom, the teacher announced, "Five minutes to clean up," and a child in the block corner looked anxiously at the fort he had built and then refused to clean up. In a third classroom, the teacher also gave a five minute warning, and a child in the block corner gave the teacher a devilish grin and then refused to clean up. (Scarlett, 1998, p. 21)

In each of these three classrooms, we see children refusing to clean up and come to circle time.

What if the teachers in each classroom matched the same method to each instance of refusing, such as providing a negative consequence or trying to help the child problem solve? Doing so may have helped one child, maybe two, but not all three because the meaning of refusing to clean up differed from one child to the next.

The first child was startled and needed a transition time, so giving him a five-minute transition time might have been the method of choice. The second child was concerned about his fort getting taken apart, so helping him save his fort by adding a "save" sign might have been what was called for. The third child was looking forward to a struggle with his teacher, so skillfully ignoring him may have been just the right method. Each of these methods is matched, then, not to the problem behavior, refusing to clean up, but to the circumstances and what refusing to clean up meant to the child.

Forrest Gathercoal (1998) gives an example of the same principle applied to adolescents: Two boys had defaced the walls of a school building. One boy willingly stayed after school to clean the wall he had defaced because he understood and agreed with the logic of the consequence. The other boy objected to this proposed consequence, saying it was the janitor's job, not his. By objecting, he indicated he had an underlying problem with authority in general and so required more time and counseling to understand his problem and to begin to see teachers in a more positive light.

As these examples indicate, matching methods also has to do with matching methods to children's or adolescents' level of maturity. As a linguistic method, saying "You need to boss your body" when young children are "out of control" works well with preschoolers but would likely invite pandemonium if used with young adolescents.

Points of Entry

Choosing the right method also depends on how complex and serious a problem is. If the problem is simple and not serious, a single method aimed at controlling

Most problems can be addressed using multiple methods applied to multiple points of entry.

a child or group might suffice, such as when a teacher remains silent until a group of fourth graders quiets down so the teacher can speak and be heard. However, if the problem is complex and serious, educators must think in terms of multiple methods applied simultaneously. Furthermore, multiple methods often need to be applied at different points of entry, as the following cartoon indicates.

Points of entry refer, then, to the different ways we can attack problems; some ways are directed at making short-term improvements, and other ways are directed toward the long term. For example, if an eighth grader is disrupting the class by continually playing the role of class clown, he may win laughs from his classmates, but he may not win their respect, and his antics probably undermine his relationships with teachers and diminish his academic potential. In this situation, a teacher may have to choose methods to respond directly to the misbehavior—to improve the short term—but other methods are likely to be needed as well, with each directed at different points of entry, such as at improving the boy's relationships with classmates as well as helping motivate the boy to focus on academics.

Points of entry also refer to how we can simultaneously employ methods designed to prevent problems, guide children or adolescents, and control problem behaviors when they occur, which brings us to the last point about choosing methods: managing dilemmas.

Managing Dilemmas

One of the many subtle characteristics distinguishing master teachers from those who are not so masterful is that master teachers always feel caught in dilemmas. Others may think that there are simple and clear-cut solutions to almost any problem, but master teachers know that the best they can do is to manage dilemmas, two in particular.

The first dilemma is between meeting short-term needs for order and safety and long-term needs for positive development. What is good for meeting short-term needs for order and safety is not always good for long-term positive development (and vice versa). For example, it may calm a particularly disruptive child to send the child to time-out after the child misbehaves, but continually doing so may have harmful long-term effects, perhaps by limiting the child's opportunities to learn alternative ways of behaving or perhaps by creating a bad-child image in the classroom community, or maybe both.

The second dilemma is between meeting the needs of the individual and meeting the needs of the group. What is good for the individual is not always good for the group (and vice versa). The previous example illustrates this dilemma as well because sending a child to time-out often restores order in the group and classroom, but it does not necessarily serve the needs of the individual child being sent to time-out. Another common dilemma occurs when a particular child receives continuous and special attention so that the child stays on task, but as a result, the group suffers.

In managing these two dilemmas, most educators intuitively follow what Fritz Redl (1966) called "the law of antisepsis." This is the guideline stating that whatever one does to address one side of a dilemma cannot be harmful (must be antiseptic) with respect to the other side. An additional aim of this book is to show how educators can follow Redl's guideline to effectively manage these dilemmas.

Review

What to consider when choosing a method to manage misbehavior:

(1) The student(s) and circumstances

(2) The most relevant points of entry

(3) The management of dilemmas

Summary

In summary, approaches to behavior and classroom management are central in this book, so the focus is on explaining the differences between approaches and methods and between approaches themselves. Approaches may be distinguished by what they feature, especially by whether they feature relationship building, learning, development, organization, or accommodating diversity.

The hope here is that by understanding approaches and methods for behavior and classroom management, the reader will be in a better position to understand how best to help children and adolescents thrive in classrooms as well as thrive in the future. Here, too, we hope that regardless of approach, all will show care; not depend heavily on rewards and punishments; accommodate diversity having to do with age, culture, and ability; and while maintaining discipline, promote positive long-term development (Evertson & Weinstein, 2006).

The subject of behavior and classroom management is especially significant today. Before the advent of public schooling in America, education meant something quite different from schooling (Cremin, 1965, 1976). To become educated meant acquiring skills and knowledge learned on the farm, in apprenticeships, in religious communities, from reading newspapers, and from engaging in discussions around potbellied stoves. In previous eras, then, there was no great need to give much thought to classroom management because so many children and adolescents were educated outside schools.

Today, however, the opposite is the case. Today, the burden on schools is not only to teach children and adolescents academic skills and subjects but also to promote positive social and emotional development and, in many cases, to address serious problems in the larger society, particularly the problems of racial and cultural prejudice, poverty, and unfair treatment of those with disabilities. As a result, the strain on schools, classrooms, and teachers is great; in some cases, it is so great that teachers find it difficult to function. To meet the many demands being placed on schools and teachers, it is imperative that we develop and implement good approaches to behavior and classroom management.

Web-Based Student Study Site

The companion Web site for *Approaches to Behavior and Classroom Management* can be found at www.sagepub.com/scarlettstudy.

Visit the Web-based student study site to enhance your understanding of the chapter content. The study materials include practice tests, flashcards, suggested readings, and Web resources.

Key Concepts

Accommodating diversity	Interpersonal (family) systems	Psychodynamic
Approaches	Just and caring	Reframing
Behavioral-learning	Learning	Relationship building
Cognitive-constructivist	Managing dilemmas	Styles of control
Control methods	Matching methods	Supporting development
Counseling approaches	Methods	System
Culture	Organic (biological) approaches	Systems approaches
Development	Organization	Teaching for learning
Developmental tasks	Points of entry	Theories of change
Ecological	Prevention methods	Types of authority
Guidance methods		Values
		Value hierarchies

Discussion Questions

1. If you did not do so at the end of the discussion on ways to categorize approaches, take a moment to reflect upon your own "natural approach." Think about the meanings, values, and assumptions that you bring to your work with children and adolescents. How does your natural approach affect how you are responsible for keeping children and adolescents safe, civil, and on task? Where does your natural approach fit within the various categories discussed in this chapter, particularly categories referring to style of control, core concepts featured, and methods featured?

2. Think of a time you used a control method, a guidance method, and a prevention method. In using these three methods, were you matching them to the child/adolescent/ group and circumstances, or were you simply using the methods you use with any child/adolescent/group and circumstance?

3. Think of a time when you were faced with having to manage the behavior of a particularly challenging child/adolescent or group. Did you manage by using a variety of "points of entry" or one point of entry only? Were there additional points of entry that you might well have used?

4. Think of a time when you consciously or semiconsciously felt caught in a dilemma when having to manage a child/adolescent or group of children/adolescents. Was the dilemma between managing for the short term versus the long term, between managing to benefit an individual versus a group, or between managing for what was best for a child/adolescent versus for you or other adults? How did you manage this dilemma? If you weren't aware at the time of there being a dilemma, looking back, can you see any dilemmas that you unwittingly managed well or that you failed to manage well?

---

1. This example is taken from the first author's experience as a supervisor of student teachers.

Chapter 2

A Historical Perspective on Behavior and Classroom Management

There has long been a strong desire to think of history as a story about our progress in becoming better educated and more civilized. A progress view of history is especially evident in discussions of school discipline; many view the 19th century as a time when educators used outdated methods, particularly corporal punishment. A progress view also shows itself in the way present-day methods are portrayed proudly as being "scientifically based." Occasionally, some tragedy, such as the shootings at Columbine High School in Colorado, makes us question our progress view—but only occasionally.

Unfortunately, this progress view distorts the record. Any careful review of the record suggests the past has given us many good ideas and approaches that are spoken of today as if they were first hatched only recently, or that have been largely forgotten or ignored. Examples can be found in the good ideas and approaches of late 19th- and early 20th-century progressive educators who linked pedagogy, curriculum, and discipline, as well as in the good ideas and approaches of mid-20th-century mental hygiene educators who provided insight into how to discipline while being sensitive to children's feelings and psychological needs.

Furthermore, the progress view overlooks the fact that there is a good deal of continuity with respect to the main debates over classroom discipline. We see this continuity even in the early 19th-century debates over corporal punishment. On the surface, the debates were about outdated methods, but underneath, they were about different assumptions regarding the nature of children and adolescents, assumptions that are also found in today's debates and that help define today's approaches to behavior and classroom management. It makes sense, then, for us to look into these earlier debates in order to better understand differences in today's approaches.

THE DEBATES OVER CORPORAL PUNISHMENT IN THE FIRST HALF OF THE 19TH CENTURY

One needs no statistical report to know that the vast majority of American educators today reject corporal punishment as an acceptable method for disciplining school children. However, our rejection of corporal punishment in the schools masks the widespread acceptance of corporal punishment (spanking) in American family life (Strauss, 1994) and the widespread acceptance of strong forms of authoritarian-coercive methods of controlling children and adolescents in schools, such as suspending and expelling misbehaving students. That is, though we may think of authoritarian-coercive ways of controlling students as relics of the 19th century, authoritarian-coercive ways are alive and well in American families and in American schools.

Furthermore, as recently as 1977 the Supreme Court upheld the right of educators to use corporal punishment as a disciplinary method, and today, 23 states still allow corporal punishment in schools. We, as a culture, may not approve of corporal punishment in schools, but we still think of at least some children and adolescents as sometimes deserving "the heavy hand."

In addition, the early 19th-century debates over corporal punishment reveal a major distinction between today's approaches. Consider the example of the debates between Horace Mann and a group of Boston schoolmasters, around the time Horace Mann was struggling to establish a public school system in Massachusetts. Mann's call for better-trained teachers brought him into conflict with the schoolmasters of that time. One focus of that conflict was corporal punishment. In 1839, Mann wrote,

> I find one party strenuously maintaining that improvement in our schools can advance only so far and so fast as bodily chastisement recedes, while the other party regards a teacher or parent, divested of his instruments of pain, as a discrowned monarch. (cited in Harris, 1928, p. 48)

In 1843, a group of Boston schoolmasters formed an association to argue their case against Mann's plan to recruit better-trained teachers with outstanding character. Their case and that of Mann's were couched in religious terms and made use of theological arguments. However, at the heart of the conflict were different images of children, which, in turn, supported different approaches to education and discipline.

The Boston schoolmasters held to a mostly Calvinist view of the world and children. Calvinism, the orthodoxy among a variety of American Protestant churches at that time, emphasized the supreme power of God and the innate sinfulness of mankind, leading to a view of children as prone to wickedness and needing to be taught to be obedient. From a Calvinist perspective, children were not to be trusted, hence the need for harsh forms of discipline such as corporal punishment.

In contrast, Horace Mann's view represented a Unitarian Protestant view, a view that held a far more positive and benign image of the divine. Furthermore, Mann's Unitarian beliefs provided a very different view of children and discipline, more in keeping with the Enlightenment's emphasis on reason. In the Unitarian view, children are innocent and vulnerable to temptation, on the one hand, but responsive to moral persuasion and the modeling of virtue, on the other. In a journal edited by Mann, one writer, S. G. Howe, wrote, "Almost all children are as pure as Eve was; but the tempting apples are left hanging so thickly about that it would be a marvel if they did not eat" (Harris, 1928, p. 56).

For Horace Mann, children were innocent, vulnerable to temptation, and responsive to moral persuasion.

According to this view, it was the teacher's task to reduce temptations and then trust children to respond to the laws of reason and duty. These laws were to be taught with words but also modeled in the character of the teacher. For Mann, making serfs of children through harsh disciplinary methods such as corporal punishment was no way to prepare children to become citizens. The combination of teachers teaching and modeling reason, duty, and virtue would, said Mann, lead children to eventually become what our democratic society demands: free men and women who can govern themselves while contributing to the common good.

Stepping back from the religious language of the debate between Mann and the Boston schoolmasters, we can identify themes among competing approaches in today's debate over discipline in schools. On the one hand, in the past several decades, and as happened in the 1840s, leading educators have argued for approaches that make controlling children or managing behavior the issue (see Canter & Canter, 1976). On the other hand, others have argued for approaches that make the issue preparing children to become moral citizens (see Butchart & McEwan, 1998). To explain this point, here is Ronald Butchart (1998a) commenting on today's talk about school discipline: "Mainstream management assumes that children are incapable of rationality and must be controlled through various forms

Whether children should be trusted has long been a debate among American educators.

of enticement and manipulation. Constructivist discipline assumes . . . they are capable of . . . mastering the intricacies of responsible behavior" (p. 11).

While Butchart may be overdrawing the distinction by referring to "mainstream management," few would disagree that today's approaches, just like approaches in Horace Mann's time, can be distinguished from one another by how much each shows trust in students and how much each advocates for strong, direct teacher control.

Review

A progress view of history overlooks the fact that in the past

(1) there have been many good ideas about how to educate children, and

(2) many of the debates among educators are the same or similar to the debates going on today.

THE DEBATES OVER SCHOOL DISCIPLINE IN THE LATE 19TH CENTURY

The debate over corporal punishment continued throughout the 19th century, but by the century's last decades, corporal punishment was largely relegated to rural schools considered to be backward. Here is one example given by the late

19th-century educator Emerson White (1893), describing and evaluating one of these "old-fashioned," rural schools:

> On the way from the railroad station, . . . we had the opportunity of visiting a school made up of some fifty white children, in the charge of a schoolmaster of the old type. The pupils, varying in age from six to sixteen years, as judged, were seated on high benches without backs or desks, and most of them with feet dangling in the air. With one exception, they were all studying Webster's Speller . . . with eyes on book; and save a gentle swaying of the body backwards and forwards, and a moving of the lips as the eyes passed from letter to letter, there was neither movement nor noise. There was a sort of rhythm of motion and silence—a silence that could be felt, an order that came up to the old "pin-drop" test. In a corner of the room were several whips from four to six feet in length. Detecting a pupil's furtive glance from his book to the strangers, the master seized one of the rods, and, darting towards the lad, brought it down across his shoulders, shouting, "Study!" and the swaying bodies and moving lips of the pupils responded with a quicker motion. (p. 56)

PREVIEW

Chapter 9 will focus on a cultural perspective for classroom behavior management.

However, late 19th-century education reformers focused not so much on corporal punishment and rural schools as on the problems caused by urbanization and the influx of immigrants from cultures quite different from mainstream American culture, then rooted in Protestant Christianity and American democratic ideals. Teaching immigrant children was a heavy burden to place on teachers—too heavy for most—and schools suffered from lack of resources and supports. The sorry plight of schools in late 19th-century urban America gave birth to the progressive education movement.

Before the mid-19th century, schooling in America was mostly divorced from children's everyday activities (Beatty, 1995). If a child attended school (most did not), he or she was expected to follow a curriculum in which the goals and methods had little to do with a child's everyday life. Rather than moving about freely, children sat still in desks or stood to recite. Rather than pursue their interests, children pursued the interests of their teachers. Rather than being inventive and inquisitive, children followed prescribed processes to get "right" answers and acquire "right" habits. If children did not conform, they were punished. The previous example illustrates all of these points.

Of course, this is only a composite sketch. There were always notable exceptions. However, the sketch defines the context in which late 19th-century progressive reform movements developed. These progressive movements were as much *against* the old mechanistic ways as they were *for* what they advocated.

What exactly did they advocate? The answer to this question can best be arrived at by focusing on four concepts: interests, activity, structure, and mentoring. With regard to *interests,* the progressive movement advocated for teachers to find ways to build curriculum around children's interests (Jones & Tanner, 1981). With regard to *activity,* the new movement followed a constructivist philosophy of knowing—a philosophy that says each of us must question, problem solve, and act on our environment if we are to understand and know. As mentioned in the previous chapter, constructivist philosophies of education all advocate for teachers finding ways to help students to actively question and reflect, whether in academic domains or in social domains such as figuring out alternatives to quarreling (Glassman, 2001). With regard to *structure,* the new movement redefined what it should mean to provide structure for children and adolescents to learn optimally. The old, authoritarian-coercive approaches had teachers structuring children through their directives, lectures, punishments, and assignments requiring rote learning. The new movement had teachers structuring in more subtle ways, such as by the way they organized time, space, materials, the built environment, and especially the curriculum.

With regard to *mentoring,* the new movement advocated for a very different vision of the teacher's relationship with children. Rather than being an authoritarian instructor, the teacher was to be a mentor who was a caring, professional guide—someone who worked to facilitate learning and stimulate thinking. Nowhere are these progressive ideas discussed more thoughtfully than in the writings of John Dewey, so Dewey will serve as the leading example.

Dewey and the Progressive Education Movement

Source: Corbis.

John Dewey

Progressive education is often associated with John Dewey, though Dewey was, in fact, only one of many who led the late 19th-century campaign for school reform. In the initial stages of school reform, progressive educators were simply trying to make schools, especially urban schools for immigrant children, more habitable. Removing head lice from children was, in some schools, as important as teaching children how to read (Cohen, 1964). However, out of their efforts to reform came an approach to curriculum, pedagogy, and discipline that countered the then-dominant approach.

More than anyone else at the time, Dewey (1963) made clear the connection between curriculum, pedagogy, and discipline, and in so doing, he defined where control should, ideally, reside. According to Dewey, it should reside not in the teacher but in the activities in which children and adolescents are engaged. He likened the ideal classroom to the ball field where the game itself is what controls the players—not only its rules, but also its goals and ability to capture players' interest and attention. In the case of Dewey and other progressive educators at the time, the old adage "The devil makes use of idle hands" might well have been followed with "And angels hover about the busy." Classrooms were, then, to be busy and productive as beehives, allowing for talk and a constant buzz necessitated by groups of children working together. No "pin-drop" rule need apply. For Dewey, then, the teacher should be an effective professional, someone who can manage a classroom so that everything about the classroom holds students' attention and stimulates in children the desire to be good and productive citizens.

Affection and the Kindergarten Movement

The emphasis on individual and group activity was also present in the kindergarten movement of the late 19th century. Influenced by European educators, particularly by Froebel in Germany (Bowen, 1893) and Pestalozzi in Switzerland (Green, 1969), this movement advocated organizing classrooms to support young children's productive self-activity and, over time, self-discipline.

However, the kindergarten movement added another emphasis not found at the heart of Dewey's progressive philosophy. Dewey helped to redefine the teacher's role as that of leader in a democratic classroom, a professional whose authority lay in representing the common good. He wrote,

> The teacher reduces to a minimum the occasions in which he or she has to exercise authority in a personal way. When it is necessary . . . to speak and act firmly, it is done in behalf of the interest of the group, not as an exhibition of personal power. (Dewey, 1963, p. 54)

In contrast, those from the kindergarten movement emphasized teachers needing to control children by becoming the object of their affection. As J. S. Hart (Harris, 1928), one educator from this period, put it, "The fact that children love their teacher gives to the teacher almost unbounded influence over them. . . . By this silken cord they can be drawn withersoever the teacher wills" (p. 102).

Character Education

Finally, with respect to classroom discipline and educational reform at the end of the 19th century, we need to mention **character education**. From the beginning,

American schools were viewed as instruments for character education, with character education seen as part and parcel of classroom discipline. In the beginning, character education meant demanding obedience. The main means for promoting good character were, then, authoritarian-coercive means, all for the purpose of instilling good habits.

The theory was then (as it is for many today) that if teachers can get children to behave, by whatever means necessary (including harsh, coercive means), then good behavior will become habitual. We might call this the **practice-to-habit theory**, one that follows the old adage, "Sow an act, and you reap a habit. Sow a habit, and you reap a character. Sow a character, and you reap a destiny." One mid-19th-century educator, Z. Richards, expressed this practice-to-habit approach as follows:

> If neither precept nor example will make the child do right, he must be forced to do it. This is a prerogative and a duty of the teacher. God in the order of His providence and by divine commission has made the parent and the teacher the dispensers of punishment when necessary. . . . [and] [u]nless the body is insensible to pain, the remembrance of the pain will remind the pupil of his sin. The fear or dread of the repetition of this pain will restrain him from repetition of his fault. This course may be followed until doing right becomes a habit, and thus reformation be effected. (cited in Harris, 1928, p. 74)

In contrast to this practice-to-habit theory and approach to character development, educators at the turn of the 20th century stressed the need to focus not so much on outward good behavior as on "inward" feelings and "right" motives. In Emerson White's (1893) words, "all true discipline with reference to conduct is *character training*, i.e., the forming of such states of feeling in the pupil, and such habitual modes of action, as make right conduct easy and pleasant" (p. 105).

With regard to character training, then, the key distinction for late 19th-century educators concerned the motives for being obedient. Obedience out of fear of being punished was not the goal. Rather, the goal was obedience that was free, voluntary, and prompted by a sense of duty (White, 1893, p. 109). In short, late 19th-century educators sought to foster in children the development of a conscience. The development of a conscience requires not authoritarian-coercive control but instruction and guidance by teachers who command affection and respect. Here, we see the forerunner of recent **constructivist approaches** aimed at "putting morality on the inside" (Kohlberg & Lickona, 1990).

The progressive education movement, which began toward the end of the 19th century, foreshadowed three debates going on today. The first debate is the debate over teachers' authority and how teachers should structure children—directly through directives and rules or indirectly through offering guidance and soliciting discussion. The second debate is the debate over character education and how best to conceive of character education—as a matter of directly instilling values or as a matter of attending to the supports needed for children to develop an internal morality. The third debate is the debate over community and how best to prepare children to be adult participants in the larger society—by creating classroom communities that mirror the values of industrial society or by creating democratic classroom communities that embody the ideals of justice and care.

In sum, the reform movement that began at the end of the 19th century made explicit the ineffectiveness of strictly authoritarian-coercive approaches to classroom discipline. The progressive educators' emphasis on curriculum and building on children's interests, as well as the kindergarten and character education movements' emphasis on children's emotions and motivation for "being good," all set the stage for a new era of debate between authoritarian and nonauthoritarian approaches to school discipline, an era influenced by developments outside the schools themselves.

REFLECT   How is this chapter's view of education in the 19th century different from the view you held prior to reading it?

On the one hand, there was the **child study movement** among academicians who developed theories of child development using the methods of science. On the other hand, there was the **mental hygiene movement** among mental health professionals who provided a new focus on children's "inner life." We turn now to discussing these two movements and how they shaped the debates over school discipline in the first half of the 20th century.

Review

In the late 19th century,

(1) progressive educators reformed the way children were taught and the way behavior and classroom management was defined,

(2) the kindergarten movement strongly emphasized providing an affectionate relationship between teacher and child, and

(3) character education moved from stressing obedience to stressing inculcating values and a conscience.

THE DEBATES OVER SCHOOL DISCIPLINE IN THE FIRST HALF OF THE 20TH CENTURY

In 18th- and 19th-century Europe and America, a new faith had taken hold and was fast becoming a faith for the mainstream. That new faith was a faith in science. We see this clearly in the writings of the principal philosophers at that time, for example, Auguste Compte, as well as in pronouncements by public officials such as the French minister of education, Condorcet, who predicted that science would soon replace religion (Condorcet, 1789/1976). It is not that people called science a faith. Rather, in speaking about science, people treated science as something to have faith in, something that ensures progress toward a better world.

This call for a faith in science had been growing steadily in the previous two centuries—the period sometimes referred to as the Enlightenment. Our founding fathers were products of the Enlightenment; Thomas Jefferson and Benjamin Franklin were both men of science as well as men who influenced how Americans came to think about public schooling (Cremin, 1965).

However, as is often the case with new faiths, faith in science took a long time to become fully integrated into the mainstream. Arguably, it was not until the first half of the 20th century that Enlightenment philosophies came to dominate discussions about schooling in general and discipline in particular. We see this clearly in the influence of the child study and mental hygiene movements.

Both movements took as their starting point the need to be scientific in order to make progress in educating children. By "scientific" they meant integrating theory and practice and deriving theory from the systematic gathering of data, careful measurement, and the testing of hypotheses. The model for many was Darwin, and G. Stanley Hall at Clark University was the leading example.

The Child Study Movement

Hall promoted empirical research for understanding children, their development, and the kind of parenting and education children need to optimally support their development. He tried to do for the study of children, and for explaining the development of children, what Darwin had done for the study of species and for explaining the development of species. Hall and his associates surveyed parents and teachers and collected mounds of data on a wide variety of subjects, including the subject of education. The main effort was to reform practice by having practice accommodate the nature of the child.

This **accommodating the nature of the child** reversed the old-fashioned insistence that the child accommodate the nature of the school and fit into whatever classroom or curriculum was offered. For example, one of Clark's doctoral students, Arnold Gesell, became famous for his maturationist theory of child development and used it to develop an assessment clinic where parents brought their children for help to determine whether their children were "ready" for school or ready to advance to the next grade. Assessing a child as not being ready meant the child should not be made to "fit in."

Out of the child study movement came no single approach to teaching and school discipline. In fact, it generated as much new controversy and disagreement as it generated agreement. For example, the development of tests to measure intelligence "objectively" generated the most hotly debated issue in the history of American schooling: the issue of whether biology (nature) or schooling (nurture) determines how far a child will advance in school. At issue for many was whether some children, because of their low intelligence (as measured by intelligence tests), could benefit from schooling or from schooling at the higher levels. This **nature-nurture debate** also pervaded discussions of school discipline; some saw bad behavior as a matter of bad breeding while others sought the causes of bad behavior in upbringing and teaching.

What the child study movement did, then, was change the rules for advancing arguments about educational practice in general and school discipline in particular. No longer could theology, philosophy, or personal experience be the sole or principal grounds for promoting a point of view about discipline. Now one needed to back up arguments with data, the results of measurement, and "scientific" theories. Today, most books on behavior and classroom management frame discussions in terms of "best practice" and which methods and approaches have been validated empirically—a direct outgrowth of the child study movement.

However, there are limitations to this scientific approach. The concept of "best practice" works well when the various approaches and methods being compared share the same goals and values. But often, this is not the case, especially when differences between approaches have to do with differences in culture. Furthermore, limiting discussion to only research-based methods and what can be measured can lead to overlooking or undervaluing wisdom gained through observation and experience.

For example, Fritz Redl and David Wineman (1965) suggested using "planned ignoring" at certain times when children are "acting up." Using Redl and Wineman's definition, planned ignoring is a method that is almost impossible to measure because the method requires that a teacher make an interpretation to distinguish between children being mildly disruptive because they are doing some "antsy" childlike thing that will peter out on its own (and so can be ignored) and some other mild disruption that is a buildup to something much more serious (and so should be attended to right away). Anyone who has worked with children knows this is a real, not false, distinction and that there is wisdom in this suggestion, so to ignore it just because it cannot be measured makes little sense. In sum, the research-driven, "scientific" way of talking about best practice and scientifically based methods can lead to undervaluing methods that rely on teachers' ability to interpret the meaning of students' behavior.

The scientific way of framing favored, then, some approaches to discipline over others—not necessarily because they were better but because they lent themselves to measurement and the gathering of data. Perhaps the best examples are behavioral-learning approaches to discipline. We will have more to say about these approaches in later chapters. However, right now, it is important to note that under the new, scientific rules for improving school discipline, there developed a bias favoring those approaches that fit most comfortably within the scientific frame or way of explaining.

PREVIEW

Chapter 5 includes a section about behavioral-learning approaches.

Furthermore, during this time, control came not just in the form of discipline. It also came in the form of institutional changes, particularly in the practice of tracking students and segregating difficult students who had been "scientifically" shown to be "deviant" in terms of intelligence and/or emotional makeup. As Seymour Sarason (1982) explained, schools were assumed to exist primarily for "normal" children who could one day make contributions to society. The "special" child was thought to be "an interference to the progress of the rest of the class" (p. 237).

The Mental Hygiene Movement

The other central, influential movement of the first half of the 20th century was the mental hygiene movement. This movement began not in the schools, nor in academia, but in the medical care given to the "mentally ill." Adolph Meyer, a physician at the Johns Hopkins Hospital in Baltimore, coined the term *mental hygiene.* Meyer's psychobiological theory changed the focus in discussions of psychopathology from treatment to prevention. This refocusing had a direct impact on how the medical community viewed children and schooling. During this period, the emerging professions of child psychiatry, clinical child psychology, social work, and school psychology became "allied" professions for teachers, by their sharing a common focus on ordinary, everyday problems such as the discipline problems occurring daily in schools.

The practical outcome of this focus on prevention was the child guidance clinic and a new kind of interdisciplinary team made up of a psychiatrist, psychologist, and social worker. The aim of these clinics was to provide guidance and promote a guidance approach to children's problems. Here is a quote from two child development specialists from this time:

> How may one discover the type of authority, which emerges . . . in respect of training and equipping the child for the use of freedom? This may be described as the authority of education in its original sense as a leading forth or drawing out of the capacities of the child, a development of his powers through use. It will be clear at once that in such a process the parent (or teacher) assumes the role as guide. (Blatz & Bott, 1930, p. 19)

Though Meyer objected to much that was central to psychoanalytic theory, he, like most clinicians at that time, was deeply influenced by the psychoanalytic view of the child. This view borrows heavily from the medical understanding of physical problems as symptoms of underlying diseases. Children's problem behaviors were taken as symptoms of underlying emotional problems that teachers may not be able to solve, but that teachers need to be aware of when disciplining children, so as to not make matters worse. As an example, Fritz Redl's "law of antisepsis" applied not just to managing dilemmas (see Chapter 1) but also to managing surface behavior in general in ways that are hygienic with respect to underlying problems or the possibility of a child's developing underlying problems. Here are Cutts and Mosely (1941) speaking about the principles governing a mental hygiene approach to educating and disciplining children:

> The principles of mental hygiene should be applied not only in dealing with children who are causing trouble, but even more in the day-by-day work of the school. In negative form, these principles may be summed up as demanding that we do nothing to hinder the physical development of the children, that we do not use shame, sarcasm, or ridicule and that we do not humiliate him in any way, that we do not ask him to do work beyond his physical and mental ability, that we do not place him where he will fail constantly, and that we avoid anger and scolding in our dealings with him. In positive form, these principles tell us to promote the child's health and happiness, to like him, to make him certain of his place in our

affections and his membership in the group, to adjust his work to his physical and mental ability to the point where effort will bring success, to express our approval of the good things he does and to praise his effort and improvement, and to be sure that he has a task for which he is responsible which he can do with interest and satisfaction. Both positive and negative statements emphasize one idea: prevention. (pp. 5–6)

Source: Corbis.

Arnold Gesell

In sum, teachers were asked to show a new kind of sensitivity to children's feelings and "inner" life. In Chapter 6, we will have more to say about Fritz Redl and the mental hygiene approach to school discipline. For now, it is enough to point out that this approach emerged as a dominant approach in the first half of the 20th century and did much to define and support a guidance and prevention approach to school discipline.

Most of the competing theories in the first half of the 20th century focused on understanding middle-class Euro-American children with two-parent families. Child development experts at the time often spoke in general terms about children at this or that age. For example, two of the leading child development experts of the time, Arnold Gesell and Benjamin Spock, spoke as if children from any given age group were all the same. Here they are talking about preschoolers: "Three, it's a nice age. Children at this age, being especially devoted to their parents, are easy to lead" (Spock, 1946, p. 280). "Four presents an interesting combination of independence and sociability" (Gesell et al., 1940, p. 50).

There was, then, relatively little discussion of differences pertaining to culture and little discussion of how to mainstream children with disabilities. These issues of culture and disability were issues still to come in debates over school discipline.

P R E V I E W

Chapter 9 discusses the role of culture in behavior management and Chapter 7 includes a section on organizing teams for children with special needs.

Review

In the first half of the 20th century,

(1) the child study movement brought the ethic and methods of science into discussions of children's development and education, and

(2) the mental hygiene movement maintained that behavior management was an important method to address children's emotional needs and to prevent serious emotional problems.

THE DEBATES OVER SCHOOL DISCIPLINE IN THE SECOND HALF OF THE 20TH CENTURY

At the beginning of the second half of the 20th century, behaviorist and psychodynamic theories dominated discussions of child development. School discipline was couched in terms of rewards and punishments or guiding children to manage their feelings. The emphasis was on what we do *to* children, not on what children do for themselves. This was not a time, then, when educators were encouraged to adopt constructivist approaches to school discipline or approaches emphasizing supporting children's becoming members of a democratic, just, and caring classroom community. Dewey's constructivist philosophy had been misinterpreted so many times that progressive education was marginalized in favor of more overtly structured, teacher-directed forms of educating children.

Constructivist Approaches in the Late 20th Century

Source: Piagetian Society.

Jean Piaget

However, during the late 1950s and early 1960s, a new wave of constructivist thinking arrived in the form of a cognitive revolution in the study of children. This cognitive revolution came about when Americans discovered the genius in the work of Jean Piaget. For decades, the Swiss psychologist Piaget had been studying children and their thinking. However, his work was largely ignored because it did not conform to the standards of experimental psychology.

By the early 1960s, Piaget's brilliance was recognized by American mainstream psychology and, for a while, the field of cognitive development became almost synonymous with Piaget's name. Furthermore, Piaget's constructivist approach influenced educators and those interested in promoting moral development in schools. Lawrence Kohlberg was the leading example. Kohlberg built on Piaget's earlier work on the development of moral judgment in childhood. Later on, we will have more to say about Kohlberg, moral judgment, and school discipline. For now, it is enough to point out how Kohlberg and his coworkers brought a constructivist approach to school discipline.

Kohlberg's aim was to show that children and adolescents develop self-control, good behavior, and an understanding of right and wrong through the daily negotiations and problems they have to solve in order to get along with others.

From this constructivist perspective, educators need to help children and adolescents think about alternative points of view in determining what is fair, right, and good. In doing so, children and adolescents can then "put morality on the inside," thereby becoming self-controlled, well-behaved, and, most important, responsible citizens of the classroom. Kohlberg and constructivist educators in the 1960s were, then, returning to late 19th-century attempts to help children and adolescents develop good character—not by demanding virtue but by helping them adopt virtue on their own.

The 1960s and 1970s also witnessed the first of several waves of school reform having to do with social justice (see Table 2.1). The civil rights movement had a direct impact on school discipline. It did so by making it the law that children and adolescents traditionally excluded from mainstream education were now to be included—particularly children and adolescents with disabilities and children and adolescents of color who were previously educated in segregated schools. Now teachers were faced with new groups of students who were challenging because of their diverse backgrounds and diverse abilities.

TABLE 2.1   Story of Desegregation in Schools

1954	Supreme Court rules that segregating on the basis of race is unconstitutional
1975	Congress passes the Education for All Handicapped Children Act (HCA) P.L. 94-142, which encouraged integrating children with special needs
1980s to Present	Several revisions of P.L. 94-142, now called the Individuals with Disabilities Education Act (IDEA)
1986	Regular Education Initiative (REI) to include (most) children with special needs in the regular classroom

 **REFLECT**   What are your thoughts about how much or how little progress we have made since the civil rights movement in the 1960s with respect to accommodating diversity?

At this time, children and adolescents were also viewed as becoming more challenging because of dramatic social changes having to do with the family. In particular, divorce rates skyrocketed and more and more women joined the work force.

As a result of the rapid changes taking place in American society, many teachers during the 1960s and 1970s felt they were losing control of their classrooms, so there was a felt need for new approaches to help teachers regain control. There were, then, a number of approaches in the 1970s specifically designed for regaining control. They fell into two quite different groups, one from the behaviorist tradition and the other from clinical work and counseling.

Behaviorist Approaches

PREVIEW

In Chapter 5, there is a major section on behavioral-learning approaches.

One of the most popular of the behaviorist "control approaches" was that of Lee and Marlene Canter (1976), who developed what they called **assertive discipline**. Echoing the political activism of the time, the Canters spoke of reemphasizing teachers' rights, particularly rights to limiting students' inappropriate behavior. For the Canters, the assertive teacher is

> One who clearly and firmly communicates her wants and needs to her students, and is prepared to reinforce her words with appropriate actions. She responds in a manner which maximizes her potential to get her needs met, but in no way violates the best interests of the students. (p. 9)

Other examples included Ivar Lovaas (1977), G. R. Patterson (1982), and their coworkers who developed new, more sophisticated behavioral-learning approaches that proved effective with even the most hard to manage children and adolescents. In Chapter 5, we will have more to say about these more sophisticated behavioral-learning approaches.

Counseling Approaches

From the counseling tradition came a softer language and references to meeting students' needs, but the focus remained on teachers regaining control of individual children and their classrooms. For example, Dreikurs and Grey (1990) promoted providing "logical consequences" rather than punishments when students misbehaved—a more positive-sounding negative consequence than punishment but, from the point of view of many students, not totally different from punishment. After all, it may be logical for a student who dawdles during study period to be made to finish homework during recess; however, to the student, missing recess is apt to feel like a punishment. The main point here is that Dreikurs and Grey, like others from the clinical and counseling professions, focused on finding ways for teachers to control individual children, albeit in positive ways.

Nowhere is this theme of controlling in positive ways more evident than in the work of William Glasser (1969), whose books were widely read during the 1970s and continue to be read today. Glasser looked at children's and adolescents' misbehavior as symptomatic of their having unmet needs and negative internal pictures of school and learning. Furthermore, Glasser saw misbehaving children as apt to be lonely—especially when teachers continue to blame and punish.

According to Glasser (1969), the job of the teacher is to become a quality manager who meets children's needs in the same way that quality managers in American corporations meet employees' needs and improve the quality of the workplace. The quality manager functions to make work meaningful, so Glasser recommended giving children choices, holding class meetings to discuss classroom issues, and using cooperative learning—all to give children a sense of control over their work, which, in turn, makes work feel more meaningful. However, close inspection of Glasser's methods reveals teachers actually retaining a good deal of control and fostering a kind of individualism that, at times, may work against classrooms becoming democratic communities (Henry & Abowitz, 1998).

During the 1960s and 1970s, and continuing the theme of control, a good many research projects focused on leadership style (Brophy, 2006), the most influential being the projects of Diana Baumrind (1970, 1971). As discussed in Chapter 1, Baumrind categorized parenting styles into three types—authoritarian, authoritative, and permissive—and others used these three to evaluate teachers' styles as well. The results of several studies showed authoritative styles to be associated with the most positive outcomes. As mentioned before, the essential point derived from these studies is that adults should be demanding but, at the same time, responsive to children.

A third development during the 1960s and 1970s that directly influenced school discipline was the development of a more refined psychiatric system for diagnosing children's problems. Whereas before the categories were broad and rooted in psychoanalytic theory, from the 1960s on, the diagnostic systems became differentiated and theory free. Of particular relevance to school discipline were the so-called disruptive disorders: attention-deficit/hyperactivity disorder (ADHD) being the most important in terms of frequency.

These new labels for **disorders of childhood** were meant to be descriptive. However, the very nature of the term *disorder* suggested an underlying biological cause, so many educators came to see discipline problems as needing a biological (medical) solution. This was particularly true in the case of ADHD, where the solution could be sought in medications. Behavior management techniques could help, but ultimately medication and organic approaches would determine a child's or adolescent's long-term fate. In Chapter 10, we will have more to say about the medical model and organic approaches to school discipline.

In sum, the last half of the 20th century ushered in a variety of approaches to discipline, some designed to control children (e.g., behaviorist approaches), some designed to guide children (e.g., counseling approaches), and some designed to support long-term development (e.g., moral-constructivist approaches).

Ecological and Systems Approaches

The most recent trend has been to adopt ecological and systems approaches to classroom management. Jacob Kounin and Paul Gump (1958) are often credited with leading the way toward adopting ecological approaches. The most-cited scholar writing about systems approaches is Urie Bronfenbrenner (1989).

As will be discussed in Chapter 7, ecological approaches treat classrooms as organisms with a purpose and headed in a particular direction to achieve the goal of learning (Doyle, 2006). An ecological approach defines misbehavior as behavior that stops or redirects the intended direction in which the classroom has been headed. As mentioned in Chapter 1, the main finding from research inspired by this perspective has been that the key to managing misbehavior is to prevent misbehavior—largely in the way a teacher monitors the group but also in the way a teacher organizes time, space, the built environment, and the curriculum (Kounin, 1970). Again, we will have more to say about ecological approaches later on.

Systems approaches treat discipline problems as problems in the larger classroom or school system or as problems in the relationship between larger systems (e.g., school and family systems). So, for example, a teacher may be having an impossible time controlling her classroom not because of the nature of her students and not because of her lack of skills, but primarily because her approach to discipline and the approach demanded by school administrators conflict with one another.

The other major and recent trend has been to emphasize relationship building. There was a focus on relationship building in previous decades, especially in the late 19th-century kindergarten movement and, later on, in the mental hygiene movement. However, now the emphasis is on community building and the open and frequent use of moral terms such as *justice* and *care*. Put another way, more and more, classroom management is seen as essentially a moral endeavor. In Chapter 4, we will have more to say about these community and moral approaches to behavior and classroom management.

By the end of the 20th century, then, school discipline seemed to have come full circle. Just as Horace Mann opposed the Boston schoolmasters for their focus on control, today's community and constructivist approaches oppose the focus on control that dominated discussion in the 1960s and 1970s.

However, today there is greater commitment to managing classrooms of children and adolescents who differ significantly from one another in ability and culture. There is also unanimity among today's leading educators that, regardless of approach, we must make use of the best that research has to offer to (1) build positive relationships, (2) teach so that children learn, (3) support children's long-term development, (4) create organized learning environments, and (5) accommodate diversity. In the next several chapters, then, we will discuss how all five operate in today's approaches to behavior and classroom management.

Review

The late 20th century brought

(1) the cognitive revolution, with its emphasis on constructivist approaches to educating children;

(2) a variety of new counseling approaches to managing children and classrooms;

(3) approaches stemming from the behavioral-learning tradition that emphasized ways to control children;

(4) ecological approaches emphasizing ways to organize classroom and school settings to prevent problem behavior; and

(5) new commitments to educate and include diverse populations of children.

Summary

In contrast to a progress view of history, this chapter has taken the view that there is much to be learned from previous educators and that there is considerable continuity between the issues and debates in previous centuries and the issues and debates today. In addition, this chapter has shown how the thoughts and theories in today's leading approaches are rooted in the thoughts and theories found in the past. For example, today's constructivist approaches have their roots in early 20th-century progressive approaches, and today's behavioral-learning approaches have their roots in the focus on being scientific that characterized the child study movement. Finally, this chapter has shown how much approaches to discipline are shaped and influenced by changes in the larger society, such as the rapid urbanization of America that occurred in the late 19th century and the rapid social changes that occurred as a result of the civil rights movement in the 1960s and early 1970s.

A historical perspective is, then, crucial for understanding what is going on today with respect to behavior and classroom management. Without a historical perspective, we would not fully appreciate the complexity of the problems. And without an appreciation of the complexity of problems, we might easily become complacent or overly confident that we can make discipline problems go away. Since good people with good ideas confronting similar problems exist in every era, it is likely that the best we can do is to do our best to be as wise as the wisest in previous generations.

Web-Based Student Study Site

The companion Web site for *Approaches to Behavior and Classroom Management* can be found at www.sagepub.com/scarlettstudy.

Visit the Web-based student study site to enhance your understanding of the chapter content. The study materials include practice tests, flashcards, suggested readings, and Web resources.

Key Concepts

Accommodating the nature of the child

Assertive discipline

Calvinist

Character education

Child study movement

Constructivist approaches

Disorders of childhood

Enlightenment

Mental hygiene movement

Nature-nurture debate

Practice-to-habit theory

Progressive education

Unitarian

Discussion Questions

1. The chapter suggests that the 20th century increasingly showed a preference for "being scientific" with regard to behavior and classroom management and that the results of this preference are mixed; that is, not 100 percent positive. Do you agree, and can you say what you mean by "being scientific"? If possible, come up with two examples, one positive example and one negative, of an educator claiming to "be scientific" when talking about managing students' behavior.

2. This chapter suggests that often major changes in schools and the way we educate students come from societal changes outside schools, such as a sudden influx of new immigrants or a large-scale civil rights movement. Such societal changes can bring about major changes in behavior and classroom management. What societal changes do you see today that are directly or indirectly changing the way we think about control issues in general and behavior and classroom management in particular?

3. Though the American democratic political system calls for a "separation of church and state" and though parents and religious leaders, not teachers, have often been given the major responsibility for influencing children morally, religion and ethics have always figured directly or indirectly into schooling, disciplining children, and managing behavior and classrooms. Can you supply at least one clear example of a discussion today of behavior and/or classroom management that directly or indirectly reflects a religious or religious-moral perspective? What influence, if any, does religion or a faith tradition play in your perspective on behavior and classroom management?

PART II

Relationship Building

Today, virtually every educator agrees that building positive relationships with students and between students is essential. The differences have to do with the meaning of relationships, what it takes to build relationships, and whether relationship building should be the proper starting point and emphasis for explaining behavior and classroom management. In these next two chapters, we look at building positive teacher-student relationships as well as at creating classroom and school communities and at approaches that make relationship building central.

Chapter 3 looks at four main questions: "Why focus on the teacher-student relationship as the starting point and linchpin of behavior and classroom management?" "What constitutes positive teacher-student relationships?" "What methods foster positive teacher-student relationships?" and "How does diversity affect the meaning of positive teacher-student relationships?" In looking for answers to these four questions in particular, it should become clear that building positive teacher-student relationships is not easy, not only because often there are no set formulas but also because teachers are being asked to be more than competent professionals. They are being asked to also be strong and caring persons. This chapter, then, is as much about the character of teachers as it is about methods.

In Chapter 4, the focus widens to include the whole classroom, and sometimes the whole school, as we focus on approaches that consider building just, caring, and democratic communities to be central. For these approaches, behavior and classroom management is, essentially, a moral endeavor in which schools bear a special responsibility for preparing students to become responsible citizens in a democratic society. Finally, for these approaches, community building is an essential point of entry for ensuring cooperation and preventing problem behavior—in short, for optimally managing both behavior and classrooms.

Chapter 3

BUILDING POSITIVE TEACHER-STUDENT RELATIONSHIPS

Mr. Harlan, my sixth-grade science teacher, knew when to joke around and when to be serious. He also was extremely good at making the material fun. When learning about physics, we shot water balloons out of slingshots. In addition, he formed personal relationships with us by making an effort to get to know each student. He would often go around the class asking how our weekend was or how our other classes were going. He made an effort to come to sporting events and school plays in order to understand and support us. At lunchtime he had an open-door policy, and his office was usually filled with students chatting with him over lunch. Mr. Harlan had high expectations of us, and we all tried extremely hard in his class because we didn't want to disappoint him. Everyone was well-behaved because we felt we would be letting him down if we acted out. Because of the strong teacher-student relationship, we learned a lot in Mr. Harlan's class, and there were very few behavior problems.

Of all the recent changes in our talk about behavior and classroom management, perhaps the most dramatic change of all has been in how current discussions focus on building positive teacher-student relationships. This focus is nothing new. As we saw in Chapter 2, which discussed the kindergarten movement toward the end of the 19th century, building positive teacher-student relationships has always been on the minds of educators. However, today's discussions of building positive

CHAPTER OVERVIEW

Influence of Age on Building Teacher-Student Relationships
Relationships With Young Children
Relationships With Older Students

Influence of Context on Building Teacher-Student Relationships

Overarching Needs for Positive Teacher-Student Relationships
Showing Care
Exercising Authority and Communicating High Expectations

teacher-student relationships are grounded in theory and in research. So, the discourse today tends to focus on theory, research, and what can be measured.

The current focus on building positive teacher-student relationships has come about, in part, as a result of educators becoming dissatisfied with the results of the obedience-oriented approaches that became fashionable in the 1960s and 1970s, the most famous example being the Canters' (Canter & Canter, 1976) assertive discipline approach, although in a more recent work, Lee Canter (1996) has made it clear that the success of assertive discipline depends on first establishing rapport with students.

One of the most frequent criticisms of obedience-oriented approaches has been that while they foster obedience, they do not foster the self-regulation we ultimately want from responsible students (Weinstein, 1999). A less frequent criticism has been that obedience-oriented approaches may become addictive. That is, if they are used early and often, teachers may come to depend on obedience-oriented approaches to keep order. In Ronald Butchart's (1998a) words,

> While more research is needed, it appears that elementary schools have increasingly adopted behaviorist modes of control, with the result that secondary schools have been forced by students to move more and more toward *defensive teaching*. . . . Behaviorist modes of control lose their effectiveness through overuse . . . leaving secondary teachers little recourse but to teach defensively. (p. 9)[1]

Perhaps the most convincing argument against obedience-oriented approaches is that they create a negative climate not conducive to motivating students to learn and contribute. Obedience-oriented approaches make teachers into what William Glasser (1986) called *boss managers*. Here is an example of one teacher **teaching defensively** and being a **boss manager,** from Sue Cowley's (2001) book on methods for managing behavior problems:

> The teacher noticed that a few students in his ninth-grade class were chewing gum, which was not allowed. On one occasion, he noticed that one boy was chewing gum, so he went to the front of the classroom, picked up a wastepaper basket and held it under the boy's mouth, directing the boy to put the gum in the basket. The boy said he swallowed the gum, so the teacher warned him of what would happen if he were caught again.
>
> Not long afterward, the same situation arose. Instead of reacting as before, the teacher got the boy to come to him, and then leaned toward him and whispered while pointing to the basket: "Put the gum in there NOW, and don't give me 'I'm not chewing,' because I saw you. Stay behind for five minutes after the lesson to clean up my room. Any more rubbish from you, you'll be in a half-hour detention." (p. 151)

Cowley (2001) commends the teacher in this example for exerting control and authority when control and authority were being openly challenged. Nevertheless, though the teacher did, indeed, need to exert control and authority, the exchange between the student and the teacher is not the kind of exchange that does much to build a positive teacher-student relationship. And while every instance of exerting control and authority need not also build positive relationships, one would hope that there would be plenty of occasions that do both. Furthermore, it is not too far-fetched to assume that if most of a teacher's interactions with students are of the type illustrated in this example, the result will be a classroom that fails to motivate students to learn and cooperate.

This last point is the central point of approaches defined by their emphasis on establishing positive teacher-student relationships. These approaches have in common the assumption that everything starts with the teacher-student relationship. If that relationship is good, then there are possibilities for learning and cooperation. If it is not good, then subsequent methods, however thoughtful, are apt to fail. A good deal of recent research backs up this assumption (for a review, see Pianta, 2006), and even Lee Canter (1996) has agreed that teachers should first work to establish rapport with students before implementing assertive discipline.

One of the clearest explanations of why it makes good sense to think of the teacher-student relationship as the starting point and linchpin for successful behavior and classroom management was provided decades ago by Larry Brendtro (1969) in his essay "Establishing Relationship Beachheads," an essay originally intended for those working with **relationship-resistant** older children and adolescents in residential treatment centers. Brendtro distinguished between

PREVIEW

Assertive discipline will be discussed in more depth in Chapter 5 and later in Chapter 8.

three kinds of learning processes: learning through social reinforcers (e.g., **praise/encouragement**), learning through insight, and learning through imitating or identifying with another. His essay explains that for those processes to be activated, the teacher must become, in the eyes of students, a source of social reinforcers, a source of insight, and a desirable model to imitate, and these three together define what we should mean by a good teacher-student relationship.

Brendtro (1969) went on to show how those working with even relationship-resistant students can make building positive relationships between teachers and students into a full-fledged approach to behavior and classroom management by developing good communication with students, by overcoming barriers that students may put between themselves and teachers, and by making teachers more attractive models for students to imitate. The key, for him, was communication.

Brendtro's (1969) most practical suggestions included showing how occasional "small talk" with students can open lines of communication needed to develop a positive relationship and showing how educators can use humor and nonthreatening reactions to defuse charged situations when students challenge authority. However, Brendtro gave no specific methods for educators to employ, implying that much depends on educators being sensitive, exercising good judgment, and having good communication skills.

Today's educators and researchers want more specifics, or so it seems. Today, the assumption seems to be that we can, at least in principle, measure what it takes to build positive teacher-student relationships. In addition, today's educators put far more stress than did Brendtro on how the meaning of building positive teacher-student relationships changes with changes in age and context (Pianta, 2006).

INFLUENCE OF AGE ON BUILDING TEACHER-STUDENT RELATIONSHIPS

There are many ways to group by age. For our purposes, we need only distinguish between young children (roughly 3 to 6 years old) and older students (roughly 7 to 17). This distinction highlights how teachers often are called upon to meet the security needs of younger children and the autonomy needs of older students.

Relationships With Young Children

Building a positive teacher-student relationship with young children can mean making a child feel secure by feeling attached to a teacher. That is, young children often require that teacher-student relationships share features associated with secure attachments between parents and children, as is evident by their occasionally using teachers as "secure bases" to check in with ("Look, I've drawn a house!") and by their using teachers as sources of comfort when hurt, guides when confused, and allies when attacked (Scarlett, 1998).

When young children do not develop secure attachment relationships, they often misbehave (Greenberg & Speltz, 1988). Take the following as an example:

> Seth, age four, entered his Head Start class at midyear. His father was in prison, and his mother worked long hours. When not in school, Seth stayed with a babysitter who, unfortunately, directed all of her affection toward her own son.
>
> In the classroom, Seth played by himself, and when other children approached him, he often said, "Go away." At times he disrupted others' play, as when he would purposely kick over a classmate's block construction. With teachers, he ignored their directives and acted as if he were totally independent.
>
> Seth's problem was he did not have a secure attachment, either at home or at school. So, one teacher was assigned to foster an attachment relationship with him—by repeatedly marking when he was playing ("Seth, I see you drawing") and by encouraging Seth to "check in" ("When you finish drawing, come get me. I want to see what you have drawn."), by going out of her way to provide him help when help was needed, by her occasionally co-playing with him, and by her doing all the little and not so little things that a sensitive parent might do for a young child.
>
> Without additional discipline or behavior management, Seth's behavior improved dramatically, and he became not only a cooperative child but also a positive leader in the class. (Scarlett, 1998, p. 37)

Does this mean that teachers of the very young should always act like parents to students? Not at all. As Lilian Katz explained (1989), there are and should be distinct differences between teaching and mothering. For example, it is fine for mothers to be focused on their individual child, but teachers must focus on the group as well as individuals. And it is fine for mothers to be intent always on optimizing their attachment with their child, but teachers must strike a balance between optimum attachment and optimum detachment. In Table 3.1, these and additional distinctions between mothering and teaching are defined.

Nevertheless, though teachers need not think of themselves as mothers or fathers, young children can treat them as mothers or fathers, and this is generally a good thing. Women teaching kindergarten and first grade often report instances when children inadvertently call them "mom," another indication that at young ages, children attach to their teachers. In Katz's (1989) words, "It may be possible for young children to feel very attached to their teachers . . . without teachers responding at the same level of intensity" (p. 54). And in special cases,

TABLE 3.1   Dimensions Distinguishing Mothering From Teaching

Role Dimension	Mothering	Teaching
Scope of functions	Diffuse and limitless	Specific and limited
Intensity of affect	High	Low
Attachment	Optimum attachment	Optimum detachment
Rationality	Optimum irrationality	Optimum rationality
Spontaneity	Optimum spontaneity	Optimum intentionality
Partiality	Partial	Impartial
Scope of responsibility	Individual	Whole group

Source: Katz (1989).

such as the case of Seth, actively fostering an attachment can be a preferred method. In any case, young children behaving in ways that indicate they feel attached to their teacher is, we can assume, generally a sign of there being a positive teacher-student relationship.

Take, for example, the well-known practice of young children checking in and announcing to their parents what they are doing at any given moment—something akin to an infant getting physically close to a parent after a period of exploring—or what the attachment theorists call "using the mother as a secure base from which to explore" (Ainsworth, Blehar, Waters, & Wall, 1978). Here is an example of a 4-year-old "checking in" and, in analogous fashion, using her teacher as a "secure base":

> Heather and Marianne, two delightful four-year-olds, busied themselves making "cookies" from Play-Doh. While pounding and shaping, they fantasized together about the party they were to give—who to ask, what to wear, and so forth. Suddenly, without warning, Heather turned in her seat and yelled to her teacher, "We're making cookies!" The teacher nodded and in an approving voice responded, "Oh, you're making cookies." Heather seemed pleased by the response and turned to resume play with Marianne. (Scarlett, 1998, p. 32)

The relevance of such observations becomes clear when it is realized that many preschoolers with behavior problems often do not "check in" and do not use teachers as a secure base, as was evident in the example of Seth. Here is a related observation made by one longtime consultant to early childhood centers:

> My experience has been that many disruptive, uncooperative children do not check in enough, do not share with teachers what they are doing and accomplishing. It simply does not occur to them that teachers might be interested. To counteract this mistaken belief and to cultivate checking in, we can do more than simply reinforce infrequent moments of checking in. We can ask a child to check in and come get us when some project is finished. We can make clear that we are interested. (Scarlett, 1998, p. 35)

However, the **attachment to teachers,** or attachment-like relationship between the teacher and the young child, is not what is called for later on. Later on, students, especially adolescents, may be defensive about cultivating a relationship with a teacher that has feelings associated with attachment. That does not, however, preclude teachers from forming positive relationships with older children and adolescents. It means, simply, that the meaning of positive teacher-student relationships changes with age.

Relationships With Older Students

Later on, the meaning of positive teacher-student relationships is captured more by a teacher's showing care for students in the way teachers challenge and guide students to learn and develop. Here is an example taken from the popular movie *Stand and Deliver* (Menendez, 1988) of a teacher, himself Hispanic, teaching a math class of mostly Hispanic high school students. Though it is an example from a movie and not real life, it nevertheless captures what goes on in classrooms of older students where teachers build good relationships with older students by teaching in positive ways:

T: (While playfully speaking in a stereotypical Mexican accent) This is basic math, but basic math is too easy for you burros—so I'm going to teach you algebra, 'cause I'm the champ, and if the only thing you know how to do is add and subtract, you'll only be prepared to do one thing—pump gas.

S: Hey, ripping off a gas station is better than working in one.

T: (While playfully sounding like a gang leader) Hey, Mozela, I'm a tough guy. Tough guys don't do math. Tough guys do deep-fried chicken for a living. You want a wing or a leg, man?

T: (A little while later) Minus two plus two equals?

S: Zero.

T: Zero, you're right, simple. That's it—minus two plus two equals zero. . . . Did you know that neither the Greeks nor the Romans were capable of using the concept of zero? It was your ancestors, the Mayans, who first contemplated the zero, the absence of value—true story. You burros have math in your blood.

In this example, the teacher's mocking style and humor wonderfully match that of his adolescent students; however, both his serious purpose and competence make clear that in adopting the students' style and humor, he remains the teacher who can make them better. All this is what adolescent students need and say they need for there to be a positive teacher-student relationship (Hoy & Weinstein, 2006).

> ## Review
>
> Age has an important influence on teacher-student relationships:
>
> (1) For young children, relationships are similar to secure attachments between parents and children.
>
> (2) For older students, relationships depend on teachers caring for, challenging, and guiding students so that they learn and develop and, often, on teachers having a sense of humor.

INFLUENCE OF CONTEXT ON BUILDING TEACHER-STUDENT RELATIONSHIPS

For material related to this concept, go to Video Clip 3.1 on the Student Resource CD bound into the back of your textbook.

The last example, from *Stand and Deliver*, also says something about how what constitutes a positive teacher-student relationship often differs from one school or cultural context to another. In some schools, it can mean being somewhat relaxed and informal. In other schools, it can mean just the opposite. Each school is apt, then, to have a preferred style, which inevitably influences how both teachers and students come to define their relationships with one another.

The above example also illustrates how culture figures into how teacher-student relationships are defined. The culture of the adolescents in the previous example demanded a tough but caring, no-nonsense approach, not the approach adopted by many middle-class teachers in suburban schools. In the following example, we see something similar.

Cynthia Ballenger (1998), a sociolinguist (someone who explains group behavior by explaining how groups use language), spent years teaching in a predominantly Haitian school. She found that when she adopted a progressive, constructivist approach to teaching that used conflicts between children to promote negotiation and verbal self-expression, her Haitian-American students reacted as if she were giving them license to misbehave, and so they misbehaved.

Cynthia Ballenger

Source: Cynthia Ballenger.

While observing Haitian teachers' classrooms, Ballenger (1998) noticed that these classrooms were orderly, and the children were well-behaved. It was at that moment that Ballenger realized that the overriding problem was not with the children but with the mismatch between her approach to discipline and what the children were used to.

In discussions with Haitian teachers and with Haitian parents, Ballenger (1998) learned that Haitians are concerned that American teachers are not controlling Haitian children adequately. This was especially evident when one Haitian teacher arrived at her school and watched a teacher telling a Haitian-American child that she needed to go to her classroom. The child refused and kicked the teacher. The Haitian teacher had had enough. She asked the school's director to bring her all the Haitian-American children right away. The director and she gathered all the children into one large common room. The following is the text of what she said to the children:

Teacher: Does your mother let you bite?

Children: No.

Teacher: Does your father let you punch kids?

Children: No.

Teacher: Do you kick at home?

Children: No.

Teacher: You don't respect anyone, not the teachers who play with you or the adults that work upstairs. You need to respect adults, even people you see on the streets. You are taking good ways you learn at home and not bringing them to school. You are taking the bad ways you are learning at school and taking them home. You are not going to do this anymore. Do you want your parents to be ashamed of you? (p. 148)

The content and form of these conversations are crucially different from what most North American teachers usually do in the same situation, and they are different from North American ways of exercising authority. Most North American teachers are concerned with the articulation of individual feelings and with being fair. In contrast, Haitian teachers are more concerned with articulating a child's connections to those who care for the child, especially parents, teachers, and God. Furthermore, Haitian teachers are less concerned with how a child is feeling and more concerned with a child's ability to follow directions and respect elders.

In Haitian reactions to misbehavior, immediate consequences are not made explicit. Haitian teachers do not explain why they are against hitting and biting. Rather, they refer to such behavior as "bad" and then explain the long-term consequences for bad behavior in general; for example, bringing shame to the family. Children are told to be good for the sake of being good. There are no larger explanations or negotiations. In contrast, American teachers often appear to be giving children new information in misbehavior situations. Furthermore, North American teachers explain misbehavior as if misbehavior is a result of feelings that the child has failed to identify and control.

Haitian teachers believe that children are able to share adults' understanding of what constitutes bad behavior. In this belief, they have high expectations for children and because of this belief, they use rhetorical questions, such as, "Does your mother let you bite kids? Does your father let you talk back?" Haitian children understand their role without difficulty; they repeat the expected answers in unison. There is no choice of response. There is no discussion about feelings.

Through our North American cultural lens, it may be difficult to see the love and warmth in the Haitian authoritarian approach to showing care, exercising authority, and building positive teacher-student relationships. However, that love and warmth is apparent in the smiles and behavior of the Haitian-American children thriving in their own communities. Different approaches to building positive teacher-student relationships may change the meaning of positive teacher-student relationships, but they do not change the need for showing care and exercising authority while communicating high expectations.

OVERARCHING NEEDS FOR POSITIVE TEACHER-STUDENT RELATIONSHIPS

Therefore, regardless of age and context, the two overarching needs that have to be met if there are to be positive teacher-student relationships are **showing care** and **exercising authority** while **communicating high expectations**. Again, these aren't just the needs mentioned by educators. They are the needs mentioned by students as well (Hoy & Weinstein, 2006). We will look more closely at what it means to show care and exercise authority while communicating high expectations so as to build positive teacher-student relationships.

Showing Care

Increasingly, showing care has become a major theme running throughout today's discussions of teacher-student relationships (Charney, 2002; Noddings, 2002; Watson & Battistich, 2006), which means that even as the emphasis has been on being research minded, there is at least a tacit recognition that good behavior and classroom management rests ultimately on something that is difficult to measure; namely, showing care.

Showing care is difficult to measure for two main reasons. First, showing care refers not to a set of methods or behaviors but to an attitude and style of the teacher and an experience of the student. Second, showing care comes in many forms, and some of these forms may, at first, appear to be the opposite of showing care, as in the previous example of Haitian teachers showing care by being tough and demanding.

Throughout this chapter, and in subsequent chapters as well, we show how care is at the core of developing positive teacher-student relationships that matter deeply, not simply for the short term, but for the long term as well. To illustrate what we mean, here is one man's account of a caring incident that happened over 40 years ago, when he was in eighth grade:

> It had been a rough grading period, especially in math, and a rough time at home. Then at recess one day, a teacher came up to me and said, "Bill, I hear you're having a hard time in math. I'm really sorry"—and then he walked away. I remember his saying this to me like it was yesterday because, I suppose, it meant a lot to me then, as it means a lot to me now.

Showing care, then, can have a powerful, positive, and lasting effect, as this example clearly shows.

Communicating Positively

Showing care can also be expressed by communicating positively. Communicating positively can mean something simple, such as making sure that when communicating with students, positive statements outnumber negative statements.

Thomas Gordon

The research shows that this matters (Becker, Engelmann, & Thomas, 1975). However, communicating positively has different meanings and different effects, including the effects of feeling known, understood, accepted, and supported.

Gordon and Teacher Effectiveness Training. Feeling known and understood comes about when teachers, from the very first time children and adolescents walk into their classrooms, address students by their names; when high school teachers take time to meet with students individually; when teachers of all grades show interest in students' passions and interests—the list is long. For many, the single most important way that students feel known and understood may be when teachers listen. Nowhere do we find this message about listening more clearly explained and emphasized than in the writings of Thomas Gordon (2003), author of the book *Teacher Effectiveness Training*, which was widely read during the 1970s and 1980s and is still referred to often today.

Gordon (2003) came from the counseling tradition associated with the "client-centered" approach of Carl Rogers (1951). The central idea in this approach is that all of us, children and adolescents included, have within ourselves the strength and wherewithal to change, grow, and develop, but we may be momentarily blocked from developing by having **conditions of worth** placed upon us by others. Conditions of worth are imposed when the message from others is that so long as we measure up to others' standards, we are worthy or fine. So, both negative judgments, such as "You are being inconsiderate," as well as praise, such as "Wonderful that you are being considerate," are messages about conditions of worth.

Given this analysis of the root cause of persistent problem behavior, the logical prescription is to communicate to children and adolescents a kind of acceptance that is almost a synonym for care. This approach does not deny the existence of problem behavior; rather, it calls for a radical reaching beyond problem behavior to continuously show respect for and trust in the person.

Gordon (2003) provided teachers with two big ideas for dealing with problem behavior by showing respect, trust, and unconditional *positive regard* (Rogers's [1951] term for acceptance). The first idea is **taking ownership of problems.** Teachers take ownership of problems when they communicate with **"I" messages** that stick to the facts and avoid negative evaluations of students. For example, if two students are whispering in the back of the room while a teacher is explaining the next assignment, following Gordon, the teacher might say, "Jimmy and Billy, when you whisper while I am explaining an assignment, I worry because I know you will miss what I am saying, and then I'll have to repeat myself."

These "I" messages have three effects: first, they locate the problem in the teacher. That is, they communicate that the teacher "owns" the problem (of feeling worried). The effect is to make the communication more personal. Second, they avoid casting students in the role of bad guys. Third, they leave the solution up to students.

This third point may not be clear enough by itself, so Gordon (2003) explains that whenever a teacher gives a "You" message (e.g., If the teacher in the previous hypothetical example were to say, "Stop whispering and pay attention"), the implicit message is that the students can't or won't find a solution on their own; they must be given the solution by someone else and made to behave. In contrast, "I" messages communicate that the teacher assumes the students, once they understand the problem that whispering causes, will find and carry out a solution on their own.

Gordon's (2003) second big idea is **active listening**. When listening actively, educators (and here we include school psychologists, reading specialists, and all those involved in helping children and adolescents in school settings) not only listen carefully with empathy and acceptance to what students are saying, they provide proof that they have understood by feeding back what students have said to them to make sure they have understood correctly. Active listening is especially important when students are upset and feel misunderstood.

The paradox Gordon (2003) points to is the fact that rather than reinforcing misbehavior or leaving students stuck in their problem, active listening often frees students to problem solve. But even if no perfect solution emerges from active listening, the experience of feeling listened to and understood can be a powerful and positive experience for students, making future cooperation more likely.

When first hearing what Gordon (2003) is suggesting, many teachers do not believe these methods of giving "I" messages and active listening can possibly succeed, so they are surprised when their initial experiments with "I" messages and active listening often help considerably. Indeed, Gordon's advice has helped many teachers regain control of their classrooms, and in positive ways, a conclusion that comes not just from anecdotes and informal observation but also from research (Carducci, 1976; Peterson, Loveless, Knapp, Basta, & Anderson, 1979).

Review

Gordon provided teachers with two big ideas for dealing with problem behavior while showing respect, trust, and unconditional positive regard:

(1) Taking ownership of problems through "I" messages

(2) Active listening

Furthermore, and consistent with the suggestion that we remove conditions of worth from classroom teaching, several studies have shown the benefits of replacing nonspecific praise with encouragement (Hitz & Driscoll, 1988). This distinction between nonspecific praise and encouragement is subtle, but real. Nonspecific praise often refers to achievements; for example, saying, "Nice picture" to a preschooler who has just completed a drawing. Encouragement often refers to specific feedback about effort and process; for example, saying "You worked hard on that picture, and I see you made different kinds of lines over here: straight lines, curvy lines, short lines, and lines that go in different directions."

As can be seen in this example, encouragement also has cognitive, and not simply emotional, meaning and value because encouragement of this sort helps provide students with a language they can use to help them describe, understand, and evaluate what they are doing. Nancy Smith (1983) makes essentially this same point in her advice to teachers on how best to provide feedback to young children about their drawings.

So, with respect to building positive teacher student relationships, Gordon (2003) gives us two methods in particular—the method of using "I" statements and the method of active listening—while he also gives us ways and reasons for using encouragement, not praise, to establish positive teacher-student relationships.

Reframing. Reframing is another method for communicating positively and for building positive teacher-student relationships. As mentioned in Chapter 1, reframing occurs when a teacher sees a student or group of students doing something negative, but first communicates something good in the situation. Doing so may be enough to get a child or adolescent to change something we normally would call a behavior problem—as we saw in Chapter 1's example of a teacher saying "Jimmy likes to dance" in response to Jimmy's jumping up at meeting time and starting to dance.

PREVIEW

We will have more to say about reframing in Chapter 8, where reframing becomes a featured method in the classroom systems approach to behavior and classroom management.

With reframing, the wording will change depending on age and situation, but the principle remains the same: to find and communicate something positive before setting limits, suggesting alternatives, or otherwise managing students' behavior. Reframing does so because central to that approach is the need to change the interpersonal system that defines some student or group as being a "problem." In using a systems approach, reframing solves this problem by redefining the situation so that there is no longer a problem or, at least, no longer a problem student.

However, when using individual-oriented approaches emphasizing positive teacher-student relationships, reframing is more important as a way to keep things positive, to make it more likely that students will want to cooperate and learn. That is, the meaning and purpose of reframing changes as we go from a systems approach to an individual-oriented approach focusing on building positive teacher-student relationships. Once again, we see that different kinds of approaches can employ the same method, but the meaning of the method is apt to change from one approach to another.

Showing Interest. Finally, with respect to developing teacher-student relationships through communicating positively, educators do well when they mark what students are interested in and passionate about and when they occasionally reverse roles and let students teach them. Here, the marking can be as simple and straightforward as when a teacher says to a 3-year-old building with blocks, "I see you made a tower" or as complex and subtle as when a teacher listens carefully to an adolescent explaining the various strategies he uses when playing his favorite video game.

Interest is also shown in actions. For example, many teachers take time to have lunch with students and, outside of school, attend students' athletic, musical, or other extracurricular events. Some visit students' homes and attend community events important to both students and their families. These and other actions all show interest in students as persons.

Whatever the occasion or child's age, getting to know a child's or adolescent's likes and interests and validating those likes and interests by **showing interest** can have a powerful and positive effect, as this cartoon is meant to convey.

One easy and effective method for cultivating a positive teacher-student relationship is the method of marking what a child is interested in or is accomplishing.

Being Playful, Interesting, and "Fun"

Although students expect teachers to control the class and exercise their authority, the research on student perspectives indicates they also hope their teachers are playful, interesting, and fun (Hoy & Weinstein, 2006). However, the meaning of being playful, interesting, and fun changes with students' age. Here is a teacher being interesting while conversing with a 3-year-old during snack time:[2]

T: I like peanut butter and jelly sandwiches. Do you like peanut butter and jelly sandwiches?

S: Yes.

T: I like them with the crust cut off. How about you?

S: I like them with the crust on.

This conversation went on for a while longer, with each participant exploring the details of eating a peanut butter and jelly sandwich, apparently a subject that the child was or became quite interested in.

Here is an example of a teacher of older students being both interesting and playful:[3]

In one middle school, the seventh-grade teacher was a big, powerful man who could intimidate with his size and power. However, in this school, he was a beloved teacher because he often intimidated playfully. For example, during an afternoon break, he and two students made a film of a skit thought up by the students. The skit involved the teacher tantruming after discovering that someone had stolen his snacks. It lasted about 10 minutes, and during most of that time, the teacher chased a student suspected of stealing his snacks. As teacher and student ran throughout the school building, the film captured the facial expressions of astonished classmates who did not know what was going on. In the end, the film became a school classic and another example of this teacher's ability to be playful and still be a professional.

Touch

Touch and physical contact used to be mentioned often among the suggestions and methods for developing positive teacher-student relationships and managing effectively. For example, in Redl and Wineman's (1965) widely read book, *Controls From Within*, they write,

> We have noticed sometimes that children, even of older ages, may retain the baby's original approach to what does and does not constitute security and ego support and protection against anxiety. Thus, putting the arm around the youngster's shoulder or patting him on the shoulder in a friendly way while making a limiting demand or accompanying the challenge to "come on, take it easy, snap out of it," by shoulder pats of a friendly nature may make all the difference between failure and success. (p. 165)

As another example, one of George Scarlett's fondest memories of high school in the 1960s is being on the wrestling team and having the wrestling coaches (who were also classroom teachers) grab his arm and playfully express how strong he was. He wasn't all that strong, but the gesture was nonetheless much appreciated, and certainly it made his relationships with teachers more positive.

However, the times have changed. During the 1980s, a series of sensational trials involving day care providers accused of abusing young children changed how educators think about touch and physical contact—even though in the vast majority of cases, the accusations proved false.

As a result of these sensational trials, educators today are wary of touching or making physical contact even with very young children—as exemplified in Joseph Tobin's (1997) account of an incident of "moral panic" that occurred while he was carrying out a research project in a class of 4-year-olds:

> One afternoon I stayed late, reading stories to the last children to be picked up. As I read, tired children leaned against me. One girl settled into my lap, with her thumb in her mouth and her eyes half closed, barely listening. Parents drifted into the room, calling out their children's names to take them home. Out of the corner of my eye, I spotted a woman entering the room who I thought was the mother of the girl in my lap. In a flash I straightened

Sensational Trials in the 1980s: The McMartin Case

In the 1980s, a number of sex abuse trials changed the way educators thought about the use of touch in schools. The most famous occurred in California and focused on the McMartin family, who ran a day care center. The family and staff were investigated and tried for sexually abusing the children in their care. The investigation was initiated because of accusations made by a parent who was later diagnosed with schizophrenia. What sustained the investigations and trial were diagnoses made by professionals not trained in diagnosing sexual abuse and professionals who used methods for interviewing young children that were later judged to be both unscientific (nonobjective) and developmentally inappropriate. Also, politicians and newspaper reporters used the investigations and trial to promote their own interests. Finally, the then-popular concept of repressed memories allowed investigators to discount the children's statements that they were never abused. In the end, and after one of the longest and most costly investigations and trials in American history, many children were falsely diagnosed as having been abused, the McMartin family was put through excruciating pain and suffering, and the main defendant, Ray McMartin, spent five years in jail—all without anyone being actually convicted of a crime because there was never the evidence needed to establish that a crime had been committed.

up and relocated the little girl on the rug in front of me. When the child ran over to greet her mother, I followed. Unsure whether this mother knew who I was and why I was there, I awkwardly introduced myself.

I was shaken by this event. A woman entering the classroom to pick up her daughter had inspired a sense of panic in me. Worse, my panicked feeling had led to a panicky reaction—pushing the girl from my lap, as if we were doing something shameful, and then explaining myself as if I were somehow suspect. I felt humiliated by having allowed myself to feel so afraid. (p. 120)

Unfortunately, Tobin's reaction is now a common reaction, and so the climate today often brings words of caution with respect to physical contact and touch, as evidenced in Vern and Louise Jones's (Jones & Jones, 2004) suggestion:

We strongly believe the professionally responsible decision is to be cautious. . . . Certainly, teachers must be careful not to touch students in ways that make students uncomfortable. . . . Additionally, teachers need to guard against situations in which students may misinterpret teacher behavior or in which the rare student may fabricate an event to obtain attention or "get back" at a teacher. One good rule of thumb is to have others around whenever you are working with a student. (p. 93)

With cautionary remarks such as this, it is no wonder that physical contact and touch are not high on today's lists of ways to show care. Perhaps in the future this will change. As the wisdom from previous eras indicates, there are reasons to hope for change.

REFLECT In your own experience as a student, can you remember a teacher who was remarkable for the way he or she developed positive relationships with students? If you can, how did this teacher develop positive relationships? What effect did the positive relationships have on behavior and classroom management? Did this teacher manage in ways described here or in different ways?

Exercising Authority and Communicating High Expectations

In Chapter 1, we said that educators today are apt to reject authoritarian approaches to behavior and classroom management—at least in the way they talk, if not in the way they actually teach. However, this does not mean that today's educators embrace permissive approaches that place few demands on students. On the contrary, students (at least students beyond the earliest grades) and educators want teachers to exercise authority and expect much from students (Hoy & Weinstein, 2006).

Exercising Authority

To exercise authority is not to mechanically apply some management method. Nor is it to threaten and be mean. To exercise authority is to lead, and to lead means, in part, to adopt a serious and confident style that commands respect, not fear. The Canters (Canter & Canter, 1976) called this "assertive discipline," but really what they were referring to is teachers who know how to exercise authority.

Exercising authority need not be done in negative, uncaring ways—as we have already seen in Cindy Ballenger's (1998) study of Haitian teachers. Here is another example, of a first-grade teacher, Kristen Willand, exercising authority in a positive, caring way with her student, Dennis:

> In the beginning, Dennis tested our relationship and agreements. For example, during the first week, once while Dennis worked at the computer with another child, he refused to give the other child a turn. And when she

pleaded her case, Dennis punched her in the arm, which prompted my instigating the usual talk about what could have been accomplished using words instead of fists. After this talk, I reminded Dennis of the agreement about leaving the room if he hurt someone. As I spoke, I tried to be as empathic as possible, with my face and tone of voice as well as with my words. And I tried to show that I was as upset as he was over his having to leave the classroom:

"Do you remember what we decided would happen if you hurt anyone?" He nodded and remained serious as I continued. "Now I have to call Mrs. Alexander because that's what we agreed to do if this happened. But this is your classroom, and this is where you belong. And we're right in the middle of math workshop. I know you really like it, and you're so good at that math computer game. And now you're going to have to miss your time there. I am very sad that you have to miss the rest of math workshop; I hope you calm down very quickly with Mrs. Alexander so that you don't miss anything else. This is where you belong."

Dennis said nothing but watched me intently. Then he followed me quietly to the telephone. We waited by the door for Mrs. Alexander; I repeated to her what I had said to him. (Scarlett, 1998, p. 177)

As is evident in this example, exercising authority and showing care can go hand in hand. Indeed, they must go hand in hand if there is to be a positive teacher-student relationship.

For material related to this concept, go to Video Clip 3.2 on the Student Resource CD bound into the back of your textbook.

This linking of positive teacher-student relationships not just to the warm and fuzzy concept of showing care but also to the not-so-warm and fuzzy concept of exercising authority has been an especially hot topic among those writing about teaching minority students from low-income families where parenting style is more likely to be authoritarian. As we have seen in the example of Cindy Ballenger's (1998) teaching, some students require more toughness from teachers than the average middle-class student. And several writers who focus on teaching African American children from low-income families have made similar points about toughness and the need to exercise greater or more explicit authority. For example, Lisa Delpit (1995) argues that, in contrast to most middle-class Euro-American children and adolescents, many African American children and adolescents from low-income families demand more direct expressions of power and authority from their teachers. She explains that these children and adolescents look for teachers to command respect through the power they demonstrate as *persons*, power earned by the way teachers conduct themselves rather than power given to them by the role they fill.

It is hard for many teachers from middle-class backgrounds to understand the very real affection held by some children and adolescents for the kind of tough but caring approach Delpit (1995) and others are advocating. And it is even harder for many to imitate this toughness because, in their minds, toughness is so closely associated with being cold and uncaring. However, the phenomenon exists, so educators need to be sensitive and respectful when a tough but caring approach is needed.

There is, though, a danger in trying to exercise more authority in order to be tough on students from a minority culture. The danger is that the students' culture can get disrespected, and the students themselves can get labeled "bad." We will have more to say about this danger in both Chapters 8 (the classroom systems approach) and Chapter 9 (cultural approaches).

Communicating High Expectations

Communicating high expectations is something positive, not negative—assuming the expectations are within the reach of students (are developmentally appropriate). After all, to expect little from someone can be the worst of insults.

Furthermore, communicating high expectations goes hand in hand with exercising authority and showing care. For example, teacher Willand communicated to Dennis that she expected him to find better solutions than hitting when he became frustrated. Her expectations of Dennis were instrumental in Dennis's managing his emotions and, as a result, in his becoming integrated into the classroom. Furthermore, they were one reason she and Dennis developed such a positive relationship.

This message about communicating high expectations is not simply a message rooted in logic and common sense. It is a message rooted in research as well. Robert Pianta (2006), when summarizing the research on the effects of teachers expecting much from their students, put it this way: "When teachers hold high, generalized expectations for student achievement, students tend to achieve more, experience a greater sense of self-esteem and competence as learners, and resist involvement in problem behaviors during both childhood and adolescence" (p. 693).

REFLECT   Have you ever experienced or observed a very tough, demanding teacher who seemed to also command the respect and even affection of students? If you have, how did this come about? How did the teacher's being tough and demanding translate into students feeling positively toward the teacher? How did this relate to behavior and classroom management?

Review

Creating positive teacher-student relationships depends on many factors, including

(1) age of the child;

(2) school and culture;

(3) showing care by communicating positively; being playful, interesting, and fun; and touch;

(4) exercising authority; and

(5) communicating high expectations.

Summary

Here, we saw how building positive teacher-student relationships can become the defining emphasis of an approach to behavior and classroom management. Here, too, we saw that despite there being differences in the way the teacher-student relationship is defined, there is general agreement that positive teacher-student relationships have to do with showing care, exercising authority, and communicating high expectations.

However, it is one thing to emphasize the need to build positive teacher-student relationships through showing care, exercising authority, and communicating high expectations and quite another to specify how, exactly, this should be done. In this chapter, we have tried to show that doing all three is a complicated process requiring not only a good many methods but also teachers who have the right attitude and style. There are, it seems, no formulas for developing positive teacher-student relationships because relationships demand something from us as persons.

That said, and as this chapter illustrates, there are plenty of examples of teachers building positive relationships with their students that we can take as guides. And, as the evidence suggests, doing so makes good sense because there is much to be said for good teacher-student relationships being featured in any approach. Without such relationships, it is hard to conceive of a teacher being successful in managing behavior and classrooms.

However, the teacher-student relationship is not the only kind of relationship that matters. Peer relations matter, as do the combined relationships in a classroom and school that create classroom and school communities. Therefore, in Chapter 4, we turn to a second focus of relationship building; namely, a focus on building classroom and school communities.

Web-Based Student Study Site

The companion Web site for *Approaches to Behavior and Classroom Management* can be found at www.sagepub.com/scarlettstudy.

Visit the Web-based student study site to enhance your understanding of the chapter content. The study materials include practice tests, flashcards, suggested readings, and Web resources.

Key Concepts

Active listening

Attachment to teachers

Boss manager

Checking in

Communicating high expectations

Conditions of worth

Exercising authority

"I" messages

Praise/encouragement

Relationship-resistant

Showing care

Showing interest

Taking ownership of problems

Teaching defensively

Discussion Questions

1. Everyone talks about the need to form positive teacher-student relationships, but often what exactly this means remains unspoken and unclear. What did *positive teacher-student relationships* mean to you before you read this chapter, and how did your previous understanding differ from the discussion and definition in this chapter?

2. Much has been made of teacher-student relationships depending on how teachers communicate with students—positively or negatively, in ways that show care or do not show care, in ways that make students feel understood or not feel understood, and in ways that say teacher and students share control. Can you identify times when a teacher communicated positively and other times when a teacher communicated negatively, in terms of showing care, making students feel understood, and sharing control? Finally, can you identify times when teachers knowing or not knowing your name made a difference—when it had some definite effect on you?

3. What is your experience of teachers using touch as a way to relate to students? In your schooling, was it a common experience or was it rare? Was it positive or negative? If it was positive, how did touch work to make things better? If it was

negative, how did touch work to make things worse? What role, if any, do you see touch playing in behavior and classroom management? If possible, find out the policy on touch at any of the schools you attended, or find some other example of policy guiding educators in the use of touch.

1. By *behaviorist*, Butchart means obedience oriented, though those using behavioral-learning approaches object to this conflating of the two, as will become evident in Chapter 5, when behavioral-learning approaches are discussed in some depth.
2. An observation made by Scarlett.
3. An observation made by Scarlett.

Chapter 4

COMMUNITY APPROACHES

During one morning meeting in Judy Lazarus's first-grade classroom, children listened intently to one another telling about their bedtime routines. Their talk was mostly about troublesome fantasies that made going to bed so difficult: fantasies of witches, monsters, snakes, and the like. But the talk was also about active empathizing and providing helpful suggestions for dealing with the fantasies: placing a flashlight under the pillow, concentrating on pleasant thoughts, and so forth. The sharing was remarkable for the way the children listened and empathized with one another, but it was hardly an accident, for in this classroom, the children were constantly encouraged to listen, share, and empathize.

The opening example describes a classroom where the approach to classroom and behavior management is best defined as one that focuses on building a classroom **community**. The children in this example were used to being encouraged to listen carefully and to respond with empathy and care. Heady stuff for young children, but professional teachers know how to make it good stuff even for the very young.

With respect to behavior problems, the premise behind this approach is that if a group of students and educators care for one another and respect one another's rights, then it is less likely that there will be serious behavior problems. In other words, building community is a way to manage behavior problems proactively.

However, community approaches aim at something higher than preventing behavior problems and maintaining order. They also aim at developing better people, with "better" defined in moral terms and in terms of active citizenship.

For material related to this concept, go to Video Clip 4.1 on the Student Resource CD bound into the back of your textbook.

Again, heady stuff, but not stuff that is above what even very young children can begin to appreciate and adopt as their own.

Here, then, the focus widens as we consider ways to foster positive relationships not simply between a particular dyad, such as between a teacher and student. Here, the focus is on building positive relationships throughout classrooms and schools, relationships that define classrooms and schools as communities.

This focus on community building treats behavior and classroom management as essentially a moral endeavor as well as an endeavor to teach students what it means to become responsible, caring citizens. The aim of citizenship links community approaches to the American ideal of a democratic community. To adopt a community approach is, then, to support children's and adolescents' learning how to behave not only in classrooms and schools but also in the larger, democratic society.

JUST, CARING, AND DEMOCRATIC (CLASSROOM AND SCHOOL) COMMUNITIES

The concern for community building and citizenship is nothing new in American public schools. You may recall the discussion in Chapter 2 of Horace Mann's concern that public schools should be for more than academic learning, that they should also be for developing free men and women who can govern themselves while contributing to the common good. From the beginning, then, American public schools have espoused the goal of supporting moral (character) development and citizenship.

Just and Caring

Over the years, what has changed is not the espoused goal so much as the meaning of the goal and the commitment and means to achieving the goal. For example, there has always been disagreement over what is the wellspring of morality and character development. Is it obedience demanded by teachers' authoritarian control? Is it teachers and parents modeling and teaching virtues such as honesty and humility? Is it students developing appreciation of rules and abstract moral principles? Or is it caring relationships that provide motivation to be moral?

Recently, more and more educators have been adopting the last option as being the most likely wellspring. Not *caring about* but *caring for* has become a central topic in discussions of moral education (Noddings, 2002, p. 215). This represents a shift in emphasis. Justice had traditionally been the main emphasis in talk about moral and character development and the development of democratic communities. Justice is about rights—rights defining individual freedom and rights defining the common good. Care is about connections. The need for care and not simply for justice comes from the fact that a community can be just but not especially caring. That is, a just community can have little warmth and bonding between members. In Kohlberg and Lickona's (1990) words, "There is not much human support or warmth in merely being fair" (p. 170). Therefore, both justice and care are needed for there to be a moral community.

While there may be reasonable clarity about the moral community needing to be both just and caring, there is little clarity about what developing a just and caring classroom or school community means for different groups of students. After all, developing a moral community can't mean the same for preschool classrooms as it does for, say, classrooms of adolescents. The meaning is also likely to change for groups differing with respect to culture.

In addition, ambiguity comes from the term *community* being impossible to define operationally. *Community* is one of those terms such as *love* and *care* that refers to something real but not to something that lends itself to precise measurement. That is, we feel we know a community when we see one, but we have difficulty measuring precisely what makes the community a community. The measures seem to change with each instance of community. For example, one first-grade teacher said she knew her class had become a community when, late in the school year, the children were working in their cooperative learning groups and broke out in quiet song. While breaking out in quiet song may,

Today, this ancient symbol of reasoned and unbiased justice is being applied to create classroom communities.

indeed, have indicated this particular group had become a community, it would be silly to use breaking out in quiet song as a universal or even common measure of community. Community, it seems, refers to an experience of oneness among group members, an experience that can manifest in multiple ways. However, for community approaches, that experience of oneness is best derived from a shared commitment to moral values (Kohlberg & Lickona, 1990).

The multiple, changing, and inherently ambiguous meanings of community partially explain why community approaches have less to say about specific methods than do other approaches. Furthermore, the few methods that are discussed in community approaches are often so general as to be more like guidelines than methods. For example, community approaches stress getting children and adolescents actively involved and participating in the governance of classrooms or schools. However, there is no clearly drawn path for a teacher to follow that makes it simple for any teacher to foster good participation. The success of community approaches depends as much or more on teachers' skills at developing positive relationships with children and at being a particular kind of leader than it does on specialized knowledge of methods. In whatever way a teacher or group of teachers succeed in creating a community, doing so seems to matter because the data suggest that successful community building has demonstrable positive effects on students, their behavior, and their learning. (Watson & Battistich, 2006, p. 253)

Democratic

Some, but not all, community approaches emphasize the need to develop democratic classroom communities, in part because American democracy gives a specific meaning to justice, caring, and community. They argue that because we live in a democratic society, we should be preparing students to be citizens in a democratic society (Butchart, 1998a). How else can we prepare students than by building classroom and school communities that are themselves democratic communities?

But what does this mean? As noted before, for some, the meaning of American democracy is not simply or mainly tied to a political system or to voting. The meaning is more centrally tied to a way of life and to an ideal, the ideal of individuals actively supporting individual rights and individual interests, on the one hand, and the common good on the other. We often remember the part about individual rights and interests and forget the part about the common good. In reality, both parts have been at the heart of American democracy from its beginnings.

The main assumption in the American democratic system is that there needs to be a way for everyone to have a voice in defining the meaning of individual rights and the common good. That is, American democracy embraces diversity—at least in principle—and opposes authoritarian control that stifles the individual voices of its citizens. In democratic classrooms and democratic schools, then, teachers have authority to the extent that they represent the common good, or, in the words of John Dewey (1963), the teacher is "the representative and agent of the interests of the group as a whole" (p. 54).

Given this description of American democracy and the teacher's role in democratic classrooms, it is no wonder that those advocating for community approaches that are also democratic approaches have been among the most outspoken critics of behaviorist approaches—at least, behaviorist approaches as found in many North American classrooms. They point out that there are two main contradictions in behaviorist approaches to classroom and behavior management. The first contradiction is between behaviorist approaches' emphasis on controlling children and American society's espousing the democratic ideal of sharing control among citizens. The second contradiction is between the constructivist philosophy that most educators use to support children academically and the nonconstructivist philosophy that most use to manage behavior problems.

With respect to the first contradiction, those advocating for democratic approaches point out that in many schools today, there is little or no discussion about the goals of classroom and behavior management. Instead, there is the tacit assumption that being efficient in establishing control and order makes good common sense because that is what "works." However, as Ronald Butchart (1998a) has pointed out,

> The question is never "What works?"—all manner of barbarity works, if the end is orderliness alone. The question is, what works to assure the sorts of civility and dignity that is essential in the short term for effective learning and vital in the long run for democratic life. (p. 3)

Therefore, by exposing its long-term implications, advocates of democratic approaches question the tacit assumption that simply controlling students is what makes good common sense. They argue that if children and adolescents are raised in environments that simply control them, they may become good workers, but they are not likely to become good citizens who know how to question authority responsibly and who are motivated to take responsibility for making life better for everyone. Echoing Horace Mann from almost a century and half before him, Forrest Gathercoal (1998) adds,

> If the management system in our public schools creates an autocratic environment, it follows that educators are preparing graduates who are unlikely to understand or function well in a participatory society. In the long run, the benefits of enabling students to think and act as responsible citizens far outweigh the disciplinary expediency of teaching blind obedience. (p. 203)

Nowhere do we see the argument for democratic approaches more forcefully presented than by Ronald Butchart (1998a), who explains that classroom discipline is inevitably a moral endeavor that should, as such, have the higher purpose of supporting moral development and equipping students with the attitudes and skills needed to sustain and foster democratic communities. He adds, "We learn what we live" (p. 14), meaning that only by being immersed in school communities where students experience justice, care, and democracy firsthand will students develop morally and as citizens.

With respect to the second contradiction, most American educators today acknowledge the need for students to actively participate in their learning under the tutelage of mentors who explain and guide. Most understand that rewards and punishments are not enough to teach children how to read, write, and progress academically. Students must puzzle and interpret; that is, find their own meaning. This is the essence of the constructivist philosophy of teaching.

However, when it comes to behavior management, many rely mostly on rewards and punishments (negative consequences) to "teach" children and adolescents how to behave. Those advocating democratic approaches criticize this switch in teaching philosophy when going from teaching academic subjects to behavior management. They point out that just as a "right" answer approach won't stimulate good thinking about academic subjects, so, too, a "right" behavior approach won't stimulate good thinking about how to be a responsible citizen in classrooms or schools (Kohn, 1996).

Again, Butchart (1998a) provides an important extension of the criticism that rules and punishment approaches deny the need for a constructivist philosophy when the subject is how to get along and work with each other in classrooms and schools. He distinguishes between pure constructivism and critical constructivism. With respect to behavior and classroom management, fostering critical constructivism is needed because a democratic approach calls for getting students to reflect on and construct their own meaning about what is right and wrong, not simply for themselves, but also for "the common good and for democratic values" (p. 6). In sum, most community approaches to classroom and behavior management take American democratic ideals to be the ideals that should shape and govern how students and classrooms are managed.

But what about learning and school work? Isn't the main function of schools to teach students and get them to work so that they become proficient in the various academic subjects such as math, history, and the sciences? What, then, is the connection between democratic approaches to behavior and classroom management, with their emphasis on developing just, caring, and democratic communities, and this central function of schooling, namely, to promote work and academic learning?

William Glasser (1986) provides a possible answer. Furthermore, his answer places his approach within the group we have defined as community approaches to behavior and classroom management, though his meaning of community differs significantly from that of Butchart (1998a), Gathercoal (1993, 1998), and others who emphasize being democratic.

PREVIEW

The criticism directed at rewards and punishment approaches by those advocating community approaches does not apply to the thoughtful, well-developed behavioral-learning approaches discussed in Chapter 5, where learning takes center stage.

William Glasser

Since the early 1970s, no one has had a greater impact on the field of behavior and classroom management than has William Glasser (1986). Glasser's work is a direct appeal to improve the quality of living in schools, to make schools places where students want to be, not only because they are pleasant places but also because they meet students' needs. For Glasser, the good school is "a place

Source: William Glasser.

William Glasser

where almost all students believe that if they do some work, they will be able to satisfy their needs enough so that it makes sense to keep working" (p. 15).

To become a good school, or what Glasser (1998) refers to as a **quality school,** Glasser provides a variety of concepts and methods for cultivating the kind of school where students are motivated to work, where students want to be, and that meets students needs. He begins with the role of the teacher. Taking a cue from the industrial psychologist Edwards Deming, Glasser says teachers must become **lead managers,** not boss managers. A lead manager is someone who listens to workers' (students') ideas, develops workers' (students') trust that he or she has their needs at heart, and includes workers (students) in evaluating both the work that is done and how to improve it.

In schools adopting Glasser's (1998) approach, one is apt to witness class meetings to discuss what is happening on any given day, but also witness community meetings where students and teachers discuss classroom and schoolwide issues more broadly and where the discussion turns on how to improve the classroom and/or school. Also, in such schools, one is apt to see teachers giving students choices—for example, choices as to what will be served for snacks and choices even about whether to have a study period or not. In giving choices, students come to feel they have part ownership in the classroom or school, and as a result, they find their school a more satisfying place to be. As Henry and Abowitz (1998) summarize,

> Glasser's theories lead to the development of caring classrooms, which foster peaceful conflict negotiation, personal accountability, learning without coercion, and open dialogue. . . . [C]ommunity meetings engage students in collaborative problem-solving, and attempt to construct a spirit of solidarity between students and teachers. (p. 181)

All this may sound like an unequivocally good way to approach behavior and classroom management that emphasizes creating a satisfying learning atmosphere in which students are internally motivated to do quality work because their individual needs are being met. However, Glasser's approach is not without critics, and many of his most severe critics come from the advocates for democratic community building. The gist of their argument is that while Glasser's approach manages to make schools better places to live and work, it does not adequately prepare students for participation in democratic life. In Glasser's schools, the focus is on meeting individual needs, and teachers, while giving choices, retain the power to determine the goals or ends. For some, Glasser's theory and approach is even manipulative, as exemplified by the following comment: "Glasser's theory and practice hides a manipulative, individualistic pedagogy behind a concern for school spirit, cooperative learning, and a humane workplace" (Henry & Abowitz, 1998, p. 160).

However, others advocating for democratic approaches see Glasser differently and more positively. For others, Glasser provides a good foundation to build on. All that is needed is to add the critical constructivist perspective and to infuse into "Glasser schools" a focus on moral issues. An example is Forrest Gathercoal's (1993) *Judicious Discipline* approach.

Forrest Gathercoal

Forrest Gathercoal (1993) offers a framework for older students and educators to think about discipline and the school community. The framework is no less than the U.S. Constitution. Except in matters of curriculum (where teachers retain control), the school community agrees to be governed by the Constitution and to struggle in true democratic fashion to balance the rights of individuals (e.g., to free speech) with those state interest rights having to do with property loss or damage, legitimate educational purpose, threat to health and safety, and serious disruption of the educational process—in short, the "common good" (Gathercoal, 1998, p. 202).

When a school employs this framework, educators promote open discussion about rights and competing rights, so when a teacher says in response to disruptive talk in class, "Is this the responsible time, place, or manner for talking?"

Tinker v. Des Moines Independent Schools

The Case That Established a Reason for Implementing Judicious Discipline

Prior to 1969, schools were generally given the same liberties as parents. In loco parentis was the phrase often used. However, in 1969, when school officials required a group of high school students to remove black armbands they were using to protest U.S. involvement in Vietnam, the courts said the school officials were violating the students' constitutional right to free speech. After that, from a legal point of view, students had the constitutional right to freedom of expression and, by extension, they had more rights and obligations than those implied under the old system of in loco parentis.

students know how to respond to the question (Gathercoal, 1998, p. 205). In short, Gathercoal provides a framework for both teachers and students to think about discipline, a framework that encourages debate about individual rights, the common good, and how, at any given moment, the community can effect the right balance between individual rights and the common good. However, this framework needs to be filled in and supplemented with other approaches, such as Glasser's. As Gathercoal emphasizes,

> Judicious Discipline is not intended to be used independently, but as a foundation upon which to build other cognitive strategies and ideas. . . . Cooperative learning and whole language, for example, will easily integrate with Judicious Discipline's philosophy and language. The real-world practicality of cooperation in a learning environment fit logically with what students are experiencing through Judicious Discipline. (p. 215)

With this overview of what constitutes a community approach to behavior and classroom management, we can focus more on the central features and methods of community approaches.

Review

As an approach to behavior and classroom management, community approaches emphasize the need to promote

(1) justice and individual rights in the classroom and schoolwide community;

(2) care for and among teachers, students, administrators, and all who work in classrooms and schools; and

(3) the democratic ideal of sharing control, giving everyone a voice in the management of classrooms and schools, and involving everyone in determining the right balance between individual rights and the common good.

 **REFLECT**

Was there ever a time when you were a member of a class or school that felt like a true community? If "yes," how did this work? How did the classroom or school community maintain itself as a community? If you can't remember experiencing a classroom or school as a community, was there anywhere else you experienced being a member of a true community? How did this work? How was it maintained as a community?

CENTRAL FEATURES AND METHODS

Like other approaches discussed in this book, community approaches begin with the observation that successful classroom and behavior management depends on teachers developing positive relationships with children and adolescents. For example, community approaches, like other approaches (including behaviorist approaches), caution against educators showing anger and using punishment when children and adolescents misbehave because anger and punishment work against the development of positive teacher-student relationships (Kohn, 1996).

However, what sets community approaches apart is their radical trust in children's and adolescents' motivation and ability to take responsibility and to respond positively to guidance around moral issues. Community approaches are, then, the descendents of Horace Mann, not of Mann's Calvinist contemporaries. But unlike Mann, advocates of today's community approaches have both theory and research to back up their trust.

Therefore, what we have in community approaches is a paradigm shift in the way children and adolescents are *seen*, a shift from mistrust to trust (Freiberg, 1999). Rather than seeing children and adolescents as being prone to mischief, community approaches see children and adolescents as being prone to doing good (Lerner, 2007). Rather than seeing children and adolescents as being limited in their ability to grasp moral issues, community approaches see children and adolescents as being capable, if given the right supports.

Community approaches also define and promote community by emphasizing *dialogue*. In community approaches, dialogue between teachers and students is more than exchanging ideas. Dialogue is also connecting to students in ways that make students feel cared for and respected because they are understood and heard. Nel Noddings (2002) expresses this view of dialogue and its functions as follows:

> Dialogue is the most fundamental component of the care model. True dialogue . . . is open ended. . . . People in true dialogue within a caring relation do not turn their attention wholly to intellectual objects, although, of course, they may do so for brief intervals. Rather, they attend nonselectively to each other. (p. 16)

This meaning of dialogue differs in subtle but important ways from the meaning given in Chapter 3, for example, in the ways Larry Brendtro (1969) and Thomas Gordon (2003) spoke of dialogue.

In the approaches discussed in Chapter 3, dialogue was used to establish positive teacher-student relationships so that students would then be more likely to

Nel Noddings

cooperate and learn. In community approaches, as Nel Noddings' (2002) work made clear, dialogue has a more ambitious, long-term goal: helping students become caring, responsible citizens who know how to function in and contribute to a democratic society.

Trust and dialogue, then, define the central ways that community approaches demonstrate care for students. Both lead logically to two other features of community approaches: sharing control and soliciting active participation in the development and maintenance of communal life in the classroom and school.

Sharing Control and Active Participation

To create a sense of community with everyone working together, community approaches advocate *sharing* control with students and soliciting students' active participation in developing and maintaining the classroom or school as a community. At first glance, it may seem simple to share control with students. It may also smack of being permissive. However, professionals who adopt community approaches show us that sharing control is not easy. It is, in fact, often easier for a teacher to maintain all the control than to share control effectively. Take the following example as an indication of what we mean:

> In one kindergarten classroom, class meeting had fallen apart. Children were poking one another, talking simultaneously, and, in general, not listening to what the teacher was trying to convey. Instead of reprimanding them or taking control directly, the teacher said, "We've fallen apart. What are we going to do?"
>
> In response to the teacher's question, one child suggested she send them all to time-out. The teacher explained she could not do that because doing so would mean they would not get anything done. Another child said the school should hire extra teachers to see to it that the children behaved. The teacher explained that this would not work either—both because the school did not have the money to hire more teachers and also because it would not solve the problem of everybody finding a way to be together at meeting time.
>
> Gradually, the teacher shaped the discussion so that everyone was talking not about how some outside force could control them but how the children in partnership with the teacher could generate good rules and routines to help them control themselves. (Scarlett, 1998, p. xvi)

Notice here that the teacher did not simply give over control to the children by accepting every idea they came up with. In true democratic fashion, she joined the debate so that the final, jointly constructed rules for running class meetings were rules that everyone could live by.

The theme of sharing control and encouraging active participation shows up in the talk of community approaches for older children as well. For example, in what came to be known as the Child Development Project (CDP), a comprehensive elementary school improvement program, significant improvements were found among schools that implemented the CDP program, which included heavy emphasis on class meetings, cooperative learning, literature-based reading, cross-grade "buddies," and whole-school community-building activities (Lewis, Watson, & Schaps, 2003). These and other methods had specific meanings within the program. For example, the kind of cooperative learning recommended by CDP ruled out intergroup competition, extrinsic group rewards, group grades, and preassigned group roles; that is, it ruled out those practices assumed to work against community building. The whole-school community-building activities included welcoming newcomers, grandparent gatherings, and schoolwide mural painting.

We see this same theme of sharing control and encouraging active participation reflected in a story told by a longtime education leader, Theodore Sizer, about a morning routine in the high school where he had his first teaching job. Each morning, the students assembled inside the school's auditorium and the faculty remained outside. Once the students were settled, one of the students came outside and announced to the faculty that the students were ready to receive them. This sharing of control and trust in students helped make the school a community where students took pride in accepting responsibility for making the community work well.

However, for some, if a classroom or school is to become a truly democratic community, sharing control cannot stop at letting students choose how they are to achieve the goals set for them by teachers, as is the case with Glasser's (1998) approach. For there to be truly democratic classrooms and democratic school communities, students must also have control over determining goals (Henry & Abowitz, 1998). What this looks like in practice is not clear, which may be a major reason why community approaches adopting a full and radical meaning of democratic classroom and school communities are not widespread.

Service Learning

Service learning is another method that fits comfortably within community approaches, especially those emphasizing the need to support the development of students as citizens in a democratic society. The aim of service learning is to have students tackle the issues and problems in the broader society—as those issues and problems are defined by community members (Kenny, Simon, Brabeck, & Lerner, 2001). So, for example, a student might work in a pediatric hospital. However, for that work to become service learning, the student must reflect on issues such as whether low-income families should be required to submit copayments.

Service learning has even greater potential when classroom work is well-integrated with what students are experiencing in the field. When this integration occurs, a more apt term for this method is *academic service learning* (Scarlett, Cox, & Matsudaira, 2001). Whatever the exact term, service learning fits logically into a democratic community approach because one of the hallmarks of an effective democracy is the initiative individuals take to intelligently take on public issues in order to foster the common good.

The findings from research on service learning are quite positive. In particular, the research suggests that service learning has positive effects on the civic attitudes of adolescents, helps reduce school absenteeism for program participants, increases high school students' school engagement, and for both high school and middle school students, correlates positively with academic achievement (Lapsley & Narvaez, 2006). Service learning is, then, an effective method for helping students develop a moral-civic identity.

These and other features and methods that define community approaches to behavior and classroom management indicate just how challenging and labor intensive community approaches have become—so much so that many schools and school systems have not been willing or able to adopt them as their own. All this reminds one of Piaget's (1977) observation that some of the best approaches and methods are, unfortunately, the most difficult to implement (p. 712).

Here is Allen Koshewa (1999), another advocate of community approaches, saying virtually the same thing, as well as pointing out that getting students to buy into community approaches is still well worth the try:

> Helping students appreciate the potential strength of a supportive community is a major challenge because many students have not experienced caring environments and have legitimate reasons for distrusting others. But the more teachers trust and respect students, the more students will seek experiences that build individual and collective success. Even more important, students who feel respected will learn to trust in the resilience of the human spirit. (p. 218)

Reactions to Misbehavior: Discipline and Community Approaches

As we have indicated before, no approach will always succeed at preventing behavior problems. So, every approach has to have a plan for disciplining and reacting to behavior problems. With respect to disciplining children, community approaches have much in common with developmental approaches. The focus in both approaches is on continuing to support a child's or adolescent's long-term development, especially through guidance.

Larry Nucci

Source: Larry Nucci.

However, community approaches have special language and emphasis. We see this clearly in Larry Nucci's (2001, 2006) having teachers match their responses to disruption according to whether or not the disruption raises moral issues. Community approaches differ from other types, then, by their moral language and their emphasis on the moral domain.

The key distinction for Nucci (2006) is between moral, conventional, and personal domains. As we have seen, the moral domain has to do with justice and caring and what may be regarded as universal. For example, regardless of culture, adults everywhere treat unprovoked hitting as wrong.

In contrast, the conventional domain has to do with the standards and procedures of a particular group, such as dress codes and whether students address teachers by their first name or last. Finally, the personal domain has to do with individual taste and private matters, such as liking hip-hop music and disliking insects.

Most responses by teachers to misbehavior are responses to violations of conventions rather than to violations in the moral domain. Nucci (2006, p. 719) suggests that classroom and behavior management would improve if educators eliminated unnecessary rules imposing conventions that do not have much to do with maintaining a learning environment, such as conventions requiring children to be absolutely silent even when quiet talk would not disrupt the class. The following observation (made by George Scarlett) illustrates what Nucci is advocating:

A member of a middle school band, the band's "first clarinet" and therefore a respected and able musician in the band, showed up for band practice wearing an enormous Mexican sombrero. Wisely, the band's director allowed the boy to wear his sombrero throughout band practice, even as the director pushed all of the band members to practice hard and perform the music as the composers intended.

In this example, the band director's giving the boy control over how he dressed during practice did not undermine the director's retaining control over the music. If anything, it increased his control because members of the band saw and respected the fact that the director was concerned about controlling the music more than he was concerned about imposing conventions such as what to wear during band practice.

However, Nucci's (2006, p. 719) main suggestion has to do with teachers responding to perceived misbehavior in **domain-concordant** ways. In response to moral transgressions, teachers act in domain-concordant ways when they point out harmful consequences and when they promote perspective taking. For example, if students hit others, teachers act in domain-concordant ways when they help students understand the ways that hitting can be damaging and when they help students resolve conflicts through coordinating perspectives and agendas rather than through hitting. In response to transgressions of conventions, teachers act in domain-concordant ways when they refer to classroom or school rules and to the disruption that transgressions may cause. For example, if children violate a rule about raising hands to speak during circle time, teachers act in domain-concordant ways when they refer to the rule about raising hands and how the rule helps organize discussion.

Using these same examples, we can better understand what it means for teachers to act in **domain-discordant** ways. They do so when they respond to hitting by referring to a rule, as if there were no moral implications of hitting. And they do so when they respond to children's breaking a rule about raising hands to speak by saying others are harmed, when that is not likely the case. Interestingly, children notice and resent when teachers act in domain-discordant ways (Nucci, 2006). In sum, a major way that community approaches react to problem behavior is by having educators act in domain-concordant ways, especially when the behavior problems indicate a student may not be sharing the moral values that make for a just and caring community.

For material related to this concept, go to Video Clip 4.2 on the Student Resource CD bound into the back of your textbook.

Review

Community approaches rely heavily on methods that

(1) stimulate dialogue,

(2) lead to sharing control,

(3) promote an ethic of service, and

(4) highlight the moral dimension in discipline and misbehavior.

SPECIAL EDUCATION AS A COMMUNITY APPROACH

In later chapters, we will have much to say about special education as it relates to behavior and classroom management. Here, though, we need to say something about special education as a community approach because from one perspective, that is exactly what it is. The present-day special education system derives from the mid-1970s Education for All Handicapped Children Act (P.L. 94-142) that came about to stop the unfair practice of segregating children with disabilities.

The law did several things, but the essentials were these: It ensured that children with disabilities received an education. It mandated that children with disabilities be educated in the "least restrictive environment" (LRE), and it ensured that parents had the opportunity to be involved in planning to provide extra supports and services.

P.L. 94-142 was the creation of lawyers and politicians, not educators. Most educators at the time had misgivings about the law. As mentioned in Chapter 2, for most educators and the general public at the time, schools were for preparing typical students to achieve and contribute to society later on (Sarason, 1982). With this understanding of the purpose of schools, the general public saw children with disabilities as threats to schools achieving their main purpose, so children with disabilities were segregated from the rest.

P.L. 94-142 challenged this understanding of the purpose of schools. Rather than making cognitive-academic achievement and future contribution to society the only core values, the law said democratic living in the present must also be a core value. It also said, in effect, that schools should approximate the ideal, inclusive society envisioned in the autobiographies of people with disabilities and in the accounts of parents of children with disabilities (Biklen, 1989). In effect, the law answered the question, "What are schools for?" with a different question, namely, "How should we live together?" (Sarason, 1982), and the answer implied in the law was "a just, caring, and inclusive democratic community."

Put another way, the special education system that emerged in the 1970s was a community approach to behavior and classroom management because, like all community approaches, it gave us a uniquely *moral* perspective on the question of how to educate students with disabilities. The special education system, and community approaches in general, bring out the moral issues implicit in behavior and classroom management. That is, rather than adding moral issues to the mix, they show us that moral issues are already in the mix. In fact, one of special education's most important contributions to community approaches may be to make us more aware and conscious of morality in managing. Educators need not make moral issues the central issues defining their overall approach, but they do need to make moral issues relevant.

BULLYING

We end this chapter on community approaches with a brief discussion of **bullying,** not only because bullying has become the focus of more and more discussions among educators but also because bullying is a problem of community (or lack of community).

Bullying refers to ongoing harassment of one child or adolescent by a peer or group of peers, though sometimes one hears of bully teachers. Bullying can be physical or verbal. Not surprisingly, boys are more apt to bully using both verbal and physical aggression, while girls are more apt to bully using verbal aggression only. Some would add a third type, namely, ignoring an individual or deliberately excluding an individual from a group (Olweus, 2001), but this type is harder to judge.

The topic of bullying is significant for several reasons. First, bullying causes significant psychological and sometimes physical harm, as evidenced by the number of cases in which children feel scarred by past experiences of being bullied and by those tragic cases in which bullying has been a significant cause of suicide or murder. The case of Columbine High School is, perhaps, the most famous.

Bullying and the Columbine Massacre

On April 20, 1999, two students, Eric Harris and Dylan Klebold, entered the Columbine High School, killed 12 students and a teacher, seriously wounded 23 others, and then shot themselves. In the aftermath of what is now generally called "the Columbine Massacre," a number of theories were put forth to explain the tragedy. One theory focused on the possibility that the two killers had been bullied, especially by the "in-groups" at the high school, such as the "jocks." While this interpretation has been challenged by many, it led to considerable discussion about school cliques and bullying and to a greater consciousness and effort on the part of educators to find ways to counter bullying.

Second, bullying is significant because it is so common. One leading expert, Dan Olweus (2004), estimated that one in seven students has been either a bully or a victim of bullying. Others give even higher figures (Nansel, Overpeck, Pilla, Ruan, Simons-Morton, & Scheidt, 2001).

Third, and most relevant for our present focus, bullying is often a symptom of problems in the school community. Bystanders and witnesses of bullying report negative perceptions of school climate and decreased school engagement (Astor, Benbenishty, Zeira, & Vinokur, 2002). We need, then, to understand this phenomenon of bullying from a community approach perspective.

Contrary to what some hypothesize, bullying of any type is apt to have serious negative effects, so it is not just physical bullying that needs attention. Also contrary to what many assume, bullies are not generally students who are masking their anxiety or low self-esteem. Most bullies are children and adolescents who, if anything, are less anxious than the average and who have higher

Bullying is more than an individual problem. It is community problem as well—calling for community-building solutions.

self-esteem. Bullies bully because they find bullying fun, a source of power, or satisfying because of the rewards they get from peer approval. In contrast, victims tend to be students who are more anxious and who have lower self-esteem (Olweus, 2004).

Most bullying occurs at school, so educators have a special responsibility to deal with bullying. To fulfill their responsibilities, educators must be (1) vigilant about bullying, (2) proactive, and (3) interventionist when bullying occurs. To be vigilant about bullying can mean several things. It can mean providing good teacher supervision at recess time. It can mean assessing a class for the telltale signs of bullying, such as students who are unusually anxious and withdrawn. Whatever the methods of being vigilant, educators clearly must have bullying on their minds.

Unfortunately, research shows that this is not often the case because many teachers tend to underestimate the prevalence of school bullying (Stockdale, Hangaduambo, Duys, Larson, & Sarvela, 2002). Research also indicates that high school teachers are less likely to intervene, in comparison to teachers of younger children (Holt & Keyes, 2004), so there is a real need for high school teachers to become more vigilant and involved around bullying.

Being proactive means discussing bullying openly, not just to make clear that bullying is wrong but also to explore the feelings and experiences of being both a bully and a victim. Furthermore, discussions should be about how to respond when a student sees someone being bullied. Here is one example of a teacher taking a community approach and being proactive, not by discussing bullying directly, but by discussing a behavior (teasing) that can lead to bullying. The example is, once again, from Judy Lazarus's classroom.

Thursday morning group discussions always focus on some group concern or interest. Each child shares his or her view and experience and is encouraged to respond to what others have to say. Often the topics are about emotional issues such as teasing and rejection—which can lead to bullying. In teacher Lazarus's words:

"Children see that some have similar feelings and some do not. And they hear an array of strategies for coping with the issues that children and adults cope with—everything from what your family does when there is a bug in your house to coping with feelings of loss, fear, or rejection. We try to look at all angles. Not just have you ever been teased but when have you teased, whom do you tease, why? (The consensus on that one is "it's fun."). Discussion topics come from the theme, kids, and parents. Seeing cliques develop might inspire a discussion on "Have you ever felt left out?" (Scarlett, 1998, p. 110)

The available research indicates that teachers should talk with bullies and victims, not simply to reprimand or console but also to inquire, understand students' experience, and guide.

Disciplining the bully should be for the purpose of helping the bully reform and possibly make reparations to a victim and to the community. The goal should be to find ways for the victim to feel secure and connected in the classroom and school community and to realize there are adaptive ways to respond to bullying. However, often the interventions that work best are those aimed at changing the school and classroom environment (Horne, Bartolomucci, & Newman-Carlson, 2003).

The best antidote to bullying may well be warm and close teacher-student relationships. This conclusion comes from observing that both bullies and victims tend to have negative relationships with their teachers (Hanish, Kochenderfer-Ladd, Fabes, Martin, & Denning, 2004). A teacher with poor relationships with students may also be out of touch with what is going on with respect to bullying. Finally, and most important, teachers set the tone of a classroom. If that tone is warm and positive, then bullying will seem to the students to be out of place and unacceptable.

In sum, bullying is a community problem and not simply a problem of individual students or groups of students. As with all community problems, the problem of bullying is essentially a moral problem calling for a moral solution that requires care shown for both the victim and the bully. And as with all community problems, bullying calls for a community approach that sees the ultimate solution for bullying being the creation of a just and caring community.

Summary

This chapter has focused on those approaches that take community building as the starting point and main focus for managing both behavior and classrooms. For some, such as William Glasser, this means making classrooms and schools into satisfying work communities. For others, it means making classrooms and schools into just, caring, and democratic communities where a major aim is to prepare students for citizenship in a democratic society. The main assumption in community approaches is that we learn what we live.

As we have seen in this chapter, community building follows no simple script. There are preferred methods, but in the end, community approaches rest on the leadership abilities of educators who know how to share control with students and promote students' motivation to reflect not only on their own best interests but on the common good. To this end, community approaches align themselves with methods also found in other kinds of approaches, methods such as holding class meetings and making heavy use of cooperative learning groups. Some methods are especially "at home" in community approaches, such as community meetings to discuss class or school issues and service learning. In the end, however, community approaches depend as much on a commitment to ideals and moral values as they do on specific methods.

For the majority of community approaches, behavior and classroom management is (or should be) essentially a moral endeavor. Therefore, community approaches take us away from focusing strictly on how to control students and return us to the themes raised by Horace Mann and earlier educators, themes about the character of students and about schools needing to prepare students to live responsibly and morally in our democratic society.

Web-Based Student Study Site

The companion Web site for *Approaches to Behavior and Classroom Management* can be found at www.sagepub.com/scarlettstudy.

Visit the Web-based student study site to enhance your understanding of the chapter content. The study materials include practice tests, flashcards, suggested readings, and Web resources.

Key Concepts

Bullying

Community

Critical constructivism

Democratic

Domain-concordant

Domain-discordant

In loco parentis

Lead managers

Quality school

Service learning

State interest rights

Discussion Questions

1. In democratic groups, members have a voice in how the group is run, and a major issue for discussion is how to balance the rights of individuals with the rights of the group (the common good). Were you ever in a classroom or school that was at least somewhat democratic? If "yes," how did it work? If "no," were you ever in a democratic group outside school? If "yes," how did it work, and could the methods used to maintain this group as a democratic group be used in classrooms and schools?

2. Community approaches emphasize that behavior and classroom management is, essentially, a moral endeavor. One way they do so is to clearly distinguish between issues that are moral issues (e.g., hitting, bullying), issues that are about conventions (e.g., dress codes, rules governing turn-taking at meetings), and issues that are about personal preferences (e.g., taste in music). Can you remember a time when an educator (teacher, school principal, etc.) treated an issue as a moral issue when it should have been treated as an issue about a convention or personal preference? Can you remember a time when a moral issue was treated as an issue about a convention or personal preference?

3. The focus on morality in community approaches is evident in the belief that the inclusion of children with special needs is the morally "right" thing to do. Where have you seen inclusion being treated as the morally right thing to do? Have you ever experienced someone arguing for excluding children with special needs because they might hold others back? Should classrooms be inclusive communities regardless of whether it is good for the academic progress of students without disabilities or special needs?

4. As the chapter explains, bullying at school is not simply an individual problem. It is also a community problem. Can you think of one or more examples of bullying reflecting problems in the larger school community? If you can, what led to or maintained a climate that allowed for bullying?

PART III

Learning and Development

Taken together, the chapters in Part III treat behavior and classroom management as being about teaching students so that they learn and develop. These chapters show the need to support both learning and development. They also show how emphasizing one or the other can define approaches to behavior and classroom management.

Learning and development have long been central concepts in approaches to educating children and adolescents. Traditionally, they have had separate meanings: *learning* refers to short-term achievements, such as acquiring information and simple skills, and *development* refers to long-term tasks and capacities such capacity for reasoning, for perspective taking, and for managing hard-to-manage emotions. And following Vygotsky's lead (1978a), learning and development have been seen as partners, with each contributing to the other. More recently, these two concepts have taken on overlapping meanings, so much so that the two have sometimes been treated as one and the same (Kuhn, 1995). In Part III, we retain the older practice of distinguishing between learning and development.

Chapter 5 explains how learning approaches emphasize knowing what needs to be learned, knowing how to make learning relevant to students, and knowing how to teach students to act in civil ways. The main assumption in learning approaches is that problem behavior reflects students' not knowing. In this chapter, too, we see how behavioral-learning approaches provide powerful ways to prevent and change problem behavior.

Chapter 6 focuses on development and on how educators do well when they accommodate students' level of maturity. However, Chapter 6 focuses on much more than being age and stage appropriate. In Chapter 6, we see the power of adopting a developmental perspective for understanding and implementing effective behavior and classroom management, by tying the present to the long term, by supporting qualitative changes in how students think and manage emotions, by supporting the development of inner processes such as perspective taking, and by helping students make progress on long-term tasks, such as the task of "putting morality on the inside." Furthermore, in Chapter 6 we discuss how constructivist methods and methods referred to as "ego supports" play central roles in developmental approaches. The main assumption in developmental approaches is that because development is the ultimate "cure" for behavior problems, supporting (long-term) development should be central to behavior and classroom management.

Chapter 5

LEARNING APPROACHES

"Ms. Davis, can I go to the bathroom?" asks Janice.

"No, I gotta use it!" demands Gary.

"Is we gonna do math or reading now?" asks Missy, politely.

"I need a Band-Aid, Ms. Davis, see." Ashley tugs at my blouse.

It is 8:02, a typical morning in a fourth-grade classroom. Teacher Davis finds herself in a Q & A session.

"Yes, you may go to the bathroom, Janice, but don't waste time. Gary, I don't know what 'it' is, but if you are referring to the bathroom, say it, and then you may use 'it' when Janice comes back, and I'd really like for you to say 'have to' instead of 'gotta,' okay? And Missy, did you say 'Is we'?"

"Are we," she says.

"Look at the schedule, sweetie. And Ashley, you said you need a Band-Aid? Well, I need to win the lotto!"

"Ms. Daaaavis, you know what I mean," whines Ashley.

"Yes, I do know what you mean, but when you would like something, ask me, don't tell me. I will get a Band-Aid in a moment, but please sit down . . ." (Davis, 2005, pp. 1–2)

Author's Note: Chapter 5 was coauthored by Yibing Li.

CHAPTER OVERVIEW

Models for Teaching

What Needs to Be Learned

Learning the Relevance of Education

Learning How to Cooperate and Act in Civil Ways

Behavioral-Learning Approaches

Increasing and Decreasing Target Behaviors

Behavior Modification: A Two-Way Street

Avoiding Traps

Putting the Behavioral-Learning Approach Into Practice: Being Scientific

Specific Discipline Approaches Using Behavioral-Learning Concepts and Principles

In the opening exchange, rather than seeing her fifth-grade students as being rude and noisy, teacher Davis sees them as needing to learn, which is how teachers often set themselves apart from others, by knowing when students need to learn, what they need to learn, and how to teach them so that they will learn. This applies as much to teaching "good behavior," such as asking politely for a Band-Aid, as it does to teaching math and English. Here, then, teacher Davis models what we are referring to as a learning approach to behavior and classroom management.

Learning approaches adopt the original meaning of discipline, which is the meaning derived from the Latin word *discere,* "to learn" (Johnson, 1981). Using this meaning, learning approaches include what are often referred to as behavioral-learning approaches, which systematically work to increase or decrease specific, "target" behaviors. However, learning approaches also include any approach in which the major emphasis is on teaching students so they learn how to behave "appropriately" or "well," as variously as "appropriately" and "well" may be defined.

In contrast to the developmental approaches in Chapter 6, learning approaches concentrate more on what can be acquired within a reasonably short period of time. Ms. Davis was not expecting her words to change the children next year. She was expecting them to change the children, if not right away, then soon thereafter.

Learning approaches also have in common the fact that they put a great deal of emphasis on motivating and explaining so that students learn. This is also the emphasis implied when many use the term "good teacher." Here, then, a main assumption is that "good teaching" goes a long way to ensure successful behavior and classroom management.

MODELS FOR TEACHING

Since the focus here is on teaching for learning, we need to be clear about the different models for teaching. To do so, we can make use of DeVries and Kohlberg's (1990) practice of dividing teaching models into three basic types. One type is teacher centered and focuses on teachers transmitting knowledge, so here we will refer to this type as the **transmission model.** Teachers using a transmission model retain the traditional role of imparting their knowledge through direct instruction, much as teacher Davis did in the opening example.

A second type is both teacher and student centered as it focuses on teachers guiding and supporting students in their actively puzzling as well as in their creating and constructing their own meaning, so we will refer to this type as the **constructivist model.** Throughout this book, there are many examples of methods following a constructivist model of teaching, methods in which the aim of the teacher is less to impart information directly and more to get children to reflect; problem solve; and, in general, construct their own interpretations and meanings, whether those interpretations and meanings have to do with an historical event, the pros and cons of using wind power to save energy, or something more directly relevant to behavior and classroom management, such as what rules should govern class meetings.

A third type is mostly student centered and focuses on teachers letting students discover and create on their own, so we will refer to this type as the **discovery model.** DeVries and Kohlberg used the word *romanticism* to characterize what is essentially a discovery model because the model is based upon 19th-century Romantic philosophy. That philosophy emphasized the natural endowment of children to learn and grow, with adults needing only to provide the bare necessities.

In books on behavior and classroom management, there are very few examples of the discovery model, but in the 1960s and 1970s, A. S. Neill's (1960) book, *Summerhill: A Radical Approach to Child Rearing* was widely cited as illustrating a discovery model and an alternative to the more control-oriented

Review

There are three basic types of teaching models:

(1) Transmission model

(2) Constructivist model

(3) Discovery model

approaches being advocated by most. In Neill's school, the role of teacher was defined primarily in terms of supporting students' interests and agendas, with little in the way of traditional structure or classroom management. That is, in Neill's school, students were expected to discover what they needed to know and how to go about learning what they needed to know. There are today only a few schools that follow Neill's discovery model, and because these few are so different in character from the vast majority of schools, and because there is no research to suggest a pure discovery model is superior or needed, we need not dwell on the discovery model.

Many, if not most, teachers employ some combination of the transmission and constructivist models, with moments for discovery as well. There seems to be good reason for doing so, as the examples in this and other chapters indicate. However, regardless of model, educators are always deciding on what students need to learn and what needs to be taught.

REFLECT   Thinking of your own experience as a student, can you identify one teacher in particular who used mostly a transmission model of teaching, another who used mostly a constructivist model, and still another who used mostly a discovery model? Which teacher taught you the most, or did each have something different to offer?

WHAT NEEDS TO BE LEARNED

Learning approaches to behavior and classroom management assume that students need to learn much more than is found in the approved curriculum—and much more than the average person might assume. For example, in one summer camp, a 6-year-old was making a big fuss (i.e., being a behavior problem) and refusing to go to archery, when his teacher suddenly asked, "Do you know what archery is?" The boy stopped his fussing and said he didn't know what archery was, so the teacher explained, indicating, through gestures, how at archery kids use bows to shoot arrows. After that, the boy eagerly ran to catch up to his group that was making its way to archery.

The point of this example should be clear by now: Someone adopting a learning approach first assumes a problem behavior may indicate a child or adolescent does not know something. Furthermore, the example shows how significant it can be to adopt a learning approach. After all, not adopting a learning approach might well have led to coercing the child into going to archery, a method not nearly as effective as was teaching the child what archery meant.

In particular, those adopting learning approaches to behavior and classroom management make two assumptions. First, they assume that students need to learn the relevance of education—how education links to their interests and to the real world outside school. Second, learning approaches assume that students need to learn how to cooperate and act in civil ways.

Learning the Relevance of Education

Here, *relevant* has three meanings, not one. First, to be relevant means to be relevant to students' interests. Second, it means linking whatever is being taught to the world outside school. Third, it means making the curriculum and learning process interesting.

Building Curriculum Around Students' Interests

The idea of building curriculum around students' interests is, as we have already seen, a central idea in John Dewey's philosophy and in progressive education in general (Jones & Tanner, 1981). As mentioned in Chapter 2, Dewey (1963) likened the ideal classroom to the ball field where the game itself is what controls the players—not only its rules, but also its ability to capture players' interest and attention.

But how does building curriculum around students' interests occur for students of different ages? Jerome Bruner (1984) provides a humorous example with very young children.

> I recall the account of a Head Start class whose teacher read them *Little Red Riding Hood*. When the story reached the climax at which the wolf, disguised as Grandmother, responds to Red Riding Hood's remark about her big teeth by proclaiming, "All the better to eat you, ho ho!" one of the children snarled, "That m-f son-of-a-bitch." This is not very highbrow metapragmatics, but the teacher was clever enough to ask the children how the story *should* have gone at that point. "She shoulda killed the wolf!" was the response. The teacher asked, "And then what?" And then there *was* a good discussion—not great, but good for four-year-olds. (p. 197)

Bruner's (1984) point is that, when it comes to encouraging young children to read or be drawn to books, it is best to link reading to young children's interest in fantasy worlds with high drama—no Dick and Jane books ("See Spot run!") will suffice. Doing so, he says, is the best way to make reading

For material related to this concept, go to Video Clip 5.1 on the Student Resource CD bound into the back of your textbook.

relevant and, we might add, the best way to prevent problem behavior. It is not too far-fetched to assume that the little boy who reacted so passionately to the big bad wolf would, if he were not so passionate about the story, be passionate about something else that might have distracted and disrupted.

As for building curriculum around older children's interests, here is an example of a fourth-grade teacher's curriculum:

> In my fourth-grade classroom, I noticed that my boys would talk incessantly about baseball. I wanted to find a way to channel this interest into our math lessons. I decided to start using a free fantasy baseball service. This was a game available on the Internet, where the children would choose players each day and then calculate their rankings based on the players' statistics. The game was a total success. Children would come into class each day having computed their players' statistics from the morning paper. Soon, the entire class got in on the act, and everybody seemed to have fun, boys as well as girls. I was happy because my students were learning valuable math skills and finding a way to apply them in their everyday lives. (Scarlett, Naudeau, Salonius-Pasternak, & Ponte, 2004, p. 179)

Linking to the Outside World

School is a formal environment where teachers often cover subjects that seem artificial to students and that require students to perform tasks different from those encountered outside school. As a result, students do not always see the relevance of what is being taught to them, and in not seeing the relevance, students can feel bored and trapped. When this happens, there is a greater chance that there will be behavior problems (Cowley, 2001).

To counter students' experience of feeling bored and trapped, teachers use a variety of methods to help students connect school to the world outside school. Here is an example of a second-grade teacher, Pam Roller, connecting her students' schoolwork to what goes on outside school.

> I want my students to know that reading is not just in books and on worksheets, so after learning all of the vowel sounds and vowel combinations, I have taken my students on a shopping trip to a local supermarket. To have money to shop with, we made our own lip balm and sold it. We went to the supermarket, and the students shopped for items using their decoding skills to purchase groceries needed for the Ronald McDonald House in Indianapolis. We were allowed to take a field trip to the Ronald McDonald House to deliver our items and see the house that love built. It had an impact on my kids. (Roller, 2005, p. 124)

Note how in this example, reading (decoding) is made relevant not only by its occurring in the supermarket and for the practical purpose of buying food, but also by its occurring for the meaningful, relevant purpose of giving to a worthy charity.

As students progress in their education, subjects become more abstract and distinct from the tasks of daily living. It becomes natural for students to wonder what academic subjects can do for them other than helping some get into college. Carey Jenkins (2001), a high school teacher in New Jersey, recalls her own school days when she would sit in class daydreaming, wondering why she needed to learn algebra, history, science, and English. Indeed, she wondered why she needed to be in school at all. Later, when she became a teacher, she pointed out,

> Most teachers assume students come to class knowing why they are there. In fact, students come to class knowing not much more than that one needs an education to better one's future life. That simply does not tell students enough. (p. 9)

Instead, she said, they have to be taught what school can do for them, both immediately and in the future.

Teaching in an urban high school, Jenkins's students were mostly from poor neighborhoods, lived in projects, and were inadequately prepared in elementary and middle schools. Many did not know why they were in school. In order to help her students understand the relevance of school, she brought professionals into her class to talk about their careers and lives. She also encouraged students to ask questions, such as questions about what the professionals liked and disliked about their jobs and careers. In these meetings, students learned from adults what they do and what educational preparation was needed to enter and succeed in a job and career. They also learned why math is important to an engineer, why biology is important to a doctor, and why other academic disciplines are important to a variety of careers.

In addition, she took her students on field trips to visit factories, supermarkets, labs, law offices, military bases, and government buildings. Students got to talk to on-site staff. They even got to shadow people doing their jobs. As a result, students learned what goes on in "real-world" jobs and why they need to stay in school and do what is needed to learn and get a diploma. In short, these experiences taught students the relevance of school and education for their future. As a result, teacher Jenkins spent less time managing her classroom because most of her students learned that they need to work hard to make education useful to them.

For material related to this concept, go to Video Clip 5.2 on the Student Resource CD bound into the back of your textbook.

Here is yet another example of teaching for relevance, again of teacher Brenner, this time teaching the relevance of math:

> Teacher Brenner is reviewing the long division of polynomials, making his way through a number of sample problems on the board, trying to extract input from a sullen, weary class. "Why do we have to do this?" calls out a girl with an exaggerated pout. "I'm going to be an actress," she says, "I'm never going to use this in my life."
>
> "You never know," says teacher Brenner. "You never know how you can use math. There was a student once, a student like you, who graduated and went to Austin and became a choreographer. She was good in math, interested in math. And she decided to base a dance on the Fibonacci sequence: 1, 1, 2, 3, 5, 8, 13. She knew from math that those numbers are mystical, that they appear in nature with strange regularity: in the rings of a pineapple and on a pinecone. And because she knew math, this choreographer could make fascinating patterns based on the sequence. . . . It was a wonderful dance. Math is the foundation of everything. Math is life." After listening, the girl and class turned back to their long division. (R. M. Cohen, 1991, p. 25)

In this example, teacher Brenner makes explicit how math can be relevant to a student's future, even when that future does not, at first, appear to involve math.

Making the Curriculum and Learning Process Interesting

However, sometimes the job does not so much concern linking curriculum to students' interests or to the outside world. Sometimes the job is making the curriculum and learning process interesting. As Colvin (2004) and Johnson (1981) explain, teachers need to keep students actively engaged and interested in order to prevent behavior problems. In a class that is busily engaged in academic tasks, there should be few disruptions, whereas in classes where students are not engaged, the opposite is likely to be the case. In other words, and as mentioned in Chapter 2, "The devil makes use of idle hands, and angels hover about the busy." Thus, those adopting a learning approach are apt to speak of their trying to "hook" students on the curriculum. Here is an example of a biology teacher doing just that, "hooking" her students on an interesting way to teach the respiratory system:

Using 3-liter Coke bottles, tubes, balloons, and rubber bands, teacher Chin has created models of the lung, one per student.

"What's the rubber on the bottom represent?" asks teacher Chin, making a slow turn around the classroom.

"A diaphragm?" responds one student.

"Yes, a diaphragm. Have you ever seen a diaphragm?" asks teacher Chin. "This is a diaphragm."

She pulls from the clutter of her desk a large tray covered with plastic. Underneath is a half-dissected cat, whose conveniently large diaphragm is intact. The students abandon their lung models and rush to the center of the room.

"Eeyew!" "Is that cholesterol in those veins?" "That's the liver! Isn't that the liver?" "That cat had kittens, right?" "Can you eat a cat?"

Teacher Chin laughs, and answers every question. Eventually, after poking one another in the diaphragm, and seeing who can hold his breath the longest, and telling stories from the *National Enquirer* about people who sold their lungs to buy bedroom furniture, the students returned to their lung models.

When the bell rang, the students reluctantly gathered their books together. "This is an excellent class," said one young man in a matter-of-fact way. "Ms. Chin is the best biology teacher in the country." The whole class is out the door, peacefully and quickly. Teacher Chin did not have to spend a minute managing misbehavior, since her students were so engaged with the lesson. (R. M. Cohen, 1991, pp. 58–59)

Here is another example of a teacher getting students actively involved and interested in learning by making the learning process itself interesting:

"Mr. Brenner would come in each morning for Calculus class," says Hallie, a former student, "He'd begin by telling us some story about an engineer he knew who needed to make a bridge over a particular river. He never wrote a formula on the board; he just told you the story, and you'd get more and more engrossed. The engineer was figuring this curve and that curve, and all of a sudden, you'd realize you'd learned the origin of an equation. Just like that. First the story, then the epiphany, then the formula. Ten years later, I can't tell you what the formulas are, but I can tell you how they're used, how they fit into the world."

"What I go for," Brenner says, "What I really teach for, is the moment of 'Aha!' The moment when it all comes together. You don't get an 'Aha!' when you're telling students the answers. It only happens when the answers come out of themselves." (R. M. Cohen, 1991, p. 16)

In sum, those adopting learning approaches emphasize the importance of **making learning relevant** to students by linking curriculum to their interests, by linking learning to the outside world, and by making learning itself interesting.

Review

Teachers using learning approaches can help students see the relevance of their education by

(1) building a curriculum around students' interests,

(2) linking the curriculum to the outside world, and

(3) making the curriculum and learning process interesting.

Learning How to Cooperate and Act in Civil Ways

Upon beginning school, children do not know how to behave in a classroom; in other words, they do not become good students simply because their parents send them to school. School and home are different. Children are not asked by parents to sit still for several hours of the day, work in groups, and get permission if they want to use the bathroom. At school, then, they need to be taught how to cooperate and act in civil ways.

As Daniel Meier (1997) demonstrates, teachers teach students how to cooperate and be civil when, for example, teachers say, "Raise your hand if you think you know the answer." During such times, teachers teach a behavior needed if students are to be cooperative and civil. In teaching students how to be cooperative and civil, teachers teach how to follow directions, make transitions from one activity to another, and get along with classmates. Here is an example of a teacher teaching older students how to work together:

In Ms. Liu's sixth-grade class, there are frequent cooperative learning activities. Before students start their group activity, Ms. Liu sets the stage and makes expectations explicit. Sometimes she asks them, "What should I see when you're working together?" They respond with comments such as "Heads together," "Leaning on your chin and elbows." She then asks, "What might I hear if you're working together?" They answer, "Talking," "Compliments," "Oh, yeah!" and "Help me." Another time she tells the class, "The skill you're working on is involvement." Indeed, she often spends time talking with the students about the group process itself and how it works best.

After one group activity, Ms. Liu asks the students to think about the kinds of participation that went on in the group: "Look at how your group participated. Did people talk together? Were heads together? Was there eye contact? Talk about that in your group. How did you come to agreement? Looks like most did. Is it OK to disagree sometimes?" (Knapp, Adelman, Marder, McCollum, & Needels, 1995, pp. 27–28)

Cooperative and civil behaviors can be taught and learned; this is a main assumption for learning approaches. For some children, cooperative and civil behaviors come so easily that they can learn them on their own. Others require a teacher's help. Here is an example of a teacher teaching her first graders how to act in civil ways.

Discouraged by the way her first-grade students failed to respond to her morning greetings, Ruth Charney (2002) set it as a task to teach them how to say "Hello." At morning meeting, she engaged the children as follows:

"Good morning, Eddie." Eddie smiles and looks around. "What might Eddie say now?" the teacher asks. "Good morning, Ms. Charney?" a student ventures. "Yes, I'd like that, Eddie." "Good morning." Eddie manages in a quiet voice. "Good morning, Justin." Justin replies with spirit. "Good morning, Ms. Charney." "I like that nice strong voice, Justin. I also like hearing my name." (p. 9)

Ruth Charney did not take her students failing to respond to her greetings as their being rude. Instead, she took their responses as their having yet to learn how to greet someone politely. Therefore, she took their not greeting as an opportunity to teach a "greeting lesson."

As illustrated in this example and with respect to civility and prosocial behaviors, students, especially young students, often have yet to learn the basics. One of the basics is how to be a good audience. Here is another first-grade teacher telling what she taught students about being a good audience:

We sit in a circle so we can see each other. We sit up to show respect. We look at the person who is talking so he or she will feel listened to. We respond to the topic seriously so people won't be embarrassed to express their feelings. We try not to do things that will take the spotlight off of the person whose turn it is because everyone needs to get their share of the group's recognition and attention. (Scarlett, 1998, p. 110)

If given the proper supports, even very young children can learn how to be a good audience, as the next example clearly shows. The example is taken from Kohlberg and Lickona's (1990) account of a class meeting in an American kindergarten classroom:

The teacher, Gloria Norton, began her first class meeting with a discussion of the word *cooperation,* introduced by reading the fable of the chicken and the wheat. She and the children then discussed the book, naming different situations in which people cooperate. The teacher reported that many of the children listened with care, whereas others were disruptive (nonattentive). The teacher waited a short time until she caught one of the children listening. This is the scene that followed:

Teacher: Mary, I saw that you were watching and listening to Susan as she shared with us. Susan, how did it feel to have Mary listen to you?

Susan: (smiling at Mary) It felt good when she listened to me.

Teacher: When you listen to me, I feel good inside, too.

The teacher continued the meeting in the same way, discussing cooperation and commenting on listening behavior. The next day she and the children had a discussion about listening. She asked them how they knew when they were being listened to. The teacher was pleased to discover that they were able to identify good listening behavior. Together, they began to construct a list of rules for the meeting time: (1) Look at people when they are speaking. (2) Be still and be silent when someone is speaking. (3) Everyone should have a chance to share. These rules were then printed on a big sheet of paper and hung in the block corner where the class had its meeting. (p. 159)

In the following exchange, we see how a high school biology teacher also teaches her students more than just biology. The student in this example had arrived late to class and informed her that that he had had a medical appointment and gave her a note to prove it:

T: You were at Mt. Sinai before 9:00?

S: Yeah.

Learning approaches assume children need to be taught how to act in civil ways.

T: I'm impressed [but it] would be nice if you were here by 9:00.

S: I could have come here first, but then I would have had to leave again.

T: Alright, a reasonable judgment. (Then said in a nonjudgmental way) You know, in the future, if you ever want to do that one thing that would make you beyond criticism, give a phone call. Very good thing, communication. (Wiseman, 1994)

In short, learning approaches assume that students have yet to learn how to act in cooperative, civil ways, making it part of the teacher's job description to teach students how to act in cooperative, civil ways.

BEHAVIORAL-LEARNING APPROACHES

What has been said so far about learning approaches relates mostly to how teaching for learning is typically understood: A teacher notes what a student needs to learn and then provides instruction and the conditions (pedagogy and curriculum) that make learning possible. Behavioral-learning approaches likewise focus on what needs to be learned (or unlearned), but they employ a conceptual system that makes the meaning of teaching and learning different from how teaching and learning are ordinarily understood. So, here we provide a separate discussion about behavioral-learning approaches and how they have served as approaches to behavior and classroom management.

In the previously discussed learning approaches, teaching for learning meant first teaching new ideas or insights (e.g., the idea that people like to hear their name and be greeted in the morning). In these approaches, then, changes in behavior follow changes in thinking. With most behavioral-learning approaches, the order is reversed—changes in thinking follow changes in behavior—similar to, but not the same as, old-fashioned habit training (see Chapter 2). Behavioral-learning approaches are, then, all about getting students to behave differently.

Behavioral-learning approaches have played a central role in helping educators teach especially challenging students, students whose behavior can disrupt classrooms and create chaos or worse. They have done so because the concepts and methods provide powerful ways to control students. In short, behavioral-learning approaches have a proven track record for putting teachers (back) in control.

Like most professional approaches, behavioral-learning approaches have often been misunderstood. For example, some see behavioral-learning approaches as overcontrolling and thereby turning students into robots. Others see behavioral-learning approaches as simplistic because they reduce problems to a matter of supplying rewards and punishments.

However, these criticisms miss the subtlety and aims of professional behavioral-learning approaches, so here we wish to make clear what those subtleties and aims are so that readers can make good use of behavioral-learning approaches or, at least, not dismiss behavioral-learning approaches without truly understanding them. We begin with what is meant by "behavior" and how this concept influences the meaning of what is to be learned.

Increasing and Decreasing Target Behaviors

Behavioral-learning approaches focus on a relatively small unit of analysis: individual behaviors. Usually, the behaviors are actions (raising a hand to be called on at meetings, individual acts of swearing, staying seated for a specified time set aside for seatwork, and so forth). However, sometimes, behaviors are individual thoughts (e.g., thinking it is not all right to make a mistake, thinking that everyone is out to "get" everyone else). Whether the behaviors focused on are actions or thoughts, they fall roughly into two groups—those an educator wishes to *increase* and those that an educator wishes to *decrease*. Behavioral-learning approaches are, then, all about increasing and decreasing specific behaviors. Doing so successfully means the student has learned.

Because it is so difficult and time consuming to change behaviors, those using behavioral-learning approaches are apt to select only one or a handful of behaviors to work on at any given time. These they call **target behaviors.** The first step in implementing a behavioral-learning approach is, then, to identify a target behavior and describe the behavior in such a way that its frequency or duration can be measured. Sometimes, this way of describing is called **defining operationally.** So, for example, instead of describing a student's behavior at meeting time as being disruptive, following a behavioral-learning approach, a teacher may describe the target behavior as "interrupts discussion without raising his hand," leading to operationally defining the goal as "During meeting time, will raise a hand and wait until called on."

From the perspective of a behavioral-learning approach, in order to change a target behavior, we must think in terms of what comes immediately before that behavior and what comes immediately after. What comes before are called *antecedent conditions* and what comes after are called *consequent conditions* (or simply *consequences)*.

However, because so much comes before and after a behavior (heart rate, the way a room is lit, noise level, etc.), behavioral-learning approaches focus on just those antecedents and consequences with conditions that an educator can control and that play an immediate and major role in determining whether a behavior will be maintained, will increase, or will decrease. For these especially relevant conditions, behavioral-learning approaches use the terms *stimuli* to refer to antecedents and *reinforcements* and *punishments (negative consequences)* to refer to consequences.

Now comes the part that most people miss when trying to employ a behavioral-learning approach. The concepts **stimulus,** reinforcement, and **punishment (negative consequence)** refer not to specific methods such as praising a child, giving food to a child, or taking away recess. Rather, they refer to *functional* relations between one thing or act and another. This means that something that may function as a reinforcer for one child may, for another, function as a punisher (negative consequence). Here is an example from George Scarlett's work with a troubled 11-year-old:

Mary occasionally liked to draw. She usually did so off to the side and away from others. Once, when she was finishing up a drawing, a teacher who happened to be passing by complimented her on her drawing—whereupon she immediately ripped it up and stomped away. It was a long while before Mary ventured to draw again.

What is normally a reinforcement (praise or complimenting) turned out to be, for Mary, a punishment or negative consequence.

This means that the concepts *stimulus, reinforcement,* and *punishment (negative consequence)* have, essentially, a mathematical meaning. Anything that increases the probability that a behavior will happen is a stimulus (if it comes before the behavior). Anything that increases the probability of a behavior increasing is a reinforcement (if it comes after). Anything that increases the probability of a behavior decreasing is a punishment or negative consequence.

One additional comment about these core concepts: Most behaviorists prefer the term *negative consequence* to the term *punishment* because of the negative connotations of the term *punishment* (e.g., harsh methods such as spanking). However, when used within the behavioral-learning approach, and because the term refers to a function rather than to any given method or set of methods, it should not matter which term is used. In this discussion, then, we give both to indicate that both are acceptable, provided the terms refer to functions and not methods.

Here is another example, again from George Scarlett's experience, showing the subtlety and power of these core concepts for explaining and determining how to intervene.

In a special program for troubled older children, one boy tantrumed frequently. His tantrums necessitated his being physically removed to the "quiet room" where he could "cool off." When a consultant asked the teachers for an example of what set off the tantrums, one teacher related an incident when the boy was trying to trade his dessert for another boy's chocolate milk. The teacher prevented the trade by reminding him *in a reasonable way* that he was lactose intolerant—whereupon he tantrumed.

The teacher relating this incident conveyed what most of the teachers felt; namely, that they were doing all that they could do because they were *acting in reasonable ways,* such as by reminding the boy of his being lactose intolerant.

What is especially interesting about this example is that the teachers, though trained to adopt a behavioral-learning approach, were actually not using this approach to understand the boy's tantrums. If they had been using the approach, they would have understood that their *acting in reasonable ways* was the stimulus setting off the tantrums, and once they realized this, they would then have thought up different ways of acting, such as by leading with empathy rather than with reason. This analysis was validated when it was noted that the boy did not tantrum when he was around one of the teachers who, during incidents such as the chocolate milk incident, led with empathy, not reason ("Gosh it must be hard to be allergic to milk. Doesn't seem fair, does it?").

We have given this example to show that it is not always self-evident what are the stimuli and **positive reinforcement** operating to maintain or increase unwanted behavior (e.g., tantruming) and not always self-evident what are the stimuli, reinforcements, and punishments (negative consequences) operating to maintain, increase, or decrease desired behavior. These have to be carefully assessed, and to do so may require taking a good deal of time to observe a student, his or her problem behavior, and the antecedents and consequences that may explain why the problem behavior persists. This observation can be done by the teacher or by someone in a supporting role, such as a school psychologist. However, whoever does the observing will likely need to set aside time to do nothing else but observe because discovering functional relationships takes a keen eye and the discernment of patterns that emerge over time.

Behavior Modification: A Two-Way Street

A second common misconception about behavioral-learning approaches is that they require thinking only about what we do or need to do *to* students, as if the arrow of influence goes in one direction only, from teacher to student. However, the arrows of influence go in two directions because students modify or influence teachers' behavior and not just the other way around (Patterson, 1982). Here is a common example from George Scarlett's observations:

> In a fifth-grade classroom, one student often disrupted lessons by making wisecracks and, in general, by being a "class clown." The teacher's first reaction was always to give a directive such as "Be quiet" and "Sit down." Then, when that did not work, she would threaten, "If you don't be quiet (sit down, etc.), you will have to go to the office," and then when that did not work, she would send the boy to the office.

Looked at from one angle, this teacher was modifying the boy's unwanted behavior—not by punishing it, because the unwanted behavior persisted and even increased, but by reinforcing it, probably because the boy gained so much attention and exerted so much control.

However, looked at from another angle, the boy was reinforcing the teacher's being coercive because when the boy left the classroom, the teacher no longer had to put up with his bad behavior. Behavioral-learning approaches call this kind of reinforcement **negative reinforcement** because removing something negative (the boy's disruptive behavior) made it more likely for the teacher's behavior (threatening and then sending the boy to the office) to be maintained or increased.

Avoiding Traps

The previous example illustrates another important concept of behavioral-learning approaches: the concept of avoiding *traps*. Since repeatedly sending a student to the office is not an ideal solution (indeed, it can create additional problems), professionals adopting a behavioral-learning approach describe this kind of situation as a teacher's falling into a trap. Here, the specific kind of trap was a **negative reinforcement trap.** Again, it was negative because something was being taken away (the disruptive presence of the boy). It was reinforcement because it increased the likelihood of the teacher being coercive and acting in the same way in the future. Negative reinforcement traps often play a central role in fostering and maintaining coercive behavior, as the work of G. R. Patterson (1982) has clearly shown.

Source: G. R. Patterson.

G. R. Patterson

With regard to the student's behavior, the trap was a **positive reinforcement trap** because he was getting the attention and gaining the control he wanted. In the example of the lactose intolerant boy, the trap was a **stimulus trap** because by acting in "reasonable ways," the teachers were unwittingly providing the stimulus that set off the boy's tantrums. In the example of the girl who stopped drawing when praised, the trap was a **punishment trap** because by praising the child, the teacher unwittingly decreased the desired behavior.

All traps have in common the fact that an educator unwittingly does something that contributes to the problem or that introduces a new problem. Therefore,

Educators must be careful to avoid the different traps or ways they can unwittingly encourage bad behavior.

another important feature of behavioral-learning approaches is the way these approaches assess for stimulus, reinforcement, and punishment traps. Once that assessment is made, educators can change their behavior to avoid traps, as when the teachers in the example of the boy who was lactose intolerant changed from being overly rational (reasonable) to being empathetic.

Putting the Behavioral-Learning Approach Into Practice: Being Scientific

Behavioral-learning approaches were first developed not in classrooms or clinics but in university laboratories. They evolved from 20th-century efforts to put the discipline of psychology on a more scientific footing. The emphasis was, then, on careful observation, operational definitions, measurement, and methods for testing hypotheses.

We see these same features defining behavioral-learning approaches. As mentioned, behavioral-learning approaches all emphasize the need to first observe carefully to discover the patterns, especially in chains of teacher-student interactions, that reveal functional relationships between antecedents, behaviors, and consequences—relationships that can then inform how best to design and implement interventions. Furthermore, and also as mentioned, behavioral-learning approaches all emphasize the need to operationalize target behaviors and goals—not "Billy will act appropriately" but "Billy will raise his hand before speaking at meeting time." And all fully developed behavioral-learning approaches record and measure for the purpose of evaluating whether or to what degree an intervention has succeeded—the equivalent of testing hypotheses.

In addition, and also in common with generally accepted definitions of "being scientific," behavioral-learning approaches attend to the mechanisms or processes of explaining change. They do so especially when giving us a variety of **schedules of reinforcement or punishment** to increase, decrease, and maintain behaviors. Thinking in terms of schedules is important for two reasons: First, different kinds of schedules are needed depending upon where one is in the process of getting a student to change. Second, different kinds are needed to wean students of having to be on a schedule; that is, to help students be well-behaved on their own.

At the beginning of an intervention, the schedules are apt to be continuous; each instance of a desired behavior receives immediate reinforcement, or each instance of an undesired behavior receives a punishment (negative consequence) or the removal of reinforcements. After a while, the schedules are apt to be discontinuous; a teacher reinforces only after certain intervals of time or only after a particular number of correct or desired responses. Finally, the schedules are apt to be random reinforcement schedules, so that a student cannot anticipate when a reinforcement or negative consequence will or will not occur. Once random reinforcement or random negative consequences are enough to maintain desired, "appropriate" behavior, a student is well on his or her way to showing desired behavior even when there is no teacher around. Like other approaches, then, behavioral-learning approaches aim at getting students to control themselves.

This brief overview of the essential concepts in behavioral-learning approaches is not meant to provide an exhaustive review. For that, readers are encouraged to read any of a number of excellent books and articles on behavioral-learning approaches (cf. Alberto & Troutman, 1999; Landrum & Kauffman, 2006; Maag, 2004; Patterson, 1982). Rather, this overview is meant to accomplish two limited goals. First, it is meant to explain the system of concepts that define the essence of behavioral-learning approaches. Second, it is meant to show how useful these approaches can be, especially for understanding and dealing with particularly problematic situations and particularly challenging students.

There are, however, dangers and risks in relying on behavioral-learning approaches. One risk has already been discussed in previous chapters; namely, the risk of giving teachers so much control that students may not learn how to function as responsible, self-regulating members in a democratic society. A second risk is that the approach may become too unwieldy for typical classrooms, resulting in teachers doing a poor job of implementing the approach. A poor job can mean several things, including not assessing for stimulus, reinforcement, and punishment traps and choosing the wrong reinforcers, wrong punishments, or wrong schedules. Whatever it means, a poor job can be worse than no job at all.

REFLECT   The discussion of professional behavioral-learning approaches distinguished such approaches from the ways that behavioral-learning approaches are often understood. What, if anything, surprised you about the discussion of professional behavioral-learning approaches? What might you realize now about how you once misunderstood professional behavioral-learning approaches?

Specific Discipline Approaches Using Behavioral-Learning Concepts and Principles

Sometimes specific discipline approaches, such as Lee and Marlene Canter's (1997) "assertive discipline" approach and Fredric Jones's (1987) "positive discipline" approach, are treated as being distinct from behavioral-learning approaches, which they are not. What makes them appear to be distinct is their focus on specific discipline problems and specific methods for addressing those problems. For example, in the case of the Canters, the specific problem is a teacher's either losing control by being nonassertive or gaining control by being hostile. The Canters' solution to this problem is to have teachers be "assertive." More will be said about assertive discipline in Chapter 8, when we discuss taking a systemic approach to behavior and classroom management. For now, assertive discipline serves simply as an example.

To become assertive in a classroom requires skill at adopting a certain style of relating to students. However, no approach relies solely on style to be effective, and the Canters' approach is no exception. Therefore, in addition to coaching teachers in ways to be assertive, the Canters also coach in ways to manage stimuli and consequences. For example, the Canters advocate a number of methods for responding to misbehavior by publicly recording instances of misbehavior, such as by writing a student's name on the blackboard and then writing checks next to the student's name each time the student repeats the misbehavior. The purpose of recording is to warn a student that there will be consequences if the misbehavior continues and to establish a record that can be used for justifying handing out particular consequences. With this method (often referred to as "names on the blackboard"), the more checks, the more substantial the negative consequences. In short, adopting an assertive teaching style, or any other style for that matter, still requires establishing consequences for misbehavior, and so the approaches of the Canters, Jones, and others are essentially behavioral-learning approaches.

Source: Marlene Canter.

Marlene Canter

Source: Lee Canter.

Lee Canter

Summary

In this chapter, we have seen how teaching so that students learn can be taken as the central feature defining learning approaches to behavior and classroom management. Here, we saw how teachers manage by teaching the relevance of school and schooling, by linking curriculum and pedagogy to students' interests and to the world outside of school, as well as by making the learning process interesting. Here, too, we saw how learning approaches teach students how to cooperate and behave in civil ways. Finally, we saw how behavioral-learning approaches manage the stimuli, reinforcements, and negative consequences that lead to students behaving "appropriately," so that the meaning of learning becomes more a matter of behavior and less a matter of thinking.

Learning approaches to behavior and classroom management build, then, on the essence of what it means to teach. They do so by focusing both on what students need to learn and on what methods are needed to foster learning. It is no wonder, then, that learning approaches are among the oldest and most widely used.

However, though learning approaches have been around for centuries and are widespread, their meaning has changed so that today's learning approaches differ significantly from those in previous eras. In particular, today's learning approaches share the assumption with other approaches that whatever is done for the purpose of managing behavior and classrooms, it is essential to keep teacher-student relationships positive. Furthermore, today's learning approaches reject the notion that teaching subject matter is distinct and separate from behavior and classroom management (Zins, Weissberg, Wang, & Walberg, 2004). Also, today's learning approaches see learning as involving much more than using conventional rewards and punishments. Finally, today's learning approaches take teaching to mean teaching *persons* and not just academic subjects. To teach for learning, then, means to teach persons whatever it is that they need to learn in order for them to thrive.

Web-Based Student Study Site

The companion Web site for *Approaches to Behavior and Classroom Management* can be found at www.sagepub.com/scarlettstudy.

Visit the Web-based student study site to enhance your understanding of the chapter content. The study materials include practice tests, flashcards, suggested readings, and Web resources.

Key Concepts

Constructivist model

Defining operationally

Discovery model

Learning approaches

Making learning relevant

Negative reinforcement

Negative reinforcement trap

Positive reinforcement

Positive reinforcement trap

Punishment (negative consequence)

Punishment trap

Schedules of reinforcement or punishment

Stimulus

Stimulus trap

Target behaviors

Transmission model

Discussion Questions

1. Can you remember a time when you or someone else took the approach that the cause of misbehavior was the child or group not knowing something or not knowing how to do something?

2. In your own history as a student, can you remember times when classroom misbehavior seemed directly related to a teacher's making the subject matter seem boring and irrelevant?

3. In your own experience, can you remember teachers who managed behavior and classrooms largely by making the subject matter of lessons both interesting and relevant?

4. From your own experience; provide one, two, or as many specific examples as you can of an educator teaching a child, adolescent, or group to act in cooperative, civil ways. If this is too difficult, try providing examples from outside school, such as examples from summer camp experience.

5. The idea that stimuli, reinforcements, and punishments (negative consequences) refer to functional relationships is a difficult idea for many to understand. To consolidate your understanding, from your own experience, can you give an example of something normally seen as serving to reinforce or increase a behavior that you once observed as serving to punish or decrease a behavior? And can you do the same for something normally seen as serving to punish that, in at least one incident, served to reinforce?

6. The term "trap" refers to caregivers (parents, teachers, etc.) unwittingly setting off or reinforcing bad behavior or unwittingly punishing good behavior. From your own experience, can you give examples of stimulus, reinforcement, and punishment traps?

Chapter **6** DEVELOPMENTAL APPROACHES

Throughout his elementary school years and into middle school, David was one of the most difficult and disruptive students—often because he cracked jokes at the most inappropriate times. Once, he made his third-grade teacher cry. However, most of the teachers saw in David something special, a boy who was essentially well-meaning and had a powerful intelligence and wonderful creativity. They were careful, then, to manage his behavior to prevent chaos but without discouraging his using his intelligence and creativity. Now David is in high school and doing just fine, using his intelligence and creativity to make positive contributions, such as his contribution as a worker at a local food co-op raising food for the homeless.

The opening example shows that what appears to be true for the present and short term may not be true for the long term. As an elementary school child, David appeared to be "up to no good" and "headed for trouble," but in the long run, he turned out fine, in large part because the majority of David's teachers took a developmental approach. What it means to take a developmental approach is the subject of this chapter.

By now, it should be clear that approaches are defined not so much by what they advocate as by what they *feature*. All approaches advocate relationship building, supporting learning, and development; being organized in order to create functioning learning environments; and accommodating diversity. So, our task in explaining developmental approaches must begin with defining not what is unique but what is featured. What is featured in developmental approaches is not so clear as one might first assume. In fact, of all the several types of approaches discussed throughout this text, developmental approaches may be the most hidden because they can't be seen in any one featured method and because they are defined as much by the patience of educators as they are by the specifics of what educators say or do.

This may surprise readers because one might reasonably assume just the opposite—that developmental approaches are easy to define. After all, isn't it true that virtually every educator, when managing behavior and classrooms, adopts a developmental approach when taking into account the age and stage of students? And isn't this taking into account the age and stage of students what is meant by adopting a developmental approach?

One answer is "yes"; a developmental approach is, indeed, any approach that emphasizes taking into account age and stage. However, this easy answer covers up what the real questions are for anyone actually engaged in figuring out what to do with students. The real questions are, "What exactly develops?" and "What do we mean by development?" and having answered these questions, "What exactly should we do to support development?" The minute we ask these questions, we realize that the answers aren't clear. On the one hand, if we fall back on abstract concepts, such as Piaget's stages of cognitive development (sensorimotor, preoperational, concrete operational,

formal operational), we find little help in figuring out specifically what to do
for students.

Piaget's Stages of Cognitive Development

Sensorimotor: A stage (normally ends by 24 months) characterized by children knowing the world more by physically exploring their surroundings than by representing (symbolizing).

Preoperational: A stage (normally ends around 6 years) characterized by children knowing the world more by representing (symbolizing) than by using logic and reasoning.

Concrete Operational: A stage (normally ends around 11 years) characterized by children knowing the world more by reasoning about what is directly in front of them than by reasoning about alternative interpretations/explanations and possibilities.

Formal Operational: A stage (normally begins around 11, but the endpoint is not set) characterized by knowing the world by reasoning about possibilities and about different plausible interpretations/explanations.

On the other hand, figuring out good methods for supporting development seems to lead in exactly the same direction as figuring out good methods to support learning—rendering the concept of development useless. In other words, if we get into the practical implications for adopting a developmental approach, the approach itself seems to disappear.

The role of Piaget in the history of education was described in Chapter 2.

USING THE CONCEPT OF DEVELOPMENT TO CONSTRUCT AN APPROACH

There are, however, good reasons for retaining the concept of development and using it to construct an approach to behavior and classroom management that is distinct from learning approaches. The reasons are many, but three, in particular, are essential.

Reason 1: Tying the Present to the Long Term

Source: Alfie Kohn.

Alfie Kohn

For material related to this concept, go to Video Clip 6.1 on the Student Resource CD bound into the back of your textbook.

First, unlike the other core concepts (relationship building, learning, organization, and accommodating diversity), development explicitly ties the present to the long term. This long-term view is nicely illustrated in Alfie Kohn's (1996) opening exercise for teachers attending his professional development workshops. He asks them, "What are your long-term goals for the students you work with? What would you like them to be—to be like—long after they've left you?" (p. 60).

Kohn (1996) reports that when asked these questions about long-term goals, teachers respond using words such as "caring," "responsible," and "curious." In other words, they respond with words that capture the character of persons rather than the content of what they know. In so doing, they reflect that to teach for development is to teach for the purpose of supporting character development and not just learning.

Furthermore, the teachers in Kohn's (1996) workshops unwittingly highlight the gap that exists between the long-term goals they have for their students and the short-term emphasis on compliance. As Kohn points out, none of the teachers in his workshops say that their long-term goal is for their students to become compliant adults. And as Ronald Butchart (1998a) and others have discussed, insisting on compliance and relying on rewards and punishments to control may have a snowball effect, resulting in secondary school teachers needing to adopt control-oriented methods and nondevelopmental approaches in order to maintain order. In Butchart's words, "Behaviorist modes of control lose their effectiveness through overuse . . . leaving secondary teachers little recourse but to teach defensively" (p. 9).

In sum, at issue for developmental approaches is not simply whether students behave themselves within any given school year and not simply whether students learn what they are supposed to learn in any given grading period. At issue is whether students develop as *persons* and progress on all of the most important **developmental tasks.**

Developmental tasks are those tasks that take years, not months or grading periods, to develop, and for many, even a lifetime may not be enough. You can't, for example, sit a 2-year-old down and say, "Listen carefully, I want to teach you the difference between real and pretend, how to think logically, and how to engage in collaborative relationships" because those distinctions and processes take years for a young child to develop. Similarly, you can't sit a 13-year-old down and say, "Listen carefully, I want to teach you how to have your own identity, be comfortable and competent in intimate-committed relationships, and have moral convictions based on universal principles." Some things, especially the most important things, take time to develop, which is why Piaget sometimes scoffed at Americans for wanting to speed up development (he called this "the American question"), and why David Elkind's (1987) book, *Miseducation,* which speaks directly to this problem of trying always to "speed up," struck such a chord. Of course, for children to progress on developmental tasks they need our support, but in supporting development, we know we must be patient in ways that differ from the way we are patient while teaching for learning.

Reason 2: Supporting Qualitative Changes in Students

Second, supporting development should be the aim of behavior and classroom management because unlike the other core concepts, development focuses on supporting qualitative changes in students, especially qualitative changes that have to do with the way students organize themselves in their efforts to master developmental tasks. This distinction between qualitative and quantitative is not clear-cut, but it is clear enough to be useful (see Table 6.1). We would, for example, be limited in describing age changes in students if all we could describe were quantitative changes, such as changes in height, size of working vocabulary, number of facts known about world geography, and so forth. We would not be so limited if we could add information about qualitative changes captured in distinctions such as the distinctions between cooperative and collaborative peer relationships (Selman & Hickey-Shultz, 1990; Sullivan, 1953), conventional and postconventional morality (Kohlberg, 1980), and impaired and healthy egos (Redl & Wineman, 1965). Adopting a developmental approach means, then, helping students develop qualitatively different and more mature ways of being in the world.

Table 6.1   Examples of Quantitative Versus Qualitative Changes

Quantitative Changes	Qualitative Changes
Growing taller	Egocentric vs. Capable of perspective taking
Increasing vocabulary	Conventional (rules oriented) vs. Principled morality
Increasing knowledge of facts about history	Defining oneself as others define oneself vs. Defining oneself independently

Reason 3: Focusing Attention on Inner Processes

Third, development should be the aim of behavior and classroom management because doing so focuses attention on **inner processes** and realities underlying appearances, realities that can lead to our evaluating students quite differently than if we were to focus only on overt behavior. Take, as an example, Piaget's experience with intelligence tests (Bringuier, 1980). Early on in his career, Piaget noticed that children who gave wrong answers to certain items on intelligence tests (e.g., saying "two mouses" when asked to give the plural of "mouse") were actually more advanced in their thinking than were some children who gave correct answers (e.g., saying "two mice"). They were more advanced because the thinking behind their mistakes was logical (e.g., "To make something plural, add an *s*.").

A more relevant example might be the irreverent humor one often finds in groups of adolescents, humor that questions society's conventions and what adults take to be sacred. While the humor may annoy and distract, within limits, it is "developmentally appropriate" and a positive sign of growth and development because it shows adolescents are defining themselves not only by identifying with adults but also by differentiating themselves from adults and their "old" ways. Therefore, a developmental approach focuses more on evaluating and supporting **inner processes** than it does on evaluating and supporting outward behavior and achievements (Werner, 1937).

Taking a Developmental Perspective: Appearance Versus Reality in Adolescent Humor

No other American president matches Abraham Lincoln for the way he is treated as a spiritual exemplar. His second inaugural address is not only one of the great speeches in American history. It is also a sermon. However, in his adolescence, Lincoln would reluctantly attend the Little Pigeon Creek Baptist Church and then, afterward, climb on a tree stump and parody the minister—much to the delight of his adolescent friends (Donald, 1995, p. 33). Therefore, though his behavior as an adolescent might seem to predict an areligious, nonspiritual, or even antireligious future, the very opposite proved to be the case.

To support the development of inner processes, those adopting developmental approaches invariably support constructivist approaches to teaching, not only with regard to academic subjects but also with regard to helping students become better friends and more responsible members of the classroom community.

They do so because constructivist approaches focus on processes and not just achievements. In a way, then, developmental approaches are to behavior and classroom management what organic farming is to gardening and farming. With developmental approaches, the focus is more on building processes such as thinking processes (akin to building good soil) than it is on implementing control methods (akin to adding chemicals).

For material related to this concept, go to Video Clip 6.2 on the Student Resource CD bound into the back of your textbook.

Developmental approached attend to cultivating the "soil" for supporting long-term growth and development.

The following is another example of a teacher taking a developmental approach with a disruptive boy in an afterschool program for "troubled" children; she developed his skill as an artist by using a behavior (making Godzilla drawings) that, on the surface, appeared to be a behavior needing to be extinguished. Here is teacher Seki's account:

One of D's favorite monsters is Godzilla, and he likes drawing it. When he draws Godzilla, he also draws people running away, their blood, and dead men. In the school program, children are not allowed to draw violence, battle, and blood. Once during free time, when he tried to talk to one of the teachers about Godzilla, she said, "I don't want to talk about Godzilla. If you talk about Godzilla, I will go—because I don't know Godzilla and am not interested in it. I also feel uncomfortable about the topic. If you will talk about another topic or do some puzzle games, I am happy to play with you." D understood that others did not like his drawing Godzilla, but because he enjoyed others' negative reactions to his Godzilla drawings, he drew them anyway—which sometimes earned him a time out.

However, after some thought, I decided to go in a different direction. I checked a website full of Godzilla pictures and Godzilla stories—to learn more about Godzilla and to practice drawing Godzilla. Then one day, when D was drawing Godzilla alone during art time, I went to his table and asked him what he was drawing.

D: "Godzilla."

T: "Um, it looks like Godzilla. But it seems that you forgot to draw a part on his face. Many people don't know it."

D.   "Wait, wait . . ." After he thought for a while, he said, "nose?" and then he added the nose.

T: "Yes, that's right. But still, you forgot to draw another part." He became very serious while trying to remember Godzilla's face.

D: "Ears?"

T: "Yes, now you know."

He was glad to know that Godzilla has ears. I explained how Godzilla's ears look, and then he added the ears. He was satisfied with his Godzilla and started to draw fire and a battle scene.

T: "Your Godzilla is getting better. Do you know how Godzilla's body is? His skin?"

D: "I know! Like this?" and then he added the ragged skin on Godzilla's body.

T: "Yes, Godzilla has a hard but ragged body, like a rock. Do you know how Godzilla walks? He walks with a big sound because he has big feet." Then I pointed to the thin feet D had drawn.

D: "Like this?" and he then he redrew Godzilla's feet.

T: "Bigger."

D listened carefully, concentrated on his drawing, and then redrew to make the feet bigger.

T: "Now, your Godzilla looks like a real Godzilla! Good job."

After this interaction, we had many opportunities to draw Godzilla. Now, when D draws Godzilla, he shows more maturity, the maturity of an artist. He doesn't dwell so much on people running away from Godzilla, nor on the blood, nor on trying to annoy others. Now he tries to capture the details of Godzilla—paying attention mostly to matters of shape and proportion. (Seki, 2005, p. 21)

The important lesson in this example is this: What may appear on the surface to be problem behaviors can, in reality, be developed, and in their development, we see the development of inner processes (e.g., capacity to symbolize as an artist symbolizes) that help a child function better.

In this chapter, then, we show how developmental approaches to behavior and classroom management work to support long-term development, qualitative changes in mastering developmental tasks, and processes such as reasoning and symbolizing. In so doing, we hope to show both the subtlety and power of developmental approaches for giving children and adolescents what they need.

Review

The following are reasons for retaining the concept of development and using it to construct an approach to behavior and classroom management:

(1) Tying the present to the long term

(2) Supporting qualitative changes in students

(3) Focusing attention on inner processes

SUPPORTING DEVELOPMENT ON DEVELOPMENTAL TASKS: THE EXAMPLE OF MORAL DEVELOPMENT

To illustrate what is meant by supporting development on developmental tasks, we give the example of moral development. We do so for two reasons: First, much has been written about moral development and moral education (Althof & Berkowitz, 2006; Kohlberg, 1980; Power, Higgins, & Kohlberg, 1989). Second, moral development ties in directly with our focus on behavior and classroom management because so much of what is aimed for when managing behavior and classrooms has a moral dimension (Nucci, 2006). We saw this in Chapter 4 when discussing community approaches. We see this again in the way individual students develop morally because developing morally often leads to students not needing external control or "management."

This last point illustrates one of the more subtle and important assumptions underlying developmental approaches: the assumption that development is the ultimate "cure" for problem behavior. After all, if students have developed capacity for reasoning and critical thinking, for collaborative friendships, and for making principled judgments about right and wrong, they are not likely to "be" behavior problems. This observation is behind Kohlberg and Mayer's (1972) famous article, "Development as the Aim of Education."

With regard to the moral development of individuals, from a developmental perspective, the main point is that moral development occurs as a series of qualitative changes made possible by children and adolescents being actively engaged in solving the many everyday problems that raise issues about what is just (fair) and caring. To support students' moral development is, then, to support their being actively engaged in problem solving in situations with a moral dimension—and from preschool through high school, there is no end to the list of situations with a moral dimension.

This constructivist perspective on moral development has been well-documented by a number of researchers, beginning with Piaget's (1932) groundbreaking research on the moral judgment of the child. However, by far the most influential researcher of moral development and moral education has been Lawrence Kohlberg (Kohlberg, 1980; Kohlberg & Lickona, 1990; Kohlberg & Mayer, 1972; Munsey, 1980), so here we will concentrate on Kohlberg's work. We do so also because Kohlberg's work has spawned a new generation of researchers and educators devoted to making behavior and classroom management a moral endeavor (Nucci, 2006).

Kohlberg began with a focus not on moral behavior but on moral judgment because, he argued, moral judgment is the only aspect of a moral act that is explicitly moral. One may, for example, give money to the poor, but solely to lower one's taxes. Or a child may share her snack with another, but solely to win the other's friendship. Therefore, the appearance of morality may mask essentially self-serving motives. However, judgments about right and wrong, fair and unfair, caring and not caring, these judgments directly relate to morality. Furthermore, though the correlation is not perfect, there is a positive and significant correlation between how one makes judgments about moral issues and how one acts (Kohlberg, 1980).

Source: Courtesy of Harvard University Archives.

Lawrence Kohlberg

Kohlberg's work has given us stages that capture the qualitative changes in the development of students' moral judgments. In the first stage, preconventional morality, children rely on what adults say is right and wrong or on the rules adults impose and that define right and wrong. That is, for children in a preconventional stage, morality is "on the outside." Somewhat paradoxically, by giving adults the authority to determine right and wrong, children often do as they wish—until some adult steps in to control them—because they have no inner moral compass to control or guide them.

In the second stage, conventional morality, what is right and wrong is determined by rules and procedures that have been internalized by the child, as evidenced by the child's seeing rules and procedures as applicable to everyone, regardless of status and authority. At the conventional stage, then, morality is "on the inside." This internalization process comes about not by passively internalizing adult morality but by wrestling with everyday problems that necessitate some sort of moral system for there to be reasonably satisfying interpersonal relationships. Even the simplest of problems, such as determining which first grader gets to be at the head of a line, can become an occasion for children to puzzle about what is the moral solution.

In the third stage, postconventional morality, the legalism of a rule-oriented morality is replaced by a moral system that relies more on universal principles and judgments about extenuating circumstances. Principles and judgments about extenuating circumstances are needed to make moral judgments in complex situations, situations where there may be painful, even terrible, dilemmas to manage, dilemmas that may lead one to break rules in order to do the right thing.

Review

Kohlberg's Stages of Morality

Stage 1: Preconventional Morality

Children rely on what adults say is right and wrong or on the rules adults impose and that define right and wrong. Morality is "on the outside."

Stage 2: Conventional Morality

What is right and wrong is determined by rules and procedures that have been internalized by the child. Morality is "on the inside."

Stage 3: Postconventional Morality

A person's moral system relies more on universal principles and judgments about extenuating circumstances to make moral judgments in complex situations.

Despite what some of his critics have said, Kohlberg (1984) was clear about the dual nature of moral development, with moral development having to do with both care and justice. For children to develop morally, then, they need support to develop the capacity for acting on what is just and fair, the capacity for showing empathy and care, and the capacity for judging what is just and fair.

Lest this brief overview of Kohlberg's stages feel so abstract as to have little practical value for working with students, consider the following observation (made by George Scarlett) of three children in a first-grade classroom.

A few years ago, while consulting for an early childhood special education program, I had the opportunity to join two boys and a girl for snack. The snack of the day was cookies, and the rule was no more than two cookies per child. As was my custom when I visited classrooms, I found a way to test the meaning of classroom rules for the children, by announcing I was going to break the rule and have three cookies.

The boy nearest me hardly looked up. His reaction to my breaking the rule suggested that, for him, rules came from the "outside" and were really no different than an adult telling children what to do. The second boy looked surprised and puzzled, but then with a shrug, he seemed to be saying I could do whatever I wanted. His behavior suggested that for a moment, at least, he was poised between two worlds: the world where those in authority rule and the world where rules govern everyone, including those in authority. He was, then, only just beginning to make the shift to having morality be on the inside.

In contrast to the boys, the girl was visibly annoyed, and after a brief pause, she announced with some irritation, "No, you can only have two!" For her, my being an adult made no difference: a rule was a rule. Her morality was definitely on the inside. (Scarlett, 1998, pp. 85–86)

This example illustrates what is meant by children **putting morality on the inside,** but it also illustrates the significance of doing so because the informal test of what rules meant to the children perfectly discriminated who was having and making more "trouble." The first boy (who was the reason for the consultant's visit) was a particularly uncooperative and disruptive boy; the second was occasionally disruptive, and the girl was quite well-behaved. This example illustrates, then, that morality on the inside, in the form of rules owned by the children themselves, does a better job regulating behavior than does morality on the outside, in the form of rules imposed by those in authority.

So, how does someone support children "putting morality on the inside" and developing morally? As just mentioned, developmentalists suggest adopting a constructivist model of teaching, one that gets students to actively problem solve around issues pertaining to rules, justice, and caring. They also suggest that educators find acceptable ways to share control—especially through discussions during class meetings about what rules should govern the classroom. We saw a clear example of this in Chapter 4 of a teacher getting children to generate rules to govern their meeting after their meeting had fallen apart. In their essay on the class meeting, Kohlberg and Lickona (1990) explain how putting morality on the inside is connected to class discussions, such as the discussion in the example in Chapter 4:

> When children feel responsibility for the rules of the classroom and part of the group that makes them, they are more likely to respect the rules in their behavior than when they have no hand in making or enforcing them. Morality begins to become internal rather than external. As a third-grade girl said to her teacher, "It feels weird to break your own rules. . . . It's like disobeying your own self!" (p. 165)

Chapter 4 also provides an example of supporting the moral development of older students, namely, the example of what Forrest Gathercoal refers to as "judicious discipline." Central to judicious discipline is the method of interviewing students following some incident of misbehavior. The purpose of the interview is to turn the incident into an educational opportunity by getting students

Developmental approaches tend to be more optimistic about the future and children's capacity to change.

to reflect on what happened, to support a process leading to their understanding what is and what is not responsible behavior. As Gathercoal (1998) puts it,

> Professional educators are usually patient and understanding with students and know that academic accomplishments take some time to develop. It would only follow, then, that the same professional approach toward behavior problems would be equally effective. (p. 206)

As an additional example of supporting the moral development of older students, Joseph Reimer (1989, p. 69) describes an incident when Kohlberg was consulting to a local high school attempting to become more democratic. The teachers there had arranged to show a film to the students, and prior to the showing, students and teachers had agreed there would be no smoking (this was the 1970s) during the film. However, once the lights dimmed and the film began, out came the cigarettes. Kohlberg had the teachers stop the film and meet with him outside, where he explained how important it is in a democracy for members to respect agreements. With that message in mind, the teachers reentered the film room and held a brief discussion with students about respecting agreements.

The moral lesson learned was neither about cigarettes nor about being obedient. Rather, it was about honoring agreements. Adolescents are likely to be transitioning from a conventional, legalistic morality to a more principled morality. Being in transition, they are apt to disrespect even those conventions that have been agreed upon, such as the convention to not smoke. They need help, then, finding justifications for following conventions and honoring agreements around conventions they do not like.

Readers may have noticed that the previous examples fit comfortably within community approaches. One might then ask, "What is the difference between community approaches and developmental approaches, since both rely on a constructivist model of teaching and both emphasize methods that promote moral development?" The difference is a matter of emphasis—as is the case for all approaches. The approaches discussed in Chapter 4 make the development of communities the emphasis. The approaches discussed in this chapter make the development of persons the emphasis.

REFLECT Developmental approaches aim to help students mature on developmental tasks that take years, not months, to master. Can you think of a time when you were helped to mature on some developmental task, and can you identify some developmental task that you have yet to master?

Resolving Conflicts: Problem Solving and Perspective Taking

The distinction between community and developmental approaches is perhaps better reflected in methods focusing not as directly on community building as on getting students to adopt more mature ways of resolving conflicts. In helping to resolve conflicts between teachers and students and between students themselves, developmental approaches encourage students to problem solve, coordinate agendas, and, when necessary, negotiate compromises. Here is one example of a teacher using a developmental approach to help resolve a conflict between three children and herself:

> Stopping by the sand table, the kindergarten teacher calls out, "Time to clean up, it's circle time." Dana and Sylvie protest and dawdle. Rather than force them to clean up, the teacher asks, "What is the problem?" "If we put the lid on the sand table, our castle will be squished!" The teacher then asks, "Can you think of a way to clean up without squashing your castles?" After some thought, the children stack up blocks to prop up the lid, then go happily to their meeting. (Scarlett, 2003, p. 93)

The teacher's response to the children was her way of working to coordinate agendas, her own agenda being for the children to come to meeting and the children's agenda being to preserve their sand castles. Her response was also a way of helping the children move (develop) from immature ways of responding to frustration (e.g., by whining, by refusing to cooperate) to more mature ways that use thinking to problem solve. Again, a developmental approach supports the development of inner processes that take years, not days, to mature. That is, the teacher in this example will have to continue to support problem solving because problem solving is not something that children learn once and for all time.

With respect to conflicts between students, often teachers find themselves having to first break up quarrels and fights and only then stimulate discussion that gets students to consider points of view other than their own. Here is Grace Mitchell, a leading American early childhood educator, advocating just that for very young children:

> (When breaking up a fight) "You might suggest that each child bring you a chair (from opposite sides of the room). That way you will divert their attention and give yourself a moment to plan. Placing the chairs so that the children are sitting facing each other, their knees touching, you might

say, 'I can see that you are both angry. When there is an argument and each person thinks that he or she is right, we need to *com-mu-ni-cate* with words instead of fists.' (It's helpful to stress each syllable when introducing a 'grown-up' word.) Help the children use words by saying, 'Joey, tell Tony why you think you are right.' . . . If Tony interrupts, explain, 'No, Tony, it's Joey's turn to talk. When he is finished, you'll have your turn.' Guide the conversation, making sure that each child has equal time to talk. Then ask, 'What do you think is the best way to settle this?'" (Scarlett, 1998, p. 4)

In the case of older students, the facilitator (sometimes someone other than the classroom teacher) will use language different from that suggested by Grace Mitchell; however, the goal will be the same. Older students in conflict with one another still need help to listen and understand one another. Unfortunately, egocentricity is found in all age groups. Here is an example of a high school principal working to get one student to see the effect and potential danger his inappropriate humor has on others. The boy (S) had been sent to the principal's office after yelling in his science teacher's class that another boy in the class had threatened to beat him up after school. S admitted that he made the whole thing up and that he was just saying it to make a joke:

P: With this joke, who did you think was going to laugh? Who did you think the joke was for?

S: It was for Nathan (the science teacher).

P: You were saying someone is going to beat you up after school.

S: Yeah.

P: I don't get it. I don't see how Nathan would think it's funny when you shout across the room that you're gonna get beat up after school.

S: I was just playing around.

P: But you said it was a joke.

S: It wasn't like a Ha-Ha joke; it was like a "I'm just kidding, Nathan."

P: Jokes and kidding and playing around all to me sound like somebody should be having fun. Is that what you meant to happen—that Nathan would have fun with this?

S: I was just playing around.

P: I think it's very inappropriate. It certainly changes the way things are in his class. You thought that by telling Nathan that Tom was threatening you and that he was going to get you after school that that would be fun for Nathan.

S: I . . .

P: It certainly changes the way things are in his class. . . . I think you're tearing his class apart by making jokes about physical violence. (Wiseman, 1994)

Of course, this exchange could also be seen as a method fitting right into a learning approach because the principal was trying to teach S something about the effects of his behavior. However, because the boy had a long-standing reputation (well-deserved) for disrupting classes and annoying others, this exchange was but a small part of an ongoing process designed to support whatever capacity the boy had for perspective taking and whatever motivation he had for contributing positively to his school. In short, this exchange was but a small part of a developmental approach to help this boy become more mature.

DEVELOPING "CONTROLS FROM WITHIN": SUPPORTING EGO DEVELOPMENT

So far, supporting the development of inner processes has referred to supporting problem solving, perspective taking, and thinking in general. However, it can also refer to supporting students in their efforts to control their impulses and develop what Redl and Wineman (1965) called controls from within. Developing "controls from within" is more than a matter of developing thinking— as anyone who has ever struggled to control his or her diet fully realizes. Self-control is, then, a complicated and subtle achievement that goes far beyond thinking.

Self-Control and the Psychodynamic Tradition

Of all the several theoretical traditions that have focused on how to help children develop self-control, the psychodynamic tradition has, perhaps, done the most. We focus, then, on this tradition in particular, both to gain further

Fritz Redl

Redl's contributions to the field are also discussed in Chapters 1 and 2.

understanding of what it means to adopt a developmental approach and also to keep alive the wisdom of the psychodynamic tradition. In recent years, the psychodynamic tradition has been neglected as other traditions have been featured, traditions that favor methods that are easy to implement and easy to measure. Methods derived from the psychodynamic tradition generally require a good deal from educators in terms of making good judgments and being sensitive to students' experience. And because the tradition values long-term effects, the effects are hard to measure.

One of the leading examples of the psychodynamic tradition is the work of Fritz Redl and his coworkers (Redl, 1966; Redl & Wattenberg, 1959; Redl & Wineman, 1965; Trieschman, Whittaker, & Brendtro, 1969). Redl worked mostly with troubled children in residential treatment centers. However, his work has direct relevance for regular classroom teachers. As Seymour Sarason (1982) has reminded us, it is wrong to think that those with disabilities require a different theory of human development than those without disabilities. We will have more to say about this in Chapter 10.

Redl used the psychoanalytic concepts of **ego supports** for **ego development** to explain his developmental approach. Roughly speaking, ego refers to that part of the personality that is involved in assessing reality—both external reality and internal reality. Ego supports refer to those actions that give support to a child's or adolescent's assessing reality correctly and acting on that assessment.

Providing ego support requires an ongoing balancing act and keen sensitivity to what a child or adolescent is *experiencing*. On the one hand, adults need to manage behavior and exert control over children and adolescents. On the other hand, they also need to provide space and opportunity for children and adolescents to manage their own behavior and exert control over themselves. We see this balancing act and sensitivity in one of Redl's suggested methods for managing behavior, **proximity control**. Here is how Redl and Wineman (1965) explain proximity control:

> We found that often the mere fact of coming close to youngsters or having them around or near the adult at the table would actually have a calming effect on the children. We want to make sure, by the way, that this proximity, as a calming ego- and superego-supportive device, is not confused with the proximity of the threatening person who is within easy reach of the youngster's head, ears, hair, or chin in an anticipation of punitive control. (p. 164)

In short, proximity control makes it easier for children to control themselves. Table 6.2 lists additional methods suggested by Redl and Wineman for providing ego support.

TABLE 6.2   Redl and Wineman's Suggested Methods for Providing Ego Support

Method	Description and Functions of Suggested Methods
Proximity control	Moving closer to a student in order to help a student feel more secure and under control
Planful ignoring	Ignoring minor incidents that will die down on their own or minor incidents of testing authority
Signal interference	Pointing or otherwise gesturing to a misbehaving child indicating he or she needs to control himself or herself—best done at early stages of misconduct
Hurdle help	Providing assistance at some phase in a child's work—when work is becoming too frustrating for the child to handle by himself or herself
Support from routines	Establishing clear group routines to help students know what is expected of them and help them control themselves
Humor	Providing humor to diffuse anxiety, especially anxiety that occurs when students challenge authority

The psychodynamic, developmental approach is even more clearly shown in Redl's (1966) insightful analysis of the child's experience of punishment—and how that experience determines whether punishment will work well or not. It is possible for punishment to lead to growth and development, says Redl, but only under the following conditions:

- The child experiences the displeasure to which we expose him.
- The child perceives the difference between the source of his predicament and its real cause (i.e., he knows he's to blame).

- The child directs his anger toward himself so that he eventually comes up with a kind of "New Year's resolution" not to get himself into trouble again.
- In future temptation situations, the child makes use of the internal image left from previous incidents to mobilize self-control before acting out.

In listing these conditions, Redl (1966) shows us how difficult it is for children to make good use of punishment. At each step in the process, something can easily go wrong, such as when children feel the cause of their predicament is the adult punishing them, not themselves. Because punishment is so difficult for children to process and use constructively, punishment often results in children experiencing adults as being mean—and, too often, the gap between the time of the punishment and the next "temptation situation" is just too long, resulting in a child forgetting whatever it is he had resolved not to do.

However, from an ego support perspective, it is possible to provide enough support during the punishment process to get children to benefit from punishment, provided that educators know what the child or adolescent is experiencing and know what to do and say at each step of the way. For example, if a child blames the teacher for his predicament, the teacher must immediately help the child to see things differently, perhaps by saying how sorry he or she is that the child has to be punished and then reminding the child what led up to his being punished. Here, once again, is the example offered in Chapter 3 of a teacher having to send her student, Dennis, out of the classroom after he had hit someone (for him, a punishment). This time, we can look at the example as an example of providing ego support.

> "Do you remember what we decided would happen if you hurt anyone?" He nodded and remained serious as I continued. "Now I have to call Mrs. Alexander because that's what we agreed to do if this happened. But this is your classroom, and this is where you belong. And we're right in the middle of math workshop. I know you really like it, and you're so good at that math computer game. And now you're going to have to miss your time there. I am very sad that you have to miss the rest of math workshop; I hope you calm down very quickly with Mrs. Alexander so that you don't miss anything else. This is where you belong." (Scarlett, 1998, p. 177)

The main point here is not about punishment but how it is not always easy to provide ego support. One has to be finely attuned to how a child or adolescent is feeling and experiencing and shape decisions, words, and actions accordingly, all with the long-term goal that the child will eventually control himself. Here is Fritz Redl and David Wineman (1965) discussing their developmental approach for times when teachers have to physically restrain children who have lost control. Even in such dramatic times, the message remains the same, that the aim is for children to develop capacity to control themselves:

> We want to make perfectly clear that what we are calling "physical constraint" has nothing whatever to do with "physical punishment." . . . [During moments of physical restraint the] adult can afford no counter aggression or an ounce more of counter force than is necessary to achieve the goal of restraint. He has to remain calm, friendly, affectionate. . . . The attitude he tries to convey, put into a mixture of the child's language and our own, would sound like this:
>
> "Listen, kid, this is nuts. There is not the slightest reason for you to act that way. . . . We like you. There is nothing to fear, but there is nothing to gain by such behavior. You didn't get us mad by it, for we know you can't help it right now. But we sure hope this will reduce as time goes on. We aren't holding it against you, either. You can't make up for it. You needn't; this behavior is too . . . unreasonable for any such thought. We want only one thing: get it over with, snap back into your more reasonable self, so we can communicate with you again." (p. 212)

The previous examples might give the impression that ego support refers only to what we say and do to students. However, ego support also refers to the many nonverbal ways educators indirectly support self-control, such as by planning daily schedules so that young children do not have to sit too long, organizing cooperative learning groups with "just the right mix" of students, and providing high school students with workshops on what constitutes plagiarism and why plagiarism is not something students should want to do. Whatever the method, the aim is always to help students to control themselves, make good decisions, and decide beforehand not to misbehave. Remember the example from Chapter 4 of Theodore Sizer describing his experience as a faculty member at a high school where faculty waited in the hallway while students in the auditorium got themselves ready for morning assembly? This was a method very much in keeping with Redl's ways of supporting the development of egos and self-control.

Providing ego support, then, is not about providing rewards and punishments. Once again, it is about providing the supports needed for students to make good decisions and exercise self-control. Here is one further example of a teacher providing ego support for very young children to control themselves. In this example, the teacher was about to use a hot-air popper to make popcorn.

She knew that as soon as she turned the machine on, the children would reach and grab. So, to prevent them from doing so, she had them practice controlling themselves:

Teacher: Are we going to touch the machine?

Children: Nooo!

Teacher: Are we going to grab the popcorn as it comes out?

Children: Nooo!

Teacher: Look at your hands (She holds out her own hands, and the children do the same.) Tell them, "DON'T TOUCH!"

Children: (in unison) "DON'T TOUCH!"

When the moment came, no one touched—because the support given the children was enough for them to control themselves. (Scarlett, 1998, p. 5)

 **REFLECT** Take a moment to evaluate the ways a classroom provides ego support—that is, support aimed at helping students manage their impulses and emotions. Can you give one example of ego support, as Redl and Wineman thought of ego support?

Reactions to Misbehavior

In Chapter 1, we discussed Forrest Gathercoal's (1998) example of the two boys who had defaced the walls of a school building. As you may remember, one boy was asked to wash the wall he had defaced because he both understood and accepted this consequence as being logical. The other boy was asked to go into counseling because in complaining that washing the wall was the janitor's job, not his, he revealed he had a clinical problem that was preventing him from forming positive relationships with those in authority. In short, we see in this example an important principle for developmental approaches: Consequences for misbehavior must be matched not to the deed but to the person and what the person needs in order to develop.

Furthermore, in this example of matching the consequence not to the outward deed but to what the child or adolescent needs, we see caring inquiry as being essential. To determine what is needed, educators who are committed to a developmental approach begin neither with prescribed consequences nor with rhetorical, negative questions such as "Why did you do that?" Instead, they begin with thoughtful, supportive questions directed at getting at a student's perception and experience of both the problem and the solution. They then evaluate that perception and experience in terms of some adopted developmental sequence that takes the task of disciplining beyond that of simply helping a student to learn.

In the case of the two boys who had defaced a school wall, we might say that the first boy could take the point of view of the school and those in authority concerning property and property damage. We might also say that by doing so, the boy had developed beyond relating to adults in terms of what they could do or not do for him, to the point where he was capable of entering into partnerships.

In contrast, the second boy could not take the point of view of the school and those in authority, and because he was not able to do so, he was not ready to form partnerships with teachers and others in authority. Furthermore, it was clear that no amount of teaching for learning would produce a change in the short term. That is, the second boy was not open to learning. In his case, then, we can interpret counseling as a method for providing the additional ego supports needed to support long-term developmental change.

DEVELOPMENTALLY APPROPRIATE PRACTICE

So far, we have discussed what is not so apparent about developmental approaches. There remains what was mentioned in the beginning about the need to adapt methods to the age and stage of students. What was not made clear is what adapting to age and stage entails. To clarify, then, we here examine the popular concept of developmentally appropriate practice and show how this concept has been both understood and misunderstood.

When used appropriately, developmentally appropriate practice helps teachers shape curriculum and choose management methods that are both age and individually appropriate (Bredekamp, 1986). The previous example of getting very young children to practice not touching popcorn is an example of what is meant by choosing a method appropriate for a particular age group. This method would not be appropriate for older children and adolescents who are more capable of using a teacher's verbal instructions to monitor their own behavior. Counseling for the older boy who defaced the school wall is an example of what is meant by choosing a method appropriate for an individual.

There are also misuses of this concept, such as when a single method is applied to a group of same-age children without regard for the fact that children of the same age are apt to differ in maturity from each other. In other words, to insure developmentally appropriate practice, teachers need to apply different methods depending on students' stage or level of maturity and not just depending on their age.

In short, when it comes to creating developmentally appropriate practice in behavior and classroom management, there are no prepackaged programs for behavior and classroom management and no programs that will fit one age group and every student within an age group.

Summary

In this chapter, we have seen how adopting a developmental approach is a lot subtler and more complex than many assume it to be. As mentioned, many assume a developmental approach means simply adapting management methods to the age and stage of a student, such as by using simplified directions for young children and humor that appeals to adolescents. This is, indeed, one meaning of taking a developmental approach, but as mentioned, there are other meanings as well. Here, we have tried to show this in the way developmental educators think in terms of the long term, support qualitative changes by supporting progress on developmental tasks, and support the development of inner processes, such as the processes of perspective taking, reasoning, and controlling impulses.

However, even with these discussions about the subtleties in developmental approaches, some readers might still assume that developmental approaches are easy to employ—or at least no more difficult to employ than any others. In fact, the opposite seems to be the case, as indicated by one teacher's comment during a workshop on developmental approaches. After the workshop leader had gone on for some time about the importance of sharing control with students, stimulating thinking, and so forth, this teacher suddenly jumped to her feet and, in an irritated voice, explained that she was alone in her classroom with too many students, many of whom had serious problems. It is all fine and dandy, she said, to talk about supporting development, except when the ship is going down (Scarlett, 1998, p. 189). Her point is well taken. To support development as a way of managing behavior and classrooms is a worthy, but not an easy, cause, which, once again, reminds us of Piaget's (1977) insightful comment about the best methods and approaches being the most difficult (p. 712).

Nevertheless, despite their being difficult to implement, developmental approaches have a great deal of merit precisely because they link what we do for the short term with what we want children to become in the long term. In so doing, they demand from us not only a trust in the process of development but also a trust in children.

By trust, developmental approaches do not mean trust that children will always behave themselves or trust that, when left unsupervised, adolescents will stay out of trouble.

Rather, developmental approaches mean trusting that persistent support for inner processes and persistent provision of opportunities for children and adolescents to exercise self-control will eventually pay off. Developmental approaches do not, then, deny that there are challenges in keeping order, keeping children safe, and achieving necessary goals for the short term. They just don't see the short term as always taking precedence.

Web-Based Student Study Site

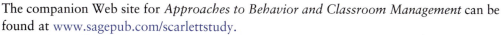

The companion Web site for *Approaches to Behavior and Classroom Management* can be found at www.sagepub.com/scarlettstudy.

   Visit the Web-based student study site to enhance your understanding of the chapter content. The study materials include practice tests, flashcards, suggested readings, and Web resources.

Key Concepts

Controls from within

Conventional morality

Developmental tasks

Ego development

Ego supports

Inner processes

Perspective taking

Postconventional morality

Preconventional morality

Proximity control

Putting morality on the inside

Qualitative changes

Discussion Questions

1. This chapter has made much of the appearance-reality distinction, both as it applies to specific behaviors and as it applies to students. Can you think of a time when a child's behavior appeared to be misbehavior, but, from a developmental perspective, it could be seen as developmentally appropriate or even as a sign of maturing? And can you think of an example of a student considered to be a "problem" who, from a developmental perspective, might be considered to be going through a developmental phase or transition or considered to be someone with a positive long-term future?

2. In this chapter, much has been made about supporting the development of inner processes, such as perspective taking, reasoning, and controlling impulses and

emotions. Can you give examples of an adult supporting the development of a child's or adolescent's inner processes, especially around problem behavior?

3. In your own efforts to manage your emotions, how do you think you have matured? If managing emotions is not a good example, choose some other process and evaluate how you have matured. Try to evaluate without using quantitative terms such as *more*. Try to evaluate so as to distinguish qualitative changes in the way you have managed emotions, reasoned, or engaged in perspective taking.

PART IV

Organization

The word *management* implies organization, and, indeed, to manage behavior and classrooms demands exceptional knowledge and organizational skill. But what exactly does *organizational skill* mean? In this section, we explore two very different meanings. The first meaning has to do with organizing time, space, the built environment, and the way both students and educators are best organized into groups. The second meaning has to do with organizing interactions into interpersonal systems. Both meanings are central to understanding how one can prevent or respond to problem behavior.

Chapter 7 explains how organizing time, space, the built environment, and groups can go a long way toward preventing problem behavior. In this chapter, we look at why organization is so central to behavior and classroom management and how educators can use organization to keep students moving in desired directions and headed toward achieving desired goals.

Chapter 8 focuses on a much-neglected approach, the classroom systems approach to behavior and classroom management. Using this approach in conjunction with others, we see how reorganizing the ways that students and educators relate to one another can provide needed help for dealing with chronic problem behavior.

Chapter 7

ORGANIZATIONAL APPROACHES

In Mrs. LeRose's classroom, the glue bottles were lined up on the shelf like soldiers on parade. Construction paper was arranged in rainbow order, and markers were in separate jars for each color. Furthermore, each morning, children arrived, took out their folders, and got right to work. The schedule printed on the blackboard indicated what the children would be doing that day, and at any moment, Mrs. LeRose might announce, "Desk check!" after which the children lifted their desktops for her to check for the following:

- · At least three pencils sharpened and ready for use
- · One eraser
- · Spelling and social studies books on the right
- · Math and science books on the left
- · Extra paper in red folders
- · NO TRASH![1]

In Mrs. LeRose's classroom, then, children knew where everything (and everyone) should go. Not surprising, few misbehaved, as children and teacher moved together like synchronized swimmers.

The opening example, though extreme, demonstrates how organization can become an approach to behavior and classroom management. Here, we focus on the approaches that lead with organization.

Organization is essential for behavior and classroom management, but when overused, it can make students feel resentful and over-controlled.

In many ways, organizational approaches try to establish control in a way that Dewey (1963) once likened to a game. He wrote, "As long as the game goes on with a reasonable smoothness, the players do not feel that they are submitting to external imposition but that they are playing the game" (p. 52). Another leading educator, Jere Brophy (1999), described the classroom that Dewey must have had in mind:

> Such a classroom has a certain look and feel. It reveals organization, planning, and scheduling. The room is divided into distinct areas equipped for specific activities. Frequently used equipment is stored where it can be accessed easily, and each item has its own place. Traffic patterns facilitate movement around the room and minimize crowding and bumping. Transitions between activities are accomplished efficiently following a brief signal or a few directions from the teacher, and students know where they are supposed to be, what they are supposed to be doing, and what equipment they will need. Students are attentive to presentations and responsive to questions. Lessons and other group activities are structured so that subparts are discernible and separated by clear transitions. When students are released to work on their own or with peers, they know what to do and settle quickly into the task. Usually, students continue the activity through to completion without difficulty and then turn to some new approved activity. If they need help, they can get it from the teacher or from some other source, and then resume working. To an observer who did not know better, this kind of learning environment seems to work automatically, without much teacher effort devoted to management. (p. 44)

No doubt, there are many classrooms in which an organizational approach leads to the kind of ideal social control described by Dewey and Brophy—in which the teacher isn't controlling (or so it feels) but rather social control is imposed by the way the classroom is organized. Furthermore, the organization makes so much sense to the students that the students buy into it and participate willingly.

Jere Brophy

Source: Jere Brophy.

No doubt, too, there are many other classrooms in which an organizational approach does not engender the feeling among students that they are buying into the classroom's programs of activity rather than being forced and cajoled. The opening example is a case in point because many of Mrs. LeRose's students felt controlled to such an extent that they disliked school.

Organizational approaches, then, can result in students feeling overcontrolled and refusing to buy into the classroom rules and routines. Furthermore, organizational approaches may run the risk of sacrificing the moral values that we associate with a democratic society for values, such as efficiency, that we associate with running businesses (Butchart, 1998a). There is, after all, nothing intrinsically moral or democratic about being organized.

However, organizational approaches need not lead to overcontrolling students or to undermining the values central to a democratic society. It is possible for educators to organize using a variety of teaching models and a variety of methods aimed at not simply keeping order but also at promoting prosocial behavior, democratic values, and good classroom communities. Put another way, when organizational approaches attend to the principles, goals, and values espoused in the other approaches discussed previously, they can work quite well.

In any case, the need to organize classrooms is self-evident. For anyone even remotely familiar with classrooms, leading with organization makes a great deal of sense. First of all, one needs to be highly organized when teaching groups of children or adolescents, in large part because there are so many forces working against organization. Put 20 or so children or adolescents together in one room for long periods of time, and you are bound to experience pressures toward disorganization, in large part because children and adolescents have so many agendas that compete with the main agendas of educators (to have fun rather than work, to impress friends rather than impress teachers, to stay focused only on activities that interest rather than focus irrespective of interest, etc.).

However, even when students and teachers share the same agenda, organization is needed to keep everyone moving together in a particular direction to achieve a particular goal. That is, organization is needed to support what some have referred to as programs of action (Doyle, 2006). To organize programs of action, teachers need to minimize interruptions and maximize flow. Programs of action, flow, and other concepts featured by organizational approaches give a different meaning to problem behavior, namely, behavior that interrupts flow.

Furthermore, in classrooms adopting organizational approaches, the main emphasis is on preventing problem behavior by maintaining flow and strengthening the main vectors in programs of action. To do so requires teachers to "stay on top of things" by spotting misbehavior or problems immediately so as to "nip them in the bud." To do so also requires skills for managing programs of action so that the group stays focused and "moves along."

In their groundbreaking research on classroom management, Jacob Kounin and his colleague, Paul Gump (1958), were the first to empirically establish the precise behaviors that interrupt flow and otherwise undermine programs of action. They identified several teacher behaviors that interrupt flow. In particular, they identified as a major source of interruption the way some teachers reprimand, either by stopping too long to reprimand or by reprimanding in an angry tone of voice. In both cases, the negative effect is to throw programs of action off course or bring them to a halt—what Kounin and Gump referred to as "negative ripple effects." This kind of research did much to shift the focus from managing individual students to managing classrooms. It also emphasized preventing problem behavior because reactions to misbehavior risk negative ripple effects.

Source: Wayne State University.

In sum, organizational approaches to behavior and classroom management are dynamic, not static. They are designed to prevent problem behavior by keeping students on track and moving in desired directions. How teachers do this is the focus of the rest of our discussion.

Jacob Kounin

REFLECT   Have you ever had a teacher who was extraordinarily well organized (the class schedule, materials, the physical environment, lessons)? If "yes," how did the organization influence whether there were behavior problems or not?

What Needs Organizing

Of course, it is one thing to suggest that students need to be kept moving in desired directions and quite another to show how this can be accomplished by being organized. To show how organization helps to establish and maintain programs of action, we need to be clear about what exactly needs organizing. Put another way, we need to organize the topic of organizing.

Organization implies differentiation and coordination of parts and wholes. The first question, then, is how are we to divide classroom organization into parts? For many, the main divisions are between organizing a classroom schedule (**organizing the temporal environment**); organizing a classroom's space, furnishings, built structures, and materials (**organizing the physical environment**); organizing how students are grouped and where, when, and how students should move and speak (**organizing the social environment**); and finally, **organizing teaching teams**. In Charles and Senter's (2008) influential book, *Elementary Classroom Management,* the authors essentially organize this way. Furthermore, if you look back at Jere Brophy's (1999) description of an ideal classroom, you will see that he, too, organizes this way. We will, then, adopt this commonly held division and discuss each in turn.

Organizing classrooms means organizing time, physical and social environments, and teaching teams.

Organizing the Temporal Environment

Organizing time means, first of all, breaking time into meaningful units. In classrooms, units of time are defined by their functions. Some units function primarily to help with transitions, such as the units at the beginning of class or the school day. Others function to restore energy depleted by continuous work, such as the unit of time set aside for recess. Still others function to get academic work done. Organizing time means, then, figuring out which functions are needed and when they are needed. Once this figuring is done, educators can construct a meaningful classroom schedule.

Scheduling

The classroom schedule includes routines for beginning classes or for beginning the school day. It also includes sequences of programs of action.

In every classroom, regardless of students' age, there is apt to be a daily routine for starting the class or starting the school day, to help students settle in. In preschool classrooms, the routines also help children separate from parents.

Teachers do this by showing children how to take control. For example, in one preschool classroom, children were encouraged to take a position at the top of an indoor climbing structure, where they could look out through a window on top of the cubbies and wave at their parents who were walking away—while waving back, of course (Scarlett, 1998, p. 125).

For elementary school children, the day often starts with morning meetings to discuss classroom news, birthdays, student activities, and the schedule for the day. Some classrooms start with quiet seat work, to prevent children from beginning the school day by racing around.

For adolescents, going directly to assigned seats and working on homework or specific tasks can help students settle in. Here's how one high school teacher described changes he made to help students settle in:

> Twenty-five students entered my algebra class. It was right after lunch so the students were not ready to focus. The first few weeks of school I was frustrated. Once the class was in their seats I would try to start my lesson. I don't think anyone was listening. Students were giggling and passing notes. A few students were even finishing their lunches. I spoke with a senior teacher about it, and she suggested that I have the students work individually on an interesting problem when they first enter the classroom. She explained to me that this helps them refocus, and then they are ready for the class lecture. I got really into it. I started to create problems about situations they would care about and that involved algebra from the lesson before. Then I allowed the students to work in groups after my lesson and told them that the more work they got done together the less they would have at home. After this change, it felt like a totally different class. (Boston public high school teacher)

Students' knowing where they are in the classroom schedule and what they can and cannot do at any given time provides an important means for keeping classroom order, which is why, from preschool through primary school, classroom schedules are often posted for all to see. Doing so has positive consequences, as a study by Yinger (1980) showed.

In Yinger's (1980) study, classrooms with clear and consistent schedules were less likely to have disruptions than were classrooms in which schedules were not so clear and consistent. The following is an example of what can happen when the classroom schedule is not so clear to very young children.

> In one Head Start classroom, the general class schedule was not made clear. At the end of breakfast, children were told, "Okay, go play," but no mention was made of what specific activities were open. It seemed as

though teachers had opened some activities and that others would be opened if children showed an interest. For example, one child put on a smock but then found that none of the art materials had been set up. The assistant teacher noticed and said to the head teacher, "I'm going to open sponge painting because I think they want to paint." As soon as she started to set up the sponges, paints, and paper, many more children came to the painting area than could be accommodated, causing a good deal of confusion, frustration, and anger among them. (Scarlett, 1998, p. 126)

In this classroom, then, the absence of a clear schedule confused and frustrated the children, which, in turn, made it hard for them to become engaged in productive play.

Absence of clear schedules and routines can have negative consequences for adolescents as well:

In the afternoon, the students would attend history class. It was typical that the students would arrive to class, and the teacher would not be prepared. The class would sometimes start off by the students reading a page from their textbook. Other days the teacher would simply ask the students what they thought of the homework. As a result of the inconsistency, very few students participated in discussions. Most kept busy by passing notes and going to the bathroom.

Problems with scheduling often occur when there are outside specialists working with children with special needs. No class can run exactly on schedule, so outside specialists need to show patience and ingenuity in finding ways to integrate their schedules with that of the classroom. Few do this perfectly, but a good specialist can create a reasonable fit. In the following example, the fit was hardly reasonable, which created problems not only for the children with special needs but for everyone else as well:

A physical therapist often visited the class to work with two children in particular, but within an inclusion model, one that encouraged other children to join in. As was often the case, this day she arrived without being prepared and without preparing the head teacher. While the children and head teacher were in a group meeting, she interrupted several times to ask for supplies and directions for carrying out her special activity. Her activity took a long time to set up, and so children had to wait much longer than usual. Naturally, they fidgeted, which elicited a good deal of reprimanding by the head teacher. (Scarlett, 1998, p. 127)

When activities run longer than expected, teachers face a dilemma. Do they cut activities short and keep to the schedule? Or do they run longer and adjust the schedule accordingly? Here is one middle school teacher discussing this dilemma:

There are two schools of thought about time organization. Some teachers go by a strict time schedule, for example, starting math at 10:30, even if reading is not totally done. Other teachers think about what needs to be done in the day and work from there, prioritizing what to do no matter how long some things takes.

Sticking to strict schedules provides predictability and consistent routines. On the other hand no classroom has every student finishing activities on time, so some flexibility in scheduling may be needed, as the following teacher's comments suggest:

I have never seen a class that finishes everything at the same time. Because of this, I think it is important to have some flexible time in the schedule. For example, maybe 30 minutes a week or 10 minutes a day of finish-up time, or 30 minutes when you finish lessons and activities that were not completed. For students who are done with everything, finish-up time can be used for enrichment, reading, writing, and peer tutoring.

There is no perfect answer to this dilemma. At times the right decision might mean allowing flexible time in a schedule, while at other times it might mean staying on schedule.

Teachers must also learn to adjust the schedule to the needs of individual students. The main complicating factor is that students differ greatly from one another on the time it takes them to finish in-class assignments. Therefore, wise teachers find ways to organize class time so that the faster students can be released from whole class instruction to work on productive individual projects while the slower students use the time they need. Here is an example of a teacher accommodating one of the faster students:[2]

In a fourth-grade classroom, one boy almost always finished his work way ahead of the rest. Rather than having him wait around (and possibly distract the others), the teacher allowed him to work on a project that was both meaningful to him and supportive of his development. As a passionate Red Sox fan, this boy took it upon himself to "redesign" Fenway Park, and for over a month, he spent the last few minutes of each period of instruction drawing and redrawing his vision of a renovated Fenway Park. In the end, his drawing was professionally framed and placed in his bedroom for all to admire, himself included.

Transitions

Organizing the temporal environment also refers to establishing routines that support transitions. We have already seen how this works in helping students settle in. Helping students "switch gears" to go to a new activity can also present challenges. Not surprising, transitions are times when behavior problems are likely to occur. Here is an example of what can happen in a classroom when there is not enough support given to a child to make a transition from play to class meeting:

> Joe and Don were making a road of blocks. Joe called to a teacher, "Look how long our road is!" The assistant teacher, Diane, replied, "Wow, that's the longest road I've ever seen! Can I play in blocks with you?" "Yes, but you have to park your car here," answered Don. Just as Diane joined them, the head teacher rang the clean-up bell. Diane and Joe began to put away the blocks, but Don refused, saying, "No! I don't want to clean up." He then started to kick and throw blocks. Diane responded, "Don, you need to help Joe clean up so we can have circle before we go on our field trip." Don smiled and then ran across the room laughing. Diane called after him, "Don, you have a choice, you can either help Joe clean up or you can stay at school while we are on our trip and clean up then." When Don continued to throw things, Diane grabbed him, whereupon he punched her. (Scarlett, 1998, p. 128)

In this example, Don could have used a five-minute warning that clean up was soon to come. He could also have used a stronger motive to clean up, such as offering to let him ring the bell that announced clean-up time.

Transitions are especially important in early childhood classrooms, and one of the interesting features of good early childhood classrooms is the way teachers often express themselves in their transition rituals. In classrooms with well-planned transitions, some teachers play music or sing. Others play games such as "freeze." Whatever the ritual, teachers often find ways to make transitions enjoyable, and by making transitions enjoyable, they prevent behavior problems.

As for transitions in middle and high school, even though bells and buzzers may clearly mark the time for transition, there still need to be clear rules and monitoring in order for students to make their way from one class to another without disruption or delay. How this is accomplished can vary from one school to another (Scarlett, 1998). Hopefully, it is accomplished without the need for methods that turn schools into military-like communities, as was the case in the high school that became the inspiration for the movie *Lean on Me* (Avildsen, 1989). In that high school, the new principal took it upon himself to become a sergeant-like hallway monitor, using a bullhorn to keep students in line.

Time and Instruction

How much time is needed for a lesson, for students to take in what is being taught, and for students to practice or apply what has been taught? In short, how much time is needed for students to learn? Determining how time, instruction, and learning relate to one another is central to the mission of schools, so it is central to organizational approaches to classroom management. In addressing this question, the central distinction has been between *time spent on instruction* and *time needed for students to engage in learning.*

Many educators and schools have responded to the question of time needed to engage in learning with a simplistic notion that the more instructional time, the better. In some cases, this has led to reorganizing the daily schedule to reduce recess time, as well as to reorganizing the school year schedule to increase the number of school days. However, research suggests that both of these "solutions" are misguided (Karweit, 1989) and that it is the time engaged in learning, not instructional time, that matters.

Research suggests that recess provides a much-needed respite from tension-producing seat work and academic tasks in general. It also suggests there may be links between play at recess and academic achievement because productive play on school playgrounds predicts academic success in the classroom (Pellegrini, 1995). Given the research, it seems clear that taking from recess to give to instructional time is not a good solution; one possible reason is that recess actually increases time spent engaged in learning.

Therefore, a more important consideration than instructional time is the amount of time students attend to lessons and are engaged in learning. Research suggests that simply extending the amount of instructional time does not ensure there will be a significant gain in the amount of time students are engaged in learning (Karweit, 1989). More research is needed to fully understand this relationship between instructional time and engaged time, but there is enough research right now to say that there are no simple answers to this question of how much instructional time is optimal.

Organizing the Physical Environment

For material related to this concept, go to Video Clip 7.1 on the Student Resource CD bound into the back of your textbook.

Organizationally minded teachers are fully aware of the importance of organizing the physical environment. Here, the focus is on how furniture is arranged, how floors are covered (or not covered), where activity centers are placed, how materials are prepared and stored, what kinds of shelving and built structures are brought into the classroom—the list is long.

Space and the Built Environment

The following example shows that attending to the physical environment is important for maintaining order:

> As a visitor entered one early childhood classroom, three boys were at the far end poised as if to take off, and take off they did. Barreling down the middle of the classroom, they seemed like racecar drivers at some local track. And like racecar drivers, they did not stop at the end of the straight-away but continued on to curve around and head back along the far edge of the classroom. Now they were no longer racecar drivers, but runners competing in the high hurdles, as they vaulted the two low risers dividing the far wall into activity areas. Once over the second riser, they again turned to make another run, but were prevented from doing so by one teacher's screams. (Scarlett, 1998, p. 132)

This is not an example of bad boys being bad. This is an example of boys taking a long open space in the middle of a classroom as an invitation to run.

Gary Moore (1987), an architect as well as a developmental psychologist, studied the effects of different architectural plans for early childhood centers. He began his research by describing three different kinds of plans: open plans (such as the classroom in the previous example) distinguished by the presence of open spaces without partitions; closed plans distinguished by separate rooms for different activities; and modified open plans distinguished by small and large activity spaces that are open enough to allow children to see the possibilities for play yet enclosed enough to give spaces specific identities (block corner, dramatic play corner, reading corner, etc.). Often, modified open plans also have meandering pathways between activity centers that allow children to see how to transition from one activity center to another, albeit circuitously. Moore's results showed that of the three, modified open plans are the best for promoting self-initiated constructive play and for minimizing behavior problems.

In higher grades, organizing space and the built environment refers especially to the arrangement of desks. Emmer, Evertson, Sanford, Clements, and Worsham (1989) discovered that where and how desks are placed can have a major impact on students' classroom experience. Specifically, they found that when students can attend to a teacher's instruction without moving from their seats, there are apt to be fewer behavior problems than when students have to move around. They also found that when desks do not face potential sources of distraction, such as windows or doors, there are fewer problems. However, their research did not determine what type of desk formation (traditional rows, horseshoe, clusters, etc.) is preferable.

Today many teachers determine how desks are arranged based on their teaching style and characteristics of their students.

> There are so many ways to set up desks. It makes me dizzy. Some teachers prefer the traditional rows, some prefer the horseshoe shape, and others prefer desks in groups. I think all of the formations are fine. It is about what you are comfortable with, what experience you want your students to have. (Boston public high school teacher)

Emmer's group also described areas of congestion, those areas in a classroom where students tend to congregate, such as by the pencil sharpener, by the trashcan, and wherever students go to get materials. They showed that it is important for teachers to minimize congestion because congestion is related to behavior problems (Emmer et al., 1989).

Materials

The two main issues with respect to materials are first, preparing or choosing materials and second, storing materials. The following example illustrates what can happen when teachers aren't careful in preparing materials:

During one of their demonstrations, the art educators introduced clay, a material that the children had never used before in the classroom (the teachers had considered clay to be too messy). Unfortunately, during this demonstration, there had not been much thought given to the texture of the clay. Initially, the clay was too hard, but then, after adding too much water, it became too soft. Soon, the mushy clay was everywhere, and everything was a mess. Children were told to hold their hands together and walk in a direct line to the bathroom while being careful not to touch anything—hardly what the project was designed to accomplish. (Scarlett, 1998, p. 130)

As Carole Weinstein (1987) observed, "A glue bottle that is clogged, paint that is too thin, or a puzzle with a piece that is missing make the completion of a task frustrating, if not impossible" (p. 163). And too much frustration can cause behavior problems, as illustrated in the following example:

In one class, the children were enthusiastically participating in making a quilt. The teachers seemed to have planned well. Each child seemed to have all the necessary tools and materials. However, when it came time for the children to cut out their pieces of cloth, they were handed children's scissors, which could not cut effectively. The result was a good deal of frustration leading to children getting up, wandering away, and becoming disruptive. (Scarlett, 1998, p. 131)

A high school teacher explained,

I try to have everything in my classroom ready. I have learned over time that if learning materials are not accessible, it can lead to disaster. Since I teach geometry, we always need rulers, models, protractors, and compasses. If my materials are not ready and I have to dig them out of my desk or cabinet, the students have an opportunity to act up. I, of course, learned this the hard way. Now, every morning I make sure that all of my materials for all of my sections are prepared and easily accessed.

Those adopting an organizational approach are likely to also pay special attention to how materials are stored. In early education classrooms, adopting an organizational approach means having shelves within children's reach and stocked with all kinds of materials. Furthermore, it means organizing materials in such a way that each piece of equipment and each type of material has its own special place. Even the art supplies will be sorted, with markers, paper, scissors, crayons, and the rest having their own, distinctive places rather than everything being thrown together in one container. Without a word spoken, the message is "Please use the equipment and materials, but take care of them and return them to their proper place." Storage areas and storage systems thus play an important role in stimulating constructive initiative and responsible behavior, as indicated by one elementary school teacher's comments:

> It is very important that there are manipulatives, tools, and supplies available to children. Labeling can help with this. I like the children to be able to replace the paper themselves and find the glue or coins when they are needed. I make sure that these things are accessible and that the cabinets and shelves are labeled. It helps with literacy, too!

Unfortunately, in many classrooms, equipment and materials are either missing, kept out of reach of children, or organized in such a way that children cannot easily find what they want and need. The result is either children not finding enough to do or teachers having to assume too much control. The following example illustrates this last point:

> In one classroom for preschool children, the head teacher stored the classroom materials behind a black curtain where children were forbidden to go. He was the sole dispenser of equipment and materials. It was his initiative, not the children's, that made this classroom go. As a result, there was order at the expense of children not taking initiative and learning self-control. This became apparent on days when he was absent. On those days, the children became wild and were often completely out of control. (Scarlett, 1998, p. 136)

In other classrooms, children may be able to access equipment and materials, but the way in which materials and equipment are stored on shelves makes it difficult for them to do so. Art supplies are often thrown together, as are all kinds of construction materials. Even unit blocks may have no clear places marking where they should go. As a result, children are apt to take less initiative and less responsibility for returning equipment and materials to their proper places.

During the middle and high school years, teachers have a new challenge. On the one hand, students are more independent and can get materials that they need to learn with very easily. On the other hand, students are sometimes given very expensive tools to work with and are tempted to keep them. In these cases, teachers have to come up with creative and efficient ways to keep track of materials in their classroom. One high school teacher had to come up with a method so that calculators wouldn't go missing.

> Every year I am provided enough graphing calculators for all of my students. They are so expensive they do not allow the students to take them home. Instead, they are to be used only during class time. If I lose any, I have to pay out of pocket. My first year teaching I wrote my name on all of the calculators with permanent marker. The students somehow figured out how to erase it. I lost five calculators that year. Now I have a special tool that lets me scratch my name into the plastic, and I also count every single calculator I hand out. At the end of class, when all of the students are in their seats, I collect them and count them again. If one is missing I don't let anyone leave the classroom. I say, "We are missing one calculator. If you return it now you will not get into trouble. I am going to leave the classroom and stand outside the door. When I come back in the room, it needs to be on my desk." This strategy has never failed, and I only needed to use it once last year. I like giving the students a chance to do the right thing.

Review

To organize the physical environment, teachers must attend to

(1) space and the built environment, and

(2) materials.

For material related to this concept, go to Video Clip 7.2 on the Student Resource CD bound into the back of your textbook.

Organizing the Social Environment

Organizing the social environment has a lot to do with organizing students to maximize learning and minimize disruption. Here, we discuss organizing the social environment in terms of grouping, rules and routines, and monitoring.

Grouping

Organizational approaches attend to when and how students are grouped, in order to maximize learning. Most educators consider different ways to group students when they feel that students in any given class are too diverse in ability. That is, most educators regroup in order to reduce the variability within any given group (Slavin, 1989b).

There are, however, times when grouping students occurs for reasons other than learning, the most notable example being forming cooperative learning groups. In cooperative learning groups, besides learning the subject matter, students are expected to gain valuable experience learning how to work together. In particular, they are expected to learn the benefits and satisfactions of helping one another.

The research on how grouping affects learning provides helpful suggestions. For example, the oft-used **tracking** system, which assigns students to classes based on ability, has not achieved what it was intended to achieve, namely, better learning for all (Slavin, 1989b). If anything, it has caused additional problems, particularly the problem of students with less ability becoming stigmatized. On the other hand, when students from the same class share most of the class together and only occasionally **regroup for targeted learning**, such as learning to read and learning mathematics, the results are positive—provided teachers change the way they teach to accommodate each group's required pace and level of challenge (Slavin, 1989b).

The research with regard to cooperative learning gives generally positive results but only when teachers provide clear guidelines for completing group projects and when teachers promote and assess *both* group goals and individual achievement (Slavin, 1989a). That is, in organizing students into cooperative learning groups, teachers must still find ways to motivate and assess the learning of each individual student.

Rules and Routines

Organizing the social environment requires establishing classroom rules, especially rules that make for good routines. For example, in preschool classrooms, it is common to have rules that establish how many children can be in the block corner at any given time. In elementary classrooms, it is common to require children seated in their desks to raise their hand if they want help, to avoid children crowding around the teachers' desk and getting into trouble while waiting for help.

Many of these rules and procedures are established early in the school year. In fact, teachers are often advised to establish good procedural rules on the first day, to ensure not only order at the beginning of the year but also the right frame of mind for the rest of the year. Indeed, there is research indicating that effective classroom managers in elementary and middle schools are those who are especially skilled at establishing rules and routines at the beginning of the school year (Emmer, Evertson, & Anderson, 1980).

Establishing rules and routines on the first day helps weave rules and routines into a workable classroom system. Expectations are clearly explained to students; signals are used to indicate when actions are to be started or stopped (e.g., blinking the classroom lights to end a segment). In addition, the most successful teachers make sure that rules are explicit, concrete, and functional.

Even in high school, establishing rules and expectations early on is important, as indicated in the following comment by a high school teacher:

> During the first week of class I hand out a sheet of paper that lists my classroom expectations, the grading rubric, and homework assignment grading. I also leave a space for students to write their expectations of me. I compile all of their comments about what kind of teacher they want me to be; we discuss and come to an agreement. After this I create a contract. All of the students read it and sign it the first week of class. I sign it too. It is our promise to each other. I find that by setting ground rules and being open about our expectations as students and teachers, then there is no confusion. It is a very mature way to approach this issue. I think students appreciate being treated like mature individuals.

Of course, how one establishes rules early on is important, as previous chapters have made clear. That is, adopting an organizational approach dictates the need to establish rules and routines. It does not dictate one way only for establishing rules and routines. And so, in adopting an organizational approach, there is nothing to prevent a teacher from using constructivist methods that solicit students' input on what should be the rules and routines.

Monitoring

Being organized also means monitoring what is going on. Furthermore, monitoring is itself a way of organizing—of keeping a reasonable level of organization intact. As one elementary school teacher put it,

> When I teach, I have to be on. That means I know what is going on in every corner of the classroom, even if I have my back turned. I might be helping an individual child, but I know where and when trouble is brewing!

In upper elementary and middle school classrooms, we see different teaching settings calling for different ways to monitor. Recitations, seat work, and small group cooperative learning are the most common. Each of these three settings has special challenges with respect to keeping the class moving along in the right direction and minimizing disruption.

Whatever the situation or setting, monitoring means **being "withit"**—to use Jacob Kounin's (1970) apt phrase. Kounin was the first to empirically establish how essential it is for teachers to be withit. To be withit, a teacher must monitor the whole class while attending to individuals, and in the process of monitoring, a teacher must be able to nip problems in the bud.

An Example of Not Being Withit

One longtime teacher related the following story about her student teaching days: She had been teaching in a suburban second-grade classroom when one day she found herself the only teacher in the classroom—the cooperating teacher was absent, and there was no substitute teacher available. During the day, she took the children to the gym, and for an hour she thought she had done a beautiful job organizing the group and seeing to it that everyone was playing constructively. At the end of the hour, she had girls and boys line up in separate lines. There wasn't a hint of disruption, which added to her sense of pride. She was now confident in her ability to organize this group and run an effective classroom.

Then she heard a whimper behind her. When she turned she saw a boy in the middle of the gym crying. "Billy, what's the matter?" she said. Billy told her the kids had been beating him up. "When?" she asked. "The whole time" was his answer.

Each type of teaching setting provides a slightly different challenge with respect to monitoring (Doyle, 2006). For example, recitations call for teachers to be especially skilled at managing turn taking (fostering in students a feeling that their turn to speak will come). Seat work calls for teachers to be especially skilled at keeping individual students on track (by hovering) while monitoring the whole class.

Although high school students are capable or working more independently, to prevent disruption, teachers still need to see when students need assistance. Emmer et al. (1989) write that even for older students, teachers who maintain clear lines of sight when setting up the physical space of the classroom have a much easier time supporting student work and deterring behavior problems. As one high school teacher put it,

I had to rearrange my classroom six times my first year teaching. I kept creating blind spots, places where I couldn't see the students. A tall bookcase, a desk out of sight—I think I did it all. It was unbelievable. The students could find these corners in a second and that is where all the trouble happened!

Organizing the Lesson

Too often, lessons and behavior management are treated separately, as if one does not relate to the other. Of course, they do relate to one another, as was explained in Chapter 5. From an organizational perspective, this comes as no surprise because lessons are programs of action requiring a great deal of organization to maintain flow.

To organize a lesson means to divide the lesson into parts that relate to the lesson's overall goal. Often, this means dividing the lesson into three parts, with the first part functioning to make goals and expectations clear. The second part is about giving students information, and the third part is about giving students the opportunity to apply what they have learned (e.g., by answering a teacher's questions).

This three-part organization is an example of what it means to organize a lesson. There are more refined ways to organize. Whether lessons are organized in this simple way or in some other more complicated way, it is clear that organizing lessons reduces the probability of there being behavior problems (Good & Brophy, 1989).

Organizing Teaching Teams

I hated the idea of teaching team meetings. I thought, "Oh geez, one more meeting to make our lives even busier." It was halfway through the year I realized how important teaching team meetings are—not only to share our curriculum but also to talk about student development and achievements. I found out that many of my students who were achieving in my class were having trouble in another. We not only talked about our lesson plans, we also discussed ways to support our students. Sharing that kind of information made my life so much easier. Teachers also shared strategies for lessons, as well as ideas for difficult students. It helped to know we were all on the same page! (A high school teacher)

Educators organizing themselves into teams is a major part of any organizational approach. Certainly, when there is more than one teacher in the classroom—such as occurs when there is a head teacher and teacher's aide—there must be coordination of roles. But as the previous example indicates, forming teams can also mean forming teams with those outside the classroom. Nowhere do we see this more clearly than with the teams formed within the present-day special education system, so these kinds of teams will receive our close attention.

Organizing Teams for Students With Special Needs

Special education requires creating teams that include parents, specialists, and classroom teachers. The degree to which these teams become well organized varies considerably, in large part because organizing a special education team is extremely difficult. To understand why it is so difficult, consider the sequence of events for constructing and implementing individualized education programs (IEPs) for students with special needs

IEPs require teachers, parents, school administrators, related services personnel, and (when appropriate) students themselves to work together. At the beginning, that means working together to come up with a plan. Then, throughout the year, it means working together to both implement the plan and assess progress as defined by the plan. At the end of the year, team members work together to review the plan and to make modifications if modifications are needed. At the end of three years, team members work together to evaluate the student and determine whether there needs to be ongoing special supports. This sequence and summary indicate how the special education system requires teams of adults to work together over long periods of time. There are many specifics and details not mentioned in this summary. However, one can see even in this summary that working together as an IEP team is challenging.

One of the main challenges for classroom teachers is the inclusion model. In the past, special educators have pulled children out of regular classrooms to provide services quite different from what goes on in classrooms. Pullout methods and segregated special education have led to children feeling isolated and confused. This has led, in turn, to the current push for classroom inclusion. However, in adopting an inclusion model, the classroom teacher has to both put the IEP into practice and organize therapists and special services—not an easy task. As one classroom teacher explained in her work with a class with an unusually high number of children with IEPs, "The difficulty arose around the logistics of providing services for eight children. The law required every effort be made to educate children in regular classrooms, but to do so created problems of coordinating services" (Scarlett, 1998, p. 170). This teacher's complaint is common. The biggest difficulty for classroom teachers is defining roles for the specialists, roles that fit well within the regular classroom.

> My coworkers in special education and I found it difficult to coordinate our efforts and provide services in an integrated way. Initially, our difficulties stemmed from our different histories providing for children with special needs. So, as might be expected, the specialists' first attempts at providing services in regular classrooms resembled those from the old, pullout model. (Scarlett, 1998, p. 171)

For this classroom teacher, scheduling, too, became a problem. The specialists in the school were expected to provide services for many students, so their schedules were tight. Sometimes they were available for different students at the same time or for different students back to back. This led to there being too many adults in the classroom, a conflict with the classroom schedule, or too much distraction for other students. The classroom teacher explained:

> Often, one of our classroom activities took longer than expected, so a specialist arrived to work with her small group only to find the children preoccupied and busy. We then had to abruptly stop what we were doing and help the children make a difficult transition. At other times, the specialist would be tied up in another classroom and arrive later than expected. These situations, in turn, would set off behavior problems. (Scarlett, 1998, p. 173)

However, organizing teams means more than organizing so that team members meet and coordinate schedules. It also means organizing to ensure good communication between team members and a willingness to problem solve together. Many schools require that classroom teachers meet weekly or biweekly with therapists. At these meetings, therapists and teachers consider ways to modify their support. These meetings do not always go as planned. Thomas Skrtic (1991) offers an insightful critique as to why.

At the heart of his critique is his distinction between a **professional bureaucracy** and what he calls an **adhocracy**. Organizations configure themselves as professional bureaucracies when the work is so complex and ambiguous that it requires roles filled by specialists—those who make subtle decisions and work independently on problems for which they have been trained. In a professional bureaucracy, specialists may sit around the same table and appear to work closely and collaboratively with one another, but, in actuality, they work alone and apart from one another because each professional remains locked within his or her own specialty. Put another way, in the professional bureaucracy, individuals puzzle and inquire the way their disciplines have taught them to puzzle and inquire. To summarize, professional organizations are organizations in which different professionals solve problems separately, and the problems they solve tend to be problems defined in special ways by their separate disciplines.

Applying the concept of a professional bureaucracy to schools, Skrtic (1991) finds that most schools function as professional bureaucracies—organizations in which problem solving occurs within but not among the various disciplines and specialties represented within the school. This means that the regular education teacher solves one set of problems in ways defined by the training given in a regular education licensing program; the reading specialist solves another set of problems in ways defined by the training given to reading specialists; the occupational therapist solves yet another set of problems in ways defined by the training given to occupational therapists—and so on and so forth.

The result, says Skrtic (1991), is standardization in the way students with special needs are served. This means that rather than being a problem-solving team, the team assembled to develop and carry out an IEP usually ends up solving mostly the mundane problem of who sees the student, when, and where. Furthermore, implementing the IEP usually ends up with standard practices (as defined by each discipline) being applied to whatever common problem has been identified (a reading problem, a behavior management problem, etc.). To Skrtic, this kind of teamwork is inadequate to the task of educating students with special needs, because the challenge of educating students with special needs calls for collective and creative problem solving in order to accommodate the uniqueness of each student.

Skrtic (1991) calls a team organized to accommodate the uniqueness of each student an adhocracy; the team inquires together to define problems creatively, in order to seek creative solutions that are not standard solutions. He gives as an example of an adhocracy the NASA program that organized itself in the 1960s to put a man on the moon. At the time, there was no standard practice for putting a man on the moon, so the NASA team had to organize itself differently. It had to let the team be open to new ways of defining problems. Later, once the space program became a matter of putting one shuttle into space after another, NASA could return to being a professional bureaucracy, in which different kinds of professionals defined problems following their profession's ways of defining problems and then implemented standard practice.

Skrtic's (1991) criticism of special education focuses on two basic questions: "Is the kind of planning occurring during special education IEP meetings based upon collaborative and creative inquiry?" and "Do the plans that result from

IEP meetings usually show innovations made necessary by a student's unique-ness?" Skrtic says the answer to both questions is "No" because IEP teams are likely to follow the professional bureaucracy model, and, hence, solutions to problems are likely to be "standard practice." What we need, says Skrtic, are IEP teams functioning as adhocracies, not professional bureaucracies.

Related to this concept of adhocracies is the concept of a transdisciplinary team. The term refers to a particular way teams of educators can be organized. Rather than organizing teams as professionals acting independently of one another, transdisciplinary teams organize themselves so that each team member teaches the others about his or her discipline—giving each team member the opportunity to implement that teaching. So, for example, a head teacher may implement a curriculum unit ordinarily carried out by a reading specialist, and a reading specialist may implement a curriculum unit ordinarily carried out by a head teacher. Therefore, in classrooms with transdisciplinary teams, it may be difficult to identify who is the regular education teacher and who is the specialist. In any case, transdisciplinary teams are examples of how teams can be organized.

REFLECT   Can you remember a time when you were a member of a teaching team or team of counselors who functioned well as a team? If "yes," how did this influence behavior management? Can you remember a time when you were a member of a team that did not function well as a team? If "yes," how did this influence behavior management?

Summary

In this chapter, we have examined how organizing time, the physical and social environment, and teaching teams play a major role in managing both behavior and classrooms. In doing so, we have tried to make clear how adopting an organizational approach need not lead to students being overcontrolled or to classrooms being without good values. Rather, we have tried to make clear how organization can provide a much-needed foundation that actually allows for and promotes the possibility of students internalizing democratic values.

In particular, we have seen here that to organize well means several things, not one. First and foremost, it means supporting programs of action and preventing problems by maintaining flow. It also means providing clear and sensible classroom schedules, supporting transitions, and being sensible when making decisions about instruction time. To organize classrooms means to organize the physical environment, which includes classroom space and the built environment as well as materials and how materials are prepared and stored. It also means organizing the social environment, in particular, determining how students are grouped, establishing rules and routines, and monitoring both individuals and the group. It means organizing lessons into meaningful and related parts, and, finally, it means organizing teams of educators so they can carry out complicated tasks such as designing and implementing IEPs for students with special needs. Given this array of meanings regarding organization, the value of organizational approaches should be clear, especially when they are tempered by the wisdom featured in other approaches.

Web-Based Student Study Site

The companion Web site for *Approaches to Behavior and Classroom Management* can be found at www.sagepub.com/scarlettstudy.

Visit the Web-based student study site to enhance your understanding of the chapter content. The study materials include practice tests, flashcards, suggested readings, and Web resources.

Key Concepts

Adhocracy

Being "withit"

Clear lines of sight

Closed plans

Flow

Inclusion model

Individualized education programs (IEPs)

Modified open plans

Open plans

Organizing teaching teams

Organizing the physical environment

Organizing the social environment

Organizing the temporal environment

Professional bureaucracy

Programs of action

Regroup for targeted learning

Time engaged in learning

Tracking

Transdisciplinary team

Discussion Questions

1. Compare your understanding of "being well organized" before reading this chapter with your understanding now. What are the similarities and differences? What about the discussion of organization was most striking/surprising to you when you were reading this chapter?

2. Have you ever had a teacher who was extraordinary for the way everything was not well organized? If "yes," how did the disorganization influence whether there were behavior problems or not?

3. How well organized are you when teaching or caring for children? Do you prepare and plan carefully, or do you mostly "wing it"? Do you take interest in planning activities, the schedule, the physical environment? Where are your weaknesses when it comes to organization?

---

1. Unless otherwise specified, examples and quotes will be from Iris Ponte's interviews or observations.

2. Observation made by George Scarlett.

Chapter 8

THE CLASSROOM SYSTEMS APPROACH

In planning for the fall, teachers who had worked with Dennis gave me descriptions of his difficult family history, his violent, impulsive behaviors, and his significant language delays. I learned about his biting teachers, his hurting peers, his classmates' fearing him, and his serious problems paying attention. And I learned of his being diagnosed as "having" attention deficit-hyperactivity disorder. (Scarlett, 1998, p. 175)

The opening example was reported by a first-grade teacher preparing in the spring to teach Dennis, a child who had frustrated his previous teachers to the point where they felt they had to isolate him from the rest of his classmates. Though this case is out of the ordinary, teachers often try their best by using methods that work with most students, but in the end they fail to prevent ongoing disruption and misbehavior. There is that one student who simply will not stop calling out answers, speaking out of turn, or getting up out of his seat despite a teacher's sitting the student down and explaining why what he is doing is wrong, changing where the student sits in the classroom, sending the student to a school administrator, holding parent conferences—the list can be long, and as the list increases, teachers can become understandably frustrated and feel stuck.

In this chapter, we show how teachers can get stuck when they strictly adhere to individual-oriented approaches, including those individual-oriented approaches detailed in this text. This is not to say that attempting to change problem behavior using individual-oriented approaches cannot help. In fact, there is a great deal of empirical evidence that the approaches and methods described so far are quite helpful. On the other hand, educators must be wary of limiting themselves to individual-oriented approaches. If they do limit themselves, they will eventually be faced with a problem that does not respond to the methods derived from individual-oriented approaches. In other words, eventually they will become stuck.

The classroom systems approach is meant for just such times when teachers feel stuck, when methods focusing on the individual student do not work, and when all the usual methods have failed. Therefore, unlike other approaches discussed thus far, the classroom systems approach is a reactive approach rather than a proactive approach. That is, it focuses on fixing problems rather than on preventing them.

Furthermore, instead of viewing problems as located "inside" individuals, the systems approach views problems as a reflection of a dysfunctional interpersonal system. Using a classroom systems approach, when you are looking at a student who continues to misbehave, you refocus as if you are looking into a mirror reflecting something wrong with the classroom system. This refocusing to throw problems back on classroom's interpersonal system not only prevents stigmatizing a student (as Dennis was stigmatized), it also leads to exploring alternative points of entry designed to confront the problem behavior indirectly.

At this point, some readers may be thinking that the classroom systems approach is starting to make sense—and are asking themselves why they have never heard of the classroom systems approach to behavior and classroom management. This would not be surprising because there is virtually no research and only one book (Molnar & Lindquist, 1989) on what we are here calling the classroom systems approach. Furthermore, the most recent and comprehensive handbook on behavior and classroom management (Evertson & Weinstein, 2006) makes no mention of the classroom systems approach. Nevertheless, as we hope to make clear, the approach can be invaluable, especially when it is used as an ancillary approach and for the special purpose of helping with chronic and difficult problem situations—that is, when teachers are apt to feel stuck.

The classroom systems approach is an outgrowth of family systems theory and was a movement in counseling and clinical psychology during the mid- to late 20th century. Critical of the then-dominant focus on individuals and their pathology, several scholar-clinicians (Bowen, 1978; Haley, 1987; Jackson, 1965; Minuchin, 1974) developed family systems theory to refocus attention on dysfunctional patterns of interaction among family members. They found doing so provided a better way to understand and treat chronic and serious problem behavior within families. Classrooms, too, develop dysfunctional patterns of interaction, so the classroom systems approach is a logical extension of family systems theory.

Source: Minuchin Center.

Salvador Minuchin

We see in the example of Dennis this process of refocusing and redefining the problem as a problem in the system. Here is what Dennis's first-grade teacher, Kristen Willand, had to say when she observed Dennis in his kindergarten classroom the previous spring:

> During free choice time, Dennis chose to use Play-Doh, but he remained the only child at a station set up for four. Chris (the aide assigned to "shadow" Dennis) sat or stood next to him, interacting warmly while he worked, and Dennis did indeed work. He pounded, rolled, cut, and sliced the Play-Doh. . . . No other children entered this play. In fact, several children walked by the table, paused, and looked as if they wanted to use the Play-Doh, but then they went away. They seemed hesitant, even afraid, to join Dennis at the table. Even when Chris invited them to stay, they went away.
>
> As sad as these observations seemed to me, my observation of Dennis's exit from the classroom seemed even sadder. The classroom teacher had called "cleanup time," and Chris said, "Okay, Dennis, you did a good job today. It's time for us to go back. You can go to the Treasure Box when we get there." While the other children and teachers busied themselves cleaning *their* classroom, Dennis and Chris just left. Apparently, since this classroom was not really Dennis's classroom, cleanup was not part of his routine. Furthermore, no one, no teacher and no child, noticed him or said good-bye. (Scarlett, 1998, p. 175)

Using the language of systems theory, in his kindergarten classroom, Dennis was the **identified problem student.** This was evident in the way Dennis was separated from the rest of the children and in the way his classmates had learned to stay away from Dennis. It was also evident in the way teachers talked about Dennis, as indicated in the conversations reported at the beginning of this chapter.

Before going further, it might be helpful to provide an operational definition of this elusive term: the system. A system develops when two or more people share some common task or group of tasks requiring them to interact over time. Interactions give rise to rules regarding when, how, and with whom one interacts, so, as time passes, members of the system interact with one another in patterned ways. These patterned ways of interacting are called **transactional patterns,** and it is transactional patterns of interaction that define systems.

Therefore, transactional patterns and systems form to carry out specific tasks needed for the group to function adequately. In Dennis's kindergarten classroom, the transactional patterns had to do with keeping Dennis occupied and isolated from his classmates. When the teacher said, "Time to clean up," everyone understood that this did not include Dennis and that it was a cue for Dennis's aide to lead him to somewhere outside the classroom. Given Dennis's disruptive behavior, teachers had developed a system to contain Dennis and segregate him from the rest of the class. From the teachers' point of view, the system worked well, so it was maintained. No one complained because the kindergarten class was relatively free of problem behavior. In other words, from the teachers' point of view, the system was functional because it made for a better-functioning classroom.

However, from the point of view of anyone thoughtfully concerned about what was best for Dennis, the system was dysfunctional. Because Dennis was not included in the larger group or given an opportunity to develop his social skills, his role as the identified problem student and his disruptive behavior were destined to go on indefinitely. Put another way, the educators who devised this kindergarten system violated Fritz Redl's *law of antisepsis,* the law that requires teachers to manage the dilemma between doing what is best for the group *and* at the same time doing what is best for the individual—or at least avoiding doing harm. And so, teacher Willand vowed to change the system when Dennis came to her first-grade classroom and to institute a new system that would place Dennis squarely inside the classroom community.

The example of Dennis in his kindergarten classroom illustrates, then, how an identified problem student's misconduct (or perceived potential misconduct) "can be assumed to be a system-maintaining or system-maintained device" (Minuchin, 1974).

To further illustrate, imagine that on the first day of school, a high school senior fails an easy chemistry test because he did not sleep well the night before. His teacher labels this student as being less able than the other students and, without realizing it, begins to treat this student differently. Perhaps the teacher pays less attention to the student or does not call on him as often. His classmates pick up on these cues and decide the boy is a bad student. Eventually, the student begins to perform poorly in the class, just as his teacher and classmates expected. This phenomenon of students performing better or worse depending on whether others expect them to perform better or worse is known as the **Pygmalion effect** (Rosenthal & Jacobson, 1968) and is well-documented in the psychological and educational literature (Rosenthal, 1987).

In the example of the chemistry student, one of the rules established in the classroom system was that the student should be treated as if he had less to contribute than his classmates. While it is possible that the student might have stopped performing well on his own, his decision to do so was still influenced by his teacher and fellow students. With this in mind, the problem must be viewed systemically and not individualistically.

REFLECT Having seen how problem behavior can be explained in terms of dysfunctional interpersonal systems, think of a student in your own experience who, on first impression, had challenging behavior that people saw as indicating problems within the student. Try, now, to explain this student's behavior using a systems perspective.

To summarize, the following text box lists the distinctive characteristics of a classroom systems approach.

The Distinctive Characteristics of a Classroom Systems Approach

1. Reacts to, rather than tries to prevent, chronic disruption and misbehavior

2. Focuses on changing transactional patterns that define interpersonal systems

3. Works to be an unconditionally positive approach to changing problem behavior by making positive, not negative, characterizations of students (Tauber, 1999)

With this list in mind, we can turn now to the main focus of a classroom systems approach: the focus on changing the system.

CHANGING THE SYSTEM

From a systems perspective, changing a system is not as complicated as one might expect. In fact, it can be fairly straightforward, even simple, because no matter how small or insignificant the change may seem, any change in a system will alter the dynamic of the entire system (Tyler & Jones, 1998).

However, in the literature on family systems, there are a number of favorite areas to change—areas that relate directly to changing classroom systems. In particular, systems approaches favor making changes in a group's power hierarchy, in the boundaries separating subsystems, and in how problems are interpreted or framed. Here, then, we will concentrate on these three.

The Power Hierarchy

Classrooms typically consist of two main classes of individuals: teachers and students. One of the most important rules that govern classroom systems, a rule that largely determines how these two groups interact, is that teachers are more *powerful* than students—or should be. Therefore, difficulties arise in the classroom system when teachers allow their students to have too much power or when it is unclear who is in charge.

This observation bears directly on Lee and Marlene Canter's (1976, 1997) work on assertive versus nonassertive teaching styles. In previous chapters, we have discussed the Canters' distinctions between assertive, nonassertive, and hostile teaching styles, but in those discussions, the distinctions were not clearly tied to the concept of a classroom system. Within other approaches, the Canters' distinctions seemed mostly to have to do with how teachers affect individual students. But within a systems approach, these distinctions take on added meaning by defining ways in which classroom systems can be either functional or dysfunctional. An analogy should help.

Biologists and veterinarians point out that for many mammalian species, dominance is a central principle governing how groups become organized into well-functioning packs. In a well-functioning pack, there is one individual who is the alpha, the individual who gives direction to the pack and who ensures that the pack members work together as a group. Using this systemic perspective, most of the current books on the behavior problems of domestic dogs put heavy emphasis on the importance of dog owners establishing dominance (see Dodman, 1996). The Canters' getting teachers to be assertive follows essentially the same idea. Assertive discipline is, then, to establish teachers as the alpha (Tauber, 1999, p. 69).

From a systems perspective, in becoming the alpha in the classroom, teachers perform a necessary role for the well-being of the group because students need someone who will give direction and lead. Assertive teachers provide needed leadership by giving direction, setting standards, explaining the consequences for not living up to standards, and otherwise being clear about the system that will enable the group to function. Teachers who are not assertive fail to give direction, do not set standards, and do not explain the consequences of not living up to standards; that is, they do not clearly describe the system for working together. One source of chronic disruption and misbehavior may, then, be a classroom system that is dysfunctional because it does not have a teacher who is alpha; that is, it does not have someone who fills a role essential for any classroom system to function properly.

Boundaries Separating Subsystems

Human animals are more complicated socially than are nonhuman animals, so we need more than the concept of dominance to evaluate interpersonal systems. We also need concepts to evaluate subsystems and the boundaries that separate subsystems from one another. This is as true for classrooms and schools as it is for families.

In classrooms and schools, the main subsystems are the subsystem of teachers and the subsystem of students. Other subsystems include the special education team (reading specialist, occupational therapist, school psychologist, or whatever team has been assembled to carry out IEPs) and school administrators (principal, assistant principal, whoever administers the school). In the wings there are parents, who make up their own subsystem.

However, under different circumstances there are apt to be different configurations of subsystems. So, for example, while the special educators and those serving as supports for classroom teachers may form a subsystem of their own, when special and regular educators work together in the same classroom, they form a single subsystem different from the student subsystem. The point, then, is that there are various ways to configure subsystems, and any one way may not be stable.

Subsystems function well or not so well depending, in part, on the boundaries that separate them from one another (Minuchin, 1974). As one might imagine, not all boundaries are created equal. Some are too rigid, making it difficult for subsystems to interact with and support one another, whereas some are too diffuse, making it difficult to tell who is in what subsystem. The ideal boundary is clear, not too diffuse and not too rigid.

In classroom systems with clear boundaries, teachers are higher in the power hierarchy than students, but their authority still allows for give-and-take discussions between teacher and student, discussions that make students feel known and supported. The development of problematic boundaries most often occurs when teachers adopt roles that create barriers between themselves and students (rigid boundaries) or when their authority erodes to the point that students are in control of the class (diffuse boundaries).

In classrooms with rigid boundaries, the teacher and students are apt to become strangers to one another. Communication between teacher and students becomes almost nonexistent, resulting in disengagement of the students from the teacher. The Canters' (1976, 1997) category of hostile teaching styles is essentially a category referring to a boundary problem because in classrooms where teachers are hostile, the boundary between teacher and students is apt to be overly rigid. Rigid boundaries prevent any real discussion or give and take between teacher and students, resulting in students disengaging and doing only the minimum to get by. While the teacher may characterize the problem of disengagement as students being lazy and unmotivated, from a systems perspective, the problem is too rigid a boundary between teacher and students.

Another area in which boundaries can become an issue is *openness* on the part of teachers. Jones and Jones (2004) give the following options:

1. Almost complete openness, in which we share a wide range of personal concerns and values with students

2. Openness related to our reactions to and feelings about the school environment, with limited sharing of aspects reflecting our out-of-school life

3. An almost exclusive focus on a role-bound relationship; that is, we share no personal feelings or reactions, but merely perform our instructional duties (p. 84)

For material related to this concept, go to Video Clip 8.1 on the Student Resource CD bound into the back of your textbook.

Using the boundary and subsystem concepts, we can say that the first and third options create unclear and overly rigid boundaries, respectively. In contrast, the middle option provides the best chance for boundaries between the teacher and student subsystems to be clear, especially with adolescent students who can become uncomfortable when adults are overly personal or overly formal and impersonal.

In schools, the concept of boundaries can be extended to evaluate relationships between other subsystems, particularly relationships between the administration, special education, parental, and teacher subsystems. Ideally, school administrators (superintendents, principals, vice-principals, etc.) provide leadership (establish boundaries) but allow for communication, dialogue, and support for teachers so that the boundary between these two subsystems is clear, not rigid or nonexistent. When this fails to happen, the overall school system can become dysfunctional, and the trickle-down effect can be behavior problems, especially if there are high rates of teacher turnover. Jackie Blount (1999) describes one such dysfunctional school system.

Blount (1999) spent several years teaching in a middle school that experienced three different principals. The first and third principals maintained a

Power hierarchies and rigid boundaries can create problems in communicating.

strict, authoritarian power structure in which teachers were expected to conform to whatever management system had been approved by the principal. In this particular school, the approved management system was the system developed by the Canters. Teachers had to "toe the line" or suffer serious negative consequences. The first and third principals established, in the language of the boundary and subsystem concepts, rigid boundaries between themselves and teachers that discouraged communication and undermined support for teachers.

In contrast, the second (interim) principal spent considerable time listening to both teachers and students, trying to understand their reasons for acting as they did and not simply evaluating their overt behavior. As a result, teachers were much happier and, more important, better teachers because they were given the support they needed to be thoughtful with their students. The interim principal established, in the language of the boundary and subsystem concepts, boundaries between herself and teachers that were clear: The principal retained authority but not at the expense of discouraging communication and undermining support for teachers to use their own good judgment when managing problem behavior and classrooms.

Rigid boundaries may also describe problematic relationships between the regular and special education subsystems. Returning once again to the case of Dennis, we see this in how the approaches of Dennis's first-grade teacher and that of his reading specialist differed from one another, so much so that they led to chronic behavior problems.

At the beginning of his first-grade school year, Dennis spent a portion of his day in a small group with a reading specialist. Unfortunately, the reading specialist and teacher Willand had little contact with one another, resulting in Dennis's going from the classroom's literature-based approach to reading to an entirely different approach. The disconnect upset Dennis to the point that he continually misbehaved when he was in the special reading group. It was only when the reading specialist and teacher Willand began to coordinate their approaches that Dennis's behavior in the special reading group improved. Here is what teacher Willand had to say about the reading program used by the reading specialist:

> The reading program was designed to give children skills that the specialist believed were not developed through the regular classroom's curriculum. The nature of this program became evident in the first session I watched, which was near Halloween. In this session, the specialist told the children that she was going to teach them important words they needed to know in order to be able to read. She asked them if they could think what these important words might be. One child said "pumpkin?" and the specialist replied, "Oh no. You're thinking about Halloween. The word pumpkin does not come up a lot in books." "How about ghost?" said another child. "No. You are not thinking. Think about words that you see a lot in books." Eventually, she told the children they would be learning the words *look, come,* and *the.* As the specialist spoke, the children became visibly frustrated, and Dennis . . . began to poke and kick. The rest of the group time was spent trying to manage his and others' problem behaviors. This separate and formal curriculum was not drawing the children in. (Scarlett, 1998, p. 172)

This is an example of a system being dysfunctional because members of different subsystems (the regular and special education subsystems) were working apart rather than together. Put another way, the boundary between the regular and special education subsystems was too rigid, resulting in each being unavailable to the other for support and coordination, which led to behavior problems.

The other main subsystem affecting behavior and classroom management is the parental subsystem. Ideally, parents and teachers have open lines of communication that allow for both subsystems to work cooperatively with one another. However, frequently such communication and cooperation does not exist, either because the two subsystems do not relate to one another or because one acts to undermine the other.

As an example of the latter situation, in an early childhood center, one little boy chronically misbehaved. The teachers tried everything, but to no avail. The boy continually challenged their authority. In conversations with and observations of the boy's mother, the teachers discovered that the mother had been undermining teachers' efforts by giving the boy the message that the teachers did not know what they were doing and that he should do whatever he wanted to do when he was in school. Only after the center's director had the mother agree to a written contract defining what the center required from her in the way of cooperation and support did the system become functional, leading to the boy's eventually behaving himself. That is, the contract provided a means for making the overall system functional.

Rigid boundaries between teacher and parental subsystems can also lead to problems for older students. Consider how parents of middle school and high school students often receive evaluations from their child's teacher that are negative, not positive. Frequently, the evaluations come in the form of report cards with low grades but no comments and occasionally in the form of brief, written comments such as "missed his appointment to go over test results" and "did not hand in homework assignment on time."

What are parents to do with such minimal and brief negative information? Many feel they can do little else than to start conversations with their teenagers, asking what the bad grades and negative comments mean. The result can be that their teenager gets less communicative, not more, thus making the whole situation worse, not better. Add to the mix disagreement between parenting couples over what methods should be employed to solve the problems, and one can see how the system can easily deteriorate and how, as a result, the student can do even poorer. In other words, the fairly rigid boundary between the teacher and parental subsystems, and the resulting absence of good teacher-parent communication and support, can set parents up for negative transactions within the family, which, in turn, can develop a dysfunctional system. Here is a similar scene described by a fourth-grade teacher:[1]

Olivia was a bright fourth grader who was generally uninterested in school. . . . She would read while others were sharing, draw on the desk when she was supposed to be collaborating with classmates, and sometimes she would miss entire math concepts because she had ignored multiple requests to work on practice problems.

Each week, I send home folders, and Olivia's folder always had positive comments about her academics but usually one or two comments about behavioral issues, such as her needing to listen better to her classmates and participate more in groups. The notes home did not help, and Olivia's behavior worsened.

I met with Olivia's mother to discuss her progress and performance a few weeks into the school year. Olivia's mother explained that when Olivia received negative comments, she became very upset and withdrawn, and that these notes exacerbated her anxiety about school. We made a plan to focus only on positive feedback in the weekly folders and to communicate about problematic behavior confidentially.

I began writing notes home that were completely positive. I made sure to note when Olivia had participated in a discussion. The good reports acted as a self-fulfilling prophecy. Olivia became much more engaged in classroom activities and instruction.

How Problems Are Interpreted or Framed

The third favored way to change systems is to reinterpret or reframe problem behavior in positive ways. How, you might ask, is this a method for changing the system? The answer is that interpreting or framing behavior negatively—as being a problem—can, by itself, develop or maintain a dysfunctional system. Already, we have seen how this works in several examples, including the last example of Olivia. So, one way to change a system is to reframe so that the behavior is no longer seen as a problem—or at least not as a problem "inside" the individual.

At first, reframing can seem strange, pointless, or even silly because we think of our ways of describing behavior problems as simply "stating the facts." Consider a student who suddenly jumps up on a desk and proceeds to walk to the other side of the classroom by walking on top of desks. Who would fault a teacher for seeing such behavior as being outrageous and communicating this to the student? However, a systems approach teaches us that it is neither pointless nor silly to consider alternative ways of framing, even when behaviors seem outrageous, as the following example clearly illustrates. The example, once again, is of teacher Willand's work with Dennis (Scarlett, 1998). The boldface indicates where she reframed.

One day, early in the school year, Dennis got up from his desk to get colored pencils kept on a shelf across the room and used for illustrating in writing journals. Rather than maneuver between desks, chairs, and people, as children usually do, Dennis took the shortest route by climbing on top of empty chairs and not-so-empty desks, seemingly unaware that his climbing might be scary. I approached him and said,

"**That's a great idea to use colored pencils for your journal. And you got them all by yourself, good thinking.** I noticed that you walked straight here from your seat, but to do that your feet had to step on chairs and desks. And I noticed that when your feet stepped on Jay's desk, he got worried."

"But I didn't hurt him," Dennis replied.

"**You didn't mean to hurt him,** but you might have hurt him by accident. Jay, were you surprised to see Dennis's feet on your desk?"

"Yeah," said Jay, who had indeed looked very surprised and scared.

"You know, Dennis was trying to find the quickest way to get the colored pencils. He didn't mean to scare you," I replied.

During this brief conversation between Jay and me, Dennis watched intently. Then I said, "Let's see if Dennis can find a short way back to his seat keeping his feet on the floor." He did so, and I praised him. He smiled. (p. 180)

Reframing, then, involves finding the positive in a problematic situation and using the positive as a platform on which to teach alternative behaviors. In this example, what was positive was mostly Dennis's intentions or motives, so, following Molnar and Lindquist (1989), we can refer to this kind of reframing as reframing in terms of the **positive connotation of motive**.

Because of his teacher's constant reframing, Dennis's role in the class changed from being the identified problem student to a much more positive role. Therefore, reframing is especially important in cases where students have been stigmatized. As another example, here is Joseph Cambone (1994) helping us reframe to better serve so-called "troubled" children, children whose behavior is so challenging it warrants their being schooled in segregated programs:

We repeatedly use words such as *disordered, impaired, maladaptive, deficient,* and *deviant* to describe our students; we argue that there is a clear need to *remediate, manage,* and *train* them. . . . Of course, given the behavior of many of these children, these are logical appellations. But equally logical are labels such as *resourceful, resilient, clever, creative,* and *tenacious,* especially when we consider how many of these students continue to function in difficult living situations, or, for instance, how they can often talk or work their way out of a jam, or how they can deftly manipulate the classroom behavioral system. We don't readily consider these strengths because they are too often mustered toward unhealthy ends. Yet, they are strengths nonetheless and, with an effort of thought on our part, can be redirected toward healthier ends. (p. 167)

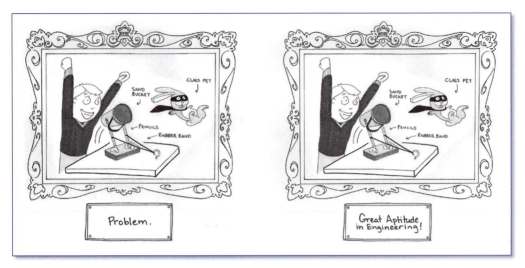

Whether a behavior is a problem all depends on how it is interpreted or framed.

For material related to this concept, go to Video Clip 8.2 on the Student Resource CD bound into the back of your textbook.

Most of the positive labels mentioned by Cambone (1994) have to do with how troubled children have managed to *function*. Faced with abusive and/or neglectful parents, some come to mistrust adults in general and survive by becoming fiercely independent, to the point that they resist any attempts to control them. Before reframing, these children are spoken of as having "oppositional defiant disorder" or worse, "conduct disorder." After reframing, they are children whose behavior serves essential functions. Cambone gives us, then, an example of what Molnar and Lindquist (1989) refer to as reframing in terms of the **positive connotation of function**.

A more common example of children needing someone to reframe in terms of the positive connotation of function may be the way some African American boys from low-income families are treated in classrooms. You may remember this as a topic of discussion in Chapter 3, about students who demand a tough but caring approach by teachers if there are to be positive teacher-student relationships. You may also remember that there is a danger in adopting a tough approach to teaching one student or group of students and a less tough approach to teaching classmates. The danger is that culture can get disrespected and students can get labeled "bad."

This essentially is Brian McCadden's (1998) observation of what some white teachers do when they take a hard-line approach to teaching African American children. McCadden provides an example in his case study of "Mrs. Hooper," a kindergarten teacher. McCadden documented how Mrs. Hooper was stricter with black boys than she was with white boys, even though, to the observer, the boys' behavior did not differ significantly from one another.

For Neil (white boy), a smart-alecky comment is either ignored or shut down quickly with a short, sharp, "Ut!" from Mrs. Hooper. . . . For Michael (black boy) . . . comments, tangents, and rule-breaking are met with direct negative discipline, such as, "Michael, what is your job at centers?" or, "Michael, you know that you are supposed to raise your hand before asking a question. Next time it's five minutes of play time." (p. 123)

McCadden (1998) goes on to point out what can happen when there is such unequal treatment: The system becomes one in which black boys are the identified problem students—not just in the eyes of teachers, but in the eyes of classmates as well.

McCadden (1998) offers no easy solutions; in fact, he is pessimistic about the abilities of many white teachers to teach black children because the cultural differences make it difficult for many white teachers to respect black culture and teach in ways that ensure that many black children will thrive. What he offers, instead, is the suggestion that white teachers find teachers who already respect black culture and who, as a result, naturally frame the behavior of black children as positive because they see their behavior as serving the positive function of fitting comfortably within black culture. For example, what to one teacher may appear to be a black child's being out of control may to another be a black child's showing energy and passion. Here is McCadden's example of a teacher showing this implicit respect for black culture and a positive way of framing black children's behavior:

Ms. Martin, a black counselor at Green End . . . came into Mrs. Hooper's class every Wednesday to discuss counseling issues with the children through the use of puppets and stories. She let the children ask many questions and often wandered with their tangents. She never, however, lost control of the class, and managed this through being intellectually nimble enough to connect the children's tangents back to her major theme for the day and through using jokes and changes in her intonation to signal to the children when they were going too far afield. Her style led to a noisy class, but it was a class in which all were engaged and in which Michael, Malik, and Dontonio were able to contribute positively. (p. 131)

We will have more to say about teaching African American children from low-income families in Chapter 9, where we focus on issues of culture. For now, it is enough to say that the phenomena just described exist and that they relate directly to our focus on problem behavior as a reflection of dysfunctional systems that require alternative, positive ways of framing misbehavior.

A third type of reframing occurs when teachers refocus by focusing on other behaviors of a student that are clearly positive. This is a method referred to by

Molnar and Lindquist (1989) as storming the back door because the positive is found by "going around back" and looking elsewhere, to put the student "in a good light."

One example of looking elsewhere to put a student or group of students in a good light is the movie *Stand and Deliver* (Menendez, 1988), a movie depicting an East Los Angeles high school math class. The movie was based on a true story. In the movie, Jaime Escalante, the math teacher, teaches a group of mostly Hispanic students who initially give the impression of being unteachable. However, in the course of the movie, both the teacher and the movie's viewers discover that outside school, many of the students live their lives as responsible, caring, and thoughtful young adults, holding down jobs, caring for family members, and so forth. As a result of this discovery, both the teacher and the viewer see how it is possible to change the old system and turn the class around, which is what happens as the students go on to receive high marks on a national Advanced Placement Calculus Exam. While this example is dramatic, it rings true because it is an example that can be found almost anywhere.

Review

Types of reframing:

(1) Positive connotation of motive: Finding a positive intent behind a student's behavior

(2) Positive connotation of function: Finding a positive function in a student's behavior

(3) Storming the back door: Looking outside the problem situation to find a student's positive interests, activities, and strengths

Summary

In this chapter, we see how stepping back to look at the larger picture can sometimes help us get unstuck. The larger picture here is classroom interpersonal systems made up of transactional patterns or regularities in the way individuals interact. We have found that often what are taken to be problems *of* students and problems *inside* students are better viewed as problems in the classroom system.

Here, too, we have found that systemic problems often have to do with power, boundaries between subsystems, and the way behavior is framed. We have concentrated, then, on ways to change dysfunctional systems by changing power relationships, changing the quality of boundaries, and changing the way behavior and students are framed. In so doing, we have seen just how useful a classroom systems approach can be, especially when teachers feel stuck.

All this leads us back to the mystery alluded to at the beginning of this chapter; namely, the mystery of why such a useful approach has been overlooked by schools and educators. The answers aren't clear, but one possible answer is worth considering.

Source: Michael Marsland/Yale University

Seymour Sarason

The classroom systems approach demands much more than implementing methods such as reframing. It also demands that we consider our beliefs and actions as derived from the larger system in which we find ourselves. Furthermore, it demands that we consider the larger system as only one among many possible systems. This is not as easy as it might seem because, most of the time, we see our beliefs and actions as coming from our perceptions of what seems right and sensible and not from some system. As such, our behavior often feels inevitable.

To make this point clear, consider Seymour Sarason's (1982) asking educators to think critically about why, in American schools, kindergarten children are rarely found making their way through school hallways unattended by a teacher. He reported that his even raising this question was met with surprise and even irritation. "Of course kindergarten children need to be supervised in hallways—they are, after all, kindergarten children." However, in other cultures, kindergarten children are given far more responsibility than simply making their way through school hallways without adult supervision. For example, in other cultures, kindergarten-age children use sharp knives to help prepare meals and look after infant siblings (Rogoff, 2003). Sarason's question about the system is not, then, as crazy as it might first appear to be.

The point here is that we may be resisting even considering a systems approach because we often don't see the possibilities for change and reframing. Following this line of reasoning, we might do better by cultivating the habit of considering alternative possibilities, even or especially when we think we are doing everything possible and everything sensible.

Web-Based Student Study Site

The companion Web site for *Approaches to Behavior and Classroom Management* can be found at www.sagepub.com/scarlettstudy.

Visit the Web-based student study site to enhance your understanding of the chapter content. The study materials include practice tests, flashcards, suggested readings, and Web resources.

Key Concepts

Boundary

Clear boundaries

Diffuse boundaries

Identified problem
student

Positive connotation of
function

Positive connotation of
motive

Power

Pygmalion effect

Reactive approach

Reframing

Rigid boundaries

Storming the back door

Subsystems

Systems theory

Transactional patterns

Discussion Questions

1. Can you think of a student in your past who was labeled a behavior problem? Now, can you think of that student as mirroring some dysfunctional system in the classroom or school? Can you use reframing to see something positive in that student's behavior? The task here is to use a systems approach to understanding problem behavior.

2. Can you come up with examples of boundary problems in a classroom or school, problems with teachers setting up boundaries between themselves and students that are either too rigid or too diffuse (unclear)?

3. In your present situation, look around you to find one, two, or several people with whom you have a difficult time and who are difficult no matter what you do to make things better. Now try reframing so that you see this person or these persons in a positive way. Can you do this sincerely? If you can, does it suggest how you might act differently?

4. Why do you think so few make use of a systems approach to understand and help with chronic behavior problems? If you had not read this chapter, would you ever have considered a systems approach? If "no," why not?

---

1. Interviewed by Iris Ponte.

PART V

Accommodating Diversity

Throughout this book we have been discussing the importance of attending to the uniqueness of individuals and groups—so much so that the following chapters on diversity may seem superfluous. However, they are not superfluous because there still is much left to discuss, especially when it comes to culture and disability. In Part V, we focus on cultural approaches and on organic approaches for students with special needs.

Chapter 9 shows how cultures differ from one another in the way they approach managing behavior and classrooms. In doing so, it shows that though cultural approaches differ from one another, they are successful in their own way, indicating that we should respect differences. In addition, the chapter on culture shows how educators teaching culturally diverse groups can accommodate cultural differences.

Chapter 10 shows how the medical model and organic approaches to disability differ from special education approaches. In focusing on differences, we show how organic and special education approaches can complement one another, provided educators understand the strengths and limitations of the medical model and organic approaches.

Chapter 9

CULTURAL APPROACHES

Culture is at the heart of all we do in the name of education. . . .
Even without our being consciously aware of it, culture determines
how we think, believe, and behave, and these, in turn, affect how
we teach and learn.

—Gay (2000, p. 14)

*Laura didn't know what to do. Everyday Kumi would pull on the classroom
door, trying to leave the classroom. Laura tried everything: talking to her, showing her that the door was closed, trying to engage her in other activities. Nothing
worked. Every morning it was the same behavior. Kumi would end up having a
full-blown tantrum and disrupt the entire preschool class throughout the morning. Kumi only spoke Japanese, so it was very difficult for Laura to explain to
her why she couldn't leave the classroom.*

*If only Laura had known that preschool children in Japan are free to move
around the school during morning hours and that Kumi was trying to visit her
little brother in another classroom during morning choice time. If she had
known, she would have been better able to support Kumi.*

Why understand different cultural approaches? The answers are several, but
two answers, in particular, seem noteworthy. First, in different cultures, there
are approaches to behavior and classroom management that, though they differ from one another, work equally well. Being aware of this is essential if we
are to respect differences in cultural approaches.

Chapter Overview

Socioeconomic Status and Culture

Urban Schools: Culture and Poverty

Behavior and Classroom Management: A Sample of Cultural Approaches
The United States: Democratic Control for Promoting Active Citizenship
Management in Minority Subcultures

Differences Between Cultures Treated as Similar: An Asian Example
Japan: Effortless Control for Promoting Harmony
China: Confucian Guan for Promoting Order

Second, we live in a time when more and more educators are faced with the task of educating culturally diverse groups of children and adolescents. American classrooms, especially those in urban schools, are becoming rainbows of race, ethnicity, and culture (Clayton, 2003). Here, then, we need to understand where children and adolescents in our classrooms are "coming from"— what cultural assumptions and practices they bring to school that might make it especially challenging for us to support them.

Here, also, we want to increase awareness of the existence of typical, North American approaches, so as to be more sensitive to just how culture may create mismatches between typical and atypical approaches to behavior and classroom management. But first, we need to say something about the different meanings of the word *culture*.

As used in both the literature and in everyday conversation, there are two main meanings of the word *culture*. One meaning has to do with what is going on within a particular geographic region, as when we refer to "American culture" or "European culture" or "Japanese culture." Using this meaning of culture, one assumes that people from the same country, region, or continent share much in common (language, food, dress, political system, etc.), and what is shared is taken to define culture.

A second meaning focuses not on geography but on those behaviors that reveal collective characteristics among people who come from similar backgrounds and who share similar values and worldviews. Using this meaning, culture is not necessarily geographically based. In this chapter, we adopt both meanings but emphasize the second.

In this chapter, too, we define culture by more than surface features such as language, dress, food, and recreational interests. We also define culture by a culture's **deep structure**. Deep structure has to do with a culture's values, ideals, and images of what individuals and communities should become. Using this distinction, we can better evaluate a culture, including our own.

The cultural diversity found in today's classrooms can present teachers with special challenges.

Our own mainstream American culture is often criticized for its surface features, such as its public displays of violence and sex in movies, television shows, and advertisements. However, the deep structure of American culture can bring out the best in us. For example, deep in American culture is the ideal that everyone should have equal opportunities to succeed and find meaning in life, and everyone, regardless of race, ethnicity, religion, or income, should have a voice in how communities are run. The challenge here will be to understand a culture's deep structure and to connect deep structure to a culture's approach to behavior and classroom management.

A word of caution: What we have to say about cultures is not intended to represent each and every member of a culture. If that were the intent, we would be guilty of stereotyping. Therefore, when we say "black culture" or "Native American culture" or any culture, for that matter, we do not mean to imply that being black, Native American, or whatever means everyone who is black, Native American, or whatever acts, believes, and values in the same or even in similar ways. Rather we mean simply that there are **ideal types**, images that people carry in their heads and that define for them what a culture takes to be

Accommodating diversity means respecting differences, not becoming someone different from who we are.

good behavior as well as what it means for individuals and communities to be mature or developed. We need to understand these ideal types both to understand the differences between cultural approaches and to fully respect those differences.

Furthermore, what we have to say about culture and how cultural differences figure into how educators manage both behavior and classrooms in no way implies that cultural differences are necessarily relevant. In many cases, they aren't relevant to how teachers teach because developmental needs and learning needs often trump whatever needs there are that may be attributed to cultural differences. And certainly one should never assume we need separate theories of human development for different groups of children, as we discussed before when discussing special education and the fallacy of treating children with disabilities as if they require a separate theory (Sarason, 1982). In particular, regardless of culture, children and adolescents everywhere need positive, caring, nurturing support.

Finally, with respect to being cautious about placing too much emphasis on culture and cultural differences, throughout this discussion of culture it will become clear that though the differences between cultures and their approaches to managing behavior and classrooms may be striking, the similarities may be even more striking. In particular, every culture tries to manage the dilemma of how to support children as unique and special individuals while also supporting their development as participants in communities. That is, though the images of self and community differ from one culture to another, the focus on developing individuals and communities is universal.

The discussion of culture also makes clear that the usual category systems for differentiating management styles are much too simplistic to encompass the variety of styles that we find in cultures. In particular, Baumrind's (1970) system for describing management styles as authoritarian, authoritative, or permissive fails to capture the variety of ways that educators and parents can be authoritarian and permissive and still function very well.

Using the restricted meanings in Baumrind's (1970) system, we are taught that authoritarian and permissive styles are bad and that authoritative styles are good. And so, when teachers and parents from other cultures use authoritarian or permissive styles, we reject them immediately.

However, if only we would notice the little details in the ways teachers and parents from other cultures are authoritarian or permissive, details that make their styles of control positive, caring, and effective, then we might be more approving. In Chapter 3, the example of a Haitian authoritarian style showed how Haitian teachers, when controlling students, remind students that they are connected to those who love them—a detail often missed by North American observers. This chapter, then, will make clear those details in cultural approaches and styles that explain their effectiveness.

It is impossible, then, to understand teachers' approaches to behavior and classroom management apart from the cultures in which they are embedded. In each of the cultures explored in this chapter, we find teachers holding different conceptions of self, authority, and community, and the different conceptions influence teachers' approaches to behavior and classroom management. These concepts of self, authority, and community are rooted in the adult world of work for which children and adolescents are being prepared, as well as in the socioeconomic status of both teachers and students.

For material related to this concept, go to Video Clip 9.1 on the Student Resource CD bound into the back of your textbook.

SOCIOECONOMIC STATUS AND CULTURE

Socioeconomic status (SES) has been explored in multiple cross-cultural studies, and the findings consistently show that culture and social class often interact to account for differences both between and within groups. For example, in her recent book, *American Individualisms*, Kusserow (2004) explored notions of individualism in the United States and showed that although individualism is valued throughout the United States, it takes a different form and meaning depending on socioeconomic class. Specifically, she found that upper-middle-class families cultivate what she called "soft individualism" while lower-class families cultivate "hard individualism." With soft individualism, the emphasis is on the delicacy of a child's self and the need for parents to provide sensitive care. With hard individualism, the emphasis is on the child's having a resilient, tough self and the need for parents to provide the supports for developing toughness (p. 170). Thus, while individualism helps define American culture, individualism takes different forms depending on social class.

Many of the combined effects of social class and culture show up in language. This is especially important for our subject of behavior and classroom management because children and adolescents from lower socioeconomic classes often are used to very different ways of speaking than the speech of their (usually) white middle-class teachers. For example, most teachers give indirect directives that are often presented as questions: "Is this a good time to be talking?" "Do you think the next person who wants to use that glue will appreciate how you left it?" Many students from lower socioeconomic classes are use to a more direct approach: "Be quiet!" "Put the glue away!" As noted sociolinguist Shirley Brice Heath (1978) explains,

> Students who come from home environments or cultures where questions— as directives, hints, or tag questions—are not used, have to learn—if they are to become acceptable members of the school's speech community—not to respond verbally. They also have to learn the values and behaviors implied in these directives. Teachers who use these devices can help by recognizing when and how often they use them and by making an effort to spell out the values and behaviors behind these routines. (p. 12)

Heath (1983) recommends, then, that teachers be aware of how their questions may confuse their students. However, because teachers' ways of speaking are the ways students need to understand if they are to function in the greater society, she also recommends that teachers explain their ways of speaking. In other words, teachers do not need to abandon their ways of speaking when speaking to students from different socioeconomic classes. Rather, they need to make their ways of speaking understandable and meaningful to all students but especially to students from subcultures and different socioeconomic classes where typical speech is quite different from the typical speech of teachers.

However, not everyone agrees with what Heath and others imply about "teacher talk" and the problem of teachers being indirect in the way they provide directives. For example, another leading sociolinguist,

Source: Shirley Brice Heath.

Shirley Brice Heath

Courtney Cazden (1988), points out that regardless of social class, compared with teachers, mothers are apt to be more direct and less polite than teachers. Cazden's observation implies that the most important point about teachers' speech and speech at home is not about SES but more generally about teachers needing to be mindful of how they speak and how students understand their speech so they can alter their speech or make its meaning more explicit when there is confusion. This, she says, is relevant for all students, not just students from lower socioeconomic classes.

Despite Cazden's (1988) caution that others may be overstating differences having to do with SES, there is enough evidence and research to suggest that SES does, indeed, matter and that the ways middle-class teachers speak and communicate with students can present special problems for students from lower socioeconomic classes (Wiener, Devoe, Runinow, & Geller, 1972). Therefore, in this chapter, SES differences will be considered alongside cultural differences. This is important because racial, ethnic, and cultural differences are often made significant by differences in socioeconomic status. Put another way, take socioeconomic status out of the equation, and many differences attributed to race, ethnicity, or culture disappear or are reduced significantly.

URBAN SCHOOLS: CULTURE AND POVERTY

Urban American schools present both challenges and opportunities for educators. On the one hand, urban schools often serve youth of color from low-income families, many with limited English fluency and greater academic, social, and emotional needs than their middle-class, suburban counterparts. Couple this with the fact that urban schools are often severely underfunded and staffed by teachers with backgrounds quite different from students' backgrounds, and the meaning of challenges becomes clear (Weiner, 2006). On the other hand, urban schools provide opportunities to address some of society's most serious issues (e.g., poverty, prejudice), and in so doing they provide work with added meaning for both teachers and students.

In the past, the challenges around behavior and classroom management in urban schools have led many teachers to quit early in their careers (Wilkins-Canter, Edwards, Young, Ramanathan, & McDougle, 2000), making for ongoing problems in behavior and classroom management. Not surprisingly, the problems have led educators and the general public to apply a "deficit paradigm" to explain urban youths' problem behavior (Weiner, 2006). Students, their families, their cultural heritage, and their community have been blamed for the problems. However, the evidence suggests that when teachers show care, teach effectively, and focus on what they can control, then teachers can have a significant impact and solve problems felt to be unsolvable (Irving, 1988).

Therefore, the main point to make about urban schools with diverse groups from poor backgrounds is that the challenges need not overwhelm. There are enough success stories to show that a school's being well run and classrooms being well taught can meet the challenges presented by problems associated with being urban, diverse, and poor. Take, for example, the Samuel Gompers Elementary School in Detroit where, in 2000, the fourth-grade students had the highest test scores of any fourth grade in Michigan (J. Comer, 2003). The high scores reflect the fact that in this urban school, administrators and teachers successfully supported children's adopting attitudes, values, and beliefs that helped them to be both confident and competent. Similar success stories can be found in every city.

REFLECT

What aspects of your upbringing reflect your culture and not simply the beliefs and styles of your parents, teachers, and other caregivers? In addition to reflecting on your cultural experience concerning control issues, reflect on your feelings about your culture's way of dealing with control issues. What works? What does not work? What are the strengths and weaknesses? And what, in your own behavior, can you now see reflects your cultural background?

BEHAVIOR AND CLASSROOM MANAGEMENT: A SAMPLE OF CULTURAL APPROACHES

Here, we provide a sample of cultural approaches to behavior and classroom management. We begin with discussions of what roughly defines mainstream U.S. approaches.

The United States: Democratic Control for Promoting Active Citizenship

Anthropologist Edward Hall (1976) wrote,

Culture hides much more than it reveals, and strangely enough, what it hides, it hides most effectively from its own participants. Years of study have convinced me that the real job is not to understand foreign culture(s) but to understand our own. (p. 30)

Thus, we begin the discussion of culture with discussion of mainstream American practices because "our own culture is often unknown to us" (Clayton, 2003, p. 3). The key concept here is the concept of **democratic practice**, as discussed at some length in Chapter 4. While democratic practice may not be the norm, for many American educators, it still is the ideal. Its meaning is captured in the following statement by Ronald Butchart (1998a):

> Classroom discipline in American schools calls on teachers to create class-rooms and schoolhouses in which young people live a curriculum of *democratic* civility . . . our hope is that young people will learn the life skills of leading courageous, just, committed, vibrant, *democratic* lives. (p. 14)

In American education, from Thomas Jefferson, to Horace Mann, to John Dewey, to the present, we find one enduring theme: the theme of democracy (Cremin, 1965). From its inception, then, the public school system in America was intended to promote the democratic way of life and to prepare students to become citizens in a democratic society. This was the stated ideal then, and it is the stated ideal now, though obviously, the ideal often does not square with reality.

However, in many, if not in most, American schools and classrooms, we see three themes that reflect what is meant by being democratic: the theme of giving everyone a "voice"; the theme of everyone being expected to consider not only his or her own perspective but also the perspectives of others; and the theme of authority deriving not from a person's status, but from how well a person represents the common good.

Democratic decision making is one way to foster the social development of students as well as foster a group's development into a just and caring community. We saw this in Chapter 4 when discussing community approaches to behavior and classroom management. In fostering democratic decision making, the teacher's authority comes not from his or her being the adult but from his or her representing the legitimate interests, rights, and needs of all the students. The teacher always retains a special responsibility for holding the group accountable to a standard of fairness and a responsibility for ensuring reasonable conformity to the rules of the wider institutional environment. But to the extent that students participate in formulating at least some of the rules, they are required to take the viewpoint of the rule maker. Many American teachers assume, then, that to construct positive classroom environments, teachers should place at least some of the decisions about behavior and classroom management in students' hands.

In the spirit of being democratic, teachers in American schools are apt to be constantly trying to balance the need to make demands on students with the need to give students freedom to choose. Furthermore, democratic teachers have simple rules and reasonable consequences for breaking rules. They spend time discussing with students the reasons for the rules, while at the same time they listen to students' ideas and concerns.

If direct intervention and teacher control is needed to stop a physical fight, teachers in American schools are apt to first stop the fight, ask for explanations, and then stimulate discussion. In a verbal altercation, teachers are apt to encourage children and adolescents to first voice their point of view and then help them come to some sort of agreement after listening to everyone's point of view.

In the following example, two children get into a verbal conflict that escalates into a physical fight.[1] After the teacher intervenes to ensure safety, she stimulates the following dialogue:

Child: (now crying) TOM WON'T GIVE ME THE GLUE!!

The teacher replies, "I don't care what he did, nothing makes hurting someone else OK! Sam, you are to come with me. We are going to have a discussion." Outside the classroom, the teacher gets down on the floor to talk to Sam, who is still crying. The teacher says, "Sam if you can calm down, you can tell me what happened. I am not angry with you, but I want you to understand why what you were doing was so dangerous. It is my job to keep all of the children in our class safe." Sam, still crying, says, "I was so mad Tom wouldn't give me the glue. I asked nice and everything, but he didn't listen." "I am going to go get Tom, and we will talk to him together," the teacher explains. She goes into the classroom and brings Tom into the hallway where they discuss what happened and how they could have handled the situation better.

During these and other instances of unsafe misbehavior, maintaining the deep structure of democracy, with its emphasis on respecting different points of view, presents a challenge. Teachers socialized in a democratic culture such as our own are apt to constantly struggle with the dilemma of how to allow children and adolescents to maintain choice and control while at the same time protecting students and keeping them safe.

Democracy is central to U.S. society, and so it should not be surprising that teachers in American schools are more apt to embrace behavior and classroom management methods that reflect the goals and desires that help define what it means to be democratic: rational debate, verbal self-expression, negotiation, ability to agree and disagree—these are among the ingredients of democratic approaches and methods. As an American, it is easy to believe that a democratic approach to behavior and classroom management is the best approach. However, this belief is debatable, as we will see when discussing alternative approaches that are equally successful in other cultures.

Management in Minority Subcultures

We begin with discussions of minority cultures within the United States and show how coming from a minority culture can present mismatches between the management practices students are used to at home and the management practices they find at school. The results can be quite negative.

African American Community: Personal Power and Positive Authority

For too long, there have been tensions when talking about race and discipline in American classrooms, forcing teachers to be overly cautious about saying anything definite when it comes to differences. This has been especially the case when talking about teaching African American students.[2] The diversity among African American students is more striking than any common characteristics. However, African Americans' unique history has led many African American families to adopt a different approach to raising children than that adopted by the majority of Euro-American, middle-class families, an approach that some think evolved in pre–Civil War times to help African American children avoid the extreme consequences of being viewed as disobedient (Butchart, 1998b).

On the surface, this different approach seems simply authoritarian, so white middle-class teachers often devalue it. However, on closer inspection, there are important subtleties that make this approach quite successful in both raising and teaching children.

As discussed in Chapters 3 and 8, there are experts who say black children from low-income families, especially black boys, often need a more authoritarian or direct approach to control them than the approach found in most classrooms taught by middle-class Euro-American teachers. Also as mentioned, these experts argue that African American children from low-income families are often confused by the indirect ways that Euro-American teachers use when trying to maintain control. As a result, they misbehave. Lisa Delpit's (1995) work has been the most influential in stressing these points.

However, as explained in Chapter 8, the issue here is not simply one of choosing a more authoritarian and direct approach when teaching those African American students who need such an approach to control them and keep them from misbehaving. The issue is how to adopt the kind of positive, nurturing authoritarian approach that many African American children and adolescents are used to at home and respond to positively—not just for the short term but for the long term as well.

This issue is explained by George Noblit (1993) in his ethnographic study of a second-grade classroom. For over a year, Noblit observed an African

For material related to this concept, go to Video Clip 9.2 on the Student Resource CD bound into the back of your textbook.

Lisa Delpit

American teacher in a predominantly African American school and found that her approach of teacher-centeredness and use of personal power worked well in helping her students succeed in schools. She expected a lot from her students and, in turn, her students performed. She, like many African American teachers, gave directives in a direct and explicit fashion, for example, by saying, "I don't want to hear it. Sit down, be quiet, and finish your work now!" This is a directive given in a style that commands respect through exhibiting personal power—power that may appear to be negative and constraining to progressive educators but is experienced by the children themselves as positive—akin to how players on sports teams sometimes experience their tough coaches as being caring by having their best interests at heart.

The distinction here is between the power of a teacher as a person and the power of the teacher's role—as already explained in Chapter 3. In Chapter 3, we saw how Noblit, Delpit, and others explain that many African American children from low-income families look for teachers to command respect through the power they demonstrate as *persons*, power earned by the way they conduct themselves. As a result, these African American children are more likely to disrespect teachers who are indirect and nonauthoritarian. In contrast, Euro-American, middle-class children are more likely to respect teachers simply because they fill the role of teacher.

However, as discussed in Chapter 8, being tough without being nurturing runs the risk of making certain students into identified problem students. It also runs the risk of disrespecting a student's culture. As Brian McCadden (1998) explains, African American children do not need simply any authoritarian approach; they need one that teaches in a positive, nurturing way what students need to understand in order to succeed in American society.

What black children, especially black boys, need is not the sort of permissive and progressive management and discipline [that middle-class white children often need]. . . . Perhaps the black boys, needing to understand a culture that is not their own, require a different, more overt form of nurturance. Success for these boys may depend on . . . teachers showing them what they need to know and be as public citizens, in a white-dominated society represented by the arena called school. (p. 119)

In sum, for reasons of culture, a significant number of African American students may need a more authoritarian approach to behavior and classroom management. However, the authoritarian approach needed is one that is also positive, nurturing, and protective of positive identity.

Hispanic Community:
Cooperation and Group-Mindedness

> "What on earth do you think you are doing?" the teacher yelled from across the room. Luis looked up with surprised eyes and said, "I am working on my math paper." "You were cheating!" shrieked the teacher. "I saw you talking to Manuel, and that is cheating!"

This exchange between teacher and child is not uncommon in a classroom with Hispanic children.[3] In Hispanic society, family or group needs take precedence over individual needs. Many Hispanics are brought up to be group-minded rather than individualistically minded, whereas U.S. classrooms typically encourage students to stand out and be individualistic. When Hispanic students work in a group, not all are expected to do their equal share. It is quite likely that if one group member does little or no work, the others won't mind (Garcia, 1991).

This group-mindedness of Hispanics can also be seen in sharing material objects and information. In the example above, sharing took the form of helping another student during a test. The students in the example were stunned and offended by the teacher's reaction because to them, they were helping each other, not cheating.

Today there are 35 million people in Spanish-speaking communities in the U.S. Like the African American community, the Hispanic community also suffers from being misunderstood. For example, a disproportionate number of Hispanic children have, over the years, been assigned to special education classrooms (Sarason, 1982). However, unlike African American students, Hispanic students are less likely to be labeled as "aggressive troublemakers." Instead, Hispanic children are more likely to be viewed as removed and quiet.

Sometimes teachers see these behaviors as covert forms of disobedience and disrespect. However, to Hispanic students, they have to do with the teacher being the authority. For this reason, the notion of conversing with a teacher can feel confusing. Take the following as an example:

> It was Michael's first day at school. During choice time Michael didn't know what to do with himself. He just stood in the middle of the floor quietly. I went over to him and knelt by his side and asked, "What would you like to do today?" He just looked at me and shrugged. I was a little frustrated; all of the other children were working and playing in the different classroom stations. I said to him, "Would you like to work on blocks, play dough, or in the art center?" He shrugged again. I was feeling a little annoyed. I brought this up to my co-teacher, and she told me to try giving him a directive. The next day I said to Michael, "Today you are going to

work on blocks. Come right over here." To my surprise he walked right over and started working.

Another challenge for Hispanic students is language. For many, English is a second language used only in school (Garcia, 1991). For some Hispanic students, the thought of speaking out in class is terrifying. When children see the faces of peers and teachers not understanding, they shut down and become introverted.

When we watch our Hispanic students during the time we teach, we will see that they are all quiet and look at us somewhat scared at the thought that we might call on them individually. When they are called upon, they will often freeze, get confused and embarrassed as they try to answer. They feel much more comfortable responding in groups, doing exercises together, and helping each other. (Teacher in Arizona)

Therefore, when teaching children from Hispanic cultures, teachers must be sensitive to what it means when students are quieter than others and what it means when students are cooperative in ways different from the way other groups are cooperative. Again, being sensitive and positive is the challenge.

Native American Community: Working Together in a State of Balance

Grown men can learn from very little children, for the hearts of the little children are pure. Therefore, the Great Spirit may show them many things which older people miss.

—Black Elk (Old Indian proverb)

Today, Native Americans account for a little less than 1 percent of the total population in the U.S. (Thornton, 2000). Despite the fact that Native Americans make up such a small percentage of the population, there have been many publications documenting problems in classrooms for Native American children. Some of the problems have to do with disruptive behavior. However, the majority of the problems have to do with students not actively participating in ways typical of white, middle-class children, so that to white, middle-class teachers, Native American students can appear to be "taciturn," "withdrawn," "lazy," or in some other way, "less than well-behaved" (McCarthy & Banally, 2003).

The majority of these complaints are made by teachers from outside Native American communities, suggesting that there are mismatches between Native

American approaches to teaching and managing and approaches typical in the larger society. For this reason, it is important that we understand Native American approaches. The key may be to understand how Native American culture favors cooperation over competition (Brown, 1980; Nuby, Ehle, & Thrower, 2001; Nuby & Oxford, 1997). Native American students find security in being a member of a group, and many feel uncomfortable being singled out. Students do not want to be shown to be either above or below others. Therefore, to be praised for personal achievement has, for many Native American students, a negative meaning. In fact, some high-achieving students stop doing good work in order to regain their place in the group. The example below explains the experience of a third-grade teacher in Arizona:

> It was time to start our book reading race. I had always loved this competition as a child. You put up a grid of all the children's names in the front of the classroom, and as they read a book and write a short report, you put a sticker on the chart. At the end of each month, as a class, we count each student's stickers to see everyone's progress. As an incentive, I told the students I would give a prize at the end of each month to the student who had read the most books.
>
> Over the next few weeks, I noticed that many of my Native American students had slowed down in their reading—students who I knew loved to read. Some didn't get a single sticker in a whole week! I had no idea what was going on. I was frustrated and confused. This game was to motivate reading, not stop it!

Other teachers of Native American students tell similar stories. In classrooms outside Native American communities, standing out and being competitive are crucial to success in classrooms. However, in many Native American communities, it is humility and being a cooperative member of the group that matters most.

Living in harmony with others and showing respect for elders are additional themes in Native American communities (Pewewardy, 2002). In these communities, to learn often means to watch and listen, not to speak up and question. And so, what to an outsider may be students being dull, uninvolved, and taciturn is, to an insider, students being alert, involved, and respectful.

So, if approaches common in the larger society do not work, what approaches and methods do work? Dehyle (1992) found that the most successful classrooms for Native American students used small groups to teach lessons. Small groups, it seemed, allowed for more sharing with classmates (Little Soldiers, 1989; Swisher & Dehyle, 1989).

Some studies indicate that Native American students are more active when class discussion is led by other students (Philips, 1983). This makes sense, given the norm of being quiet when an elder speaks.

Still others recommend teachers getting to know students' families and community. For example, Jones and Jones (2004, p. 90) observed while working on a Native American reservation that one high school teacher in the local school was especially successful at motivating students to do well in school because he was the only teacher in the school to attend cultural events, visit with families, and, in general, get to know students and their lives outside school.

In sum, in classes where there are Native American students, approaches that work to stimulate competition, reward individual achievement, and employ teacher-led discussion are likely to fail. In contrast, approaches that stimulate cooperation in small groups, reward everyone for participating, and employ student-led discussion are likely to succeed. Furthermore, it may be especially important for non–Native American teachers to do whatever they can to get to know students' families and community life outside school.

REFLECT Much has been made of the problems created when there are mismatches between the culture represented by a student's parents and the culture represented by a student's teacher and school. Have you ever experienced or observed a cultural mismatch, either at school or elsewhere? If "yes," what problem or problems did the mismatch cause? What would have helped prevent the problem(s)?

DIFFERENCES BETWEEN CULTURES TREATED AS SIMILAR: AN ASIAN EXAMPLE

We end this discussion on culture and behavior and classroom management with a contrast between typical Japanese and Chinese approaches.[4] We do so for three reasons: first, to continue to demonstrate that there are cultural approaches to behavior and classroom management; second, to continue to demonstrate that the terms *authoritarian, authoritative,* and *permissive* do not begin to capture the subtleties in cultural differences; and third, to bring attention to the fact that cultural groups that are often lumped together on the basis of something shared can differ considerably in their approach to behavior and classroom management.

Japanese and Chinese cultures are often lumped together as being **collectivist cultures;** that is, cultures emphasizing children's "fitting in" rather than "standing out." However, when it comes to approaches to behavior and classroom management, these two cultures are opposites. We begin with a discussion of typical Japanese approaches.

Japan: Effortless Control for Promoting Harmony

American teachers believe that an approach will succeed if teachers are available, if they model and stimulate discussion, and if they provide guidance for children to negotiate conflict. However, Japanese teachers believe that children should manage difficult situations without teachers' help (Zahn-Waxler, Cole, Mizuta, & Hiruma, 1996).

Japanese teachers are likely to see childhood as a pure time of life. To them, "A child is like a small angel from heaven that can do no wrong."[5] With this image of the child, it is easy to understand how teachers can allow children to figure things out on their own.

> In Japan, you give children a wide range of freedom, and you assume that they will stay in it. You assume that children will be children, but that they are inherently good and sensible and that they will monitor themselves and stay within a wide range of acceptable behavior. They do, and you leave them alone. (Walsh, 1999, p. 104)

In Japan, children learn early on that they are to be trusted and that they can still be children and run about shouting and wrestling. This social contract comes from the deep structure of Japanese society. In Japanese society, creating harmonious relations with others through reciprocity and the fulfillment of social obligations is more important than promoting one's own agenda. Living in harmony with others and feeling a sense of obligation toward others are, then, values central to explaining the way Japanese interact.

At a remarkably early age, Japanese children learn that their responsibility is to the group. Lewis (1995), an expert on Japanese early education, explains, "Peers are extensively involved in managing misbehavior, and adult (teacher) authority is muted" (p. 125). As a result, children learn to work and play with other children without the assistance of an adult. One Japanese teacher explained that "to intervene in children's disputes is to be doing them a disservice because then they will only rely on you." Here is an example of just how "hands off" this Japanese approach can seem to an outsider:

> It was a spring day at a preschool in Kyoto, Japan. Group exercises had just ended, and the children lined up to return to their classrooms for prayer time. As the classroom organ played a quieting tune, the children went to

their marked spot on the floor. With their legs folded under them, eyes closed, and hands pressed together, the classroom was silent. Suddenly, a little boy jumped out of his spot and made a mad dash for the classroom door.

An American observer was already up and out of her seat to go after him when she felt a hand push down on her shoulder. "Let him go," the classroom teacher told her. The observer watched anxiously as the little boy made it into the play yard and began to climb up the tall steps of a slide. After about 5 minutes the boy came quietly back to his spot on the classroom floor. The little boy next to him leaned over and said, "Hiro, why did you run outside? You know that this is a time for prayer." For the rest of the school year, Hiro never ran out of the classroom again.

Japanese teachers use the word *doryokumasen* to define the methods that they use. Roughly translated, it means *without effort* or effortless control. According to the teachers, methods for managing students and classrooms should appear easy and as if the teacher is doing nothing. However, the reality is that these methods demand considerable effort and thought.

As noted above, Japanese teachers are more concerned with children developing a sense of being obligated to others. In helping children develop this sense, Japanese teachers use the approach of effortless control to subtly manipulate the context so that students work through their problems seemingly on their own. As one Japanese teacher put it,

> To be a good teacher is to create a context where children need to work through problems, where children need to fight and cry and yell. Of course, if a situation gets too violent, a teacher will step in. However, how are children to learn how to be with others if I am constantly telling them what to do and how to resolve problems? (First-grade teacher in Kyoto, Japan)

In a typical Japanese classroom (even early childhood classrooms) there are approximately 30 to 35 children to one teacher. This large number of children is crucial, in that even if a teacher wanted to, it would be impossible to provide individual supports and attention for each and every child. One principal explained,

> It is natural for a teacher to want to help a child in a difficult situation; however, it would be selfish. The child is here to learn, and the most important lesson is how to be with others. How can we teach a child that lesson if the class is too small or if the teacher is always around? These numbers prevent this from happening.

Therefore, children do not seek out teachers to solve their problems. Rather, they work out problems on their own, as is evident in the following example:

In one middle school classroom, a teacher was running a cooperative activity where the students were responsible for designing a math problem together. A boy in one of the groups began to fool around by laughing, throwing erasers, and telling jokes. The teacher ignored the boy even though he began to disturb the others by laughing loudly. Another boy in the group became very annoyed and asked the misbehaving boy to stop. When that didn't work, the boy and a friend walked over and said, "Stop telling jokes. It is not ok. You are keeping us from getting our work done—ok—STOP!"

Although the teacher was fully aware of the situation, he did not intervene, neither during the disturbance nor afterward. What is striking here is not the boy's misbehavior, which has its counterpart in almost any culture. What is striking is his responding to his peers' show of disapproval. In this Japanese culture, with its emphasis on maintaining harmony, the boy was sensitive to what his peers wanted from him.

In sum, in Japan, group harmony becomes important not just to teachers and parents but also to children; it is a central part of being socialized in Japan. And because group harmony is important to children, teachers and parents can count on children to play a central role in managing themselves and each other.

China: Confucian Guan for Promoting Order

By nature, people are nearly alike; by practice, they get to be wide apart.

—Confucius

We lined up every day before going outside. The boys would be on one side, and the girls would be on the other. We spent hours learning how to line up effectively and quietly. We would move down the stairs into our school courtyard. As the line moved through the doorway to the school, we would begin to run. We wouldn't just run into the play yard the way children do here in the United States. We would run on the painted line of the soccer field. If any child ran off the line, even missed the line with one foot, we would all have to start over. This was an important lesson according to our teachers—a lesson that taught us the core values of our Chinese society: discipline, control, respect for ourselves and for others. (A young man remembering his childhood in China)

Confucians of the early Han dynasty believed that once education was made available to all, the Chinese people would experience an era of peace and high civilization. In China, education and morality have always been linked. The Han intellectuals believed that at birth a child could be good or bad, both good and bad, or morally indeterminate. However, regardless of what children are at birth, they are malleable (Fairbank & Goldman, 1992).

With these ideas and images of children, it is easier to understand what is going on in the above example. To Westerners, Chinese teachers appear harsh and overcontrolling. However, to the Chinese themselves, they are doing what is best for the child. The Chinese, then, do not believe in a democratic, authoritative approach to behavior and classroom management, nor do they believe in the kind of laissez-faire, seemingly permissive approach characteristic of Japanese classrooms. Rather, they believe in an approach we call authoritarian (Chao, 1994, 2001). Schools in China typically follow regimented schedules and routines, to place children on the "pathway to righteousness." This is not a gentle process nor one that is done gradually. Rather, it is quick and powerful.

Though standard teaching practice in China seems, to Americans, to be both harsh and unforgiving, there is love and warmth behind it. This is difficult for Americans to understand because we do not normally see an authoritarian approach as warm and caring. However, the Chinese consider authoritarian control to be an expression of care. There is a word in the Chinese language that embodies this idea: **guan**, which means to govern to care. The excerpt below captures the essence of guan:

> Mei Li was pulling a toy away from a boy at her activity table. "Give it to me," she said. The boy would not let go and held onto the toy tightly. Mei Li was about to hit the boy when a teacher came over and said in a stern voice, "Mei Li, you are not to pull toys from other children. He had it first." Mei Li glanced up at her teacher and let the toy go.

In this moment, it is obvious that the teacher is not concerned with helping Mei Li discuss the situation. The focus is on telling Mei Li what should be done, and right away. No rationale is provided.

In China, authoritarian behavior management is especially evident in the method of shaming. China still embodies the collectivist society, one in which shaming is an accepted method for controlling and guiding children. Chinese

FIGURE 9.1   The Chinese Character for *Guan*

society values group life above solitude, so removing a child from group life or shunning him or her is the ultimate punishment (Fung, 1999). Here is one situation exemplifying this point, as noted by a Chinese middle school teacher:

> During a math exam I caught one of my students cheating. I stopped the exam and announced to the class that there was a student who was cheating. I looked at the student with a harsh look. I asked the student to stand and apologize to the class for what he had done. He slowly rose to his feet and said, "Class, I am the cheater, and I am sorry." I knew this was the worst punishment I could have given him. And I know he will never cheat again.

According to this teacher, that day his peers shunned the student. Everyone refused to speak to him. Even though he tried to apologize, no one wanted to have anything to do with him. "Cheating is very serious, and for this reason it takes a serious punishment to correct it," explained the teacher. "If this child was not corrected, it would have resulted in pain in the future."

Although the teacher expressed sorrow over punishing the child so harshly, he explained that he did this out of love for the child.

> What if I didn't do this, if I took the child aside and said why are you cheating? That would not have had the same effect. I would have taken that pathway because it was easier for me, not because it was better for

the child. If I had done that, I would have been selfish. I care greatly about this child's success; it had to be done.

As this last example indicates, using the Chinese value of being connected to the group, teachers will often use ostracism and shaming to threaten separation when children misbehave, and they publicly reward when children conform to norms and demands. Furthermore, teachers will often publicly compare students to one another. For example, during a group meeting, a teacher said, "Hui Yen, look at how you are sitting. You need to sit straight when we are in a meeting with the class. Look at how nicely Li Pan is sitting! Can't you sit like Li Pan?" In addition, because in Chinese culture conformity and obedience mean something different than they mean in mainstream American culture, a child's impolite look or subtle gesture can, in a Chinese classroom, be the equivalent of a full-blown tantrum in an American classroom, as is evident in the following example of nap time in one Chinese preschool:

> There were 47 children in beds in a large room, with one teacher watching over them.

(American) Observer:	How do you get 47 children to behave so well?
Teacher:	What do you mean? They are misbehaving so much today!
Observer:	(Looking over the room of children, all laying in their beds quietly) I don't understand.
Teacher:	Look at her (pointing to a child). She is being very disobedient!
	The observer looks over at the child. She is laying in her bed under the covers not making a sound. However, she is holding her eyes wide open and has a wide smile on her face.
Teacher:	She knows that it is a time to sleep. But look at how she smiles at me with her open eyes!

In short, for all the reasons mentioned, the Chinese meaning of misbehavior and the consequent meaning of behavior and classroom management differ greatly from the meanings found in typical Japanese and typical American classrooms.

Summary

In this chapter, we have seen how culture figures centrally in the experience of students and in how teachers manage both behavior and classrooms. In particular, we have seen how the hidden, "deep" structure of cultures, the values and ideals that influence how cultures raise and teach children, manifests itself in the classroom.

The home is still the primary place where culture influences child rearing, so one of the central issues in teaching is how to teach children coming from homes where the culture at home and the culture at school present mismatches. Here, we have seen how mismatches can lead not only to dysfunctional classrooms but also to minority children being treated poorly.

Finally, we have seen how cultures grouped together for sharing one major characteristic can be quite different from one another with respect to how they manage behavior and classrooms. Realizing the subtlety and complexity of cultural differences can, then, prevent stereotyping.

As our society and schools become more and more diverse, it will be essential to use a variety of approaches to manage children's behavior problems effectively. We must come to terms with the fact that although we may be comfortable with our democratic approaches and authoritative styles, there are other approaches and styles that are more successful with children and adolescents from cultures different from our own. This chapter, then, has brought to the forefront the fact that when it comes to behavior and classroom management, no one size fits all. Furthermore, even when we cannot bring to classrooms more than one approach, it is still possible to be sensitive and positive when teaching and disciplining students from different cultures so that no culture or group of students is disrespected. Simply being aware of cultural differences can, therefore, go a long way toward providing positive supports for all.

Web-Based Student Study Site

The companion Web site for *Approaches to Behavior and Classroom Management* can be found at www.sagepub.com/scarlettstudy.

Visit the Web-based student study site to enhance your understanding of the chapter content. The study materials include practice tests, flashcards, suggested readings, and Web resources.

Key Concepts

American
  individualisms

Collectivist cultures

Deep structure

Democratic
  practice

Effortless control

Group-mindedness

Guan

Ideal types

Indirect
  directives

Discussion Questions

1. This chapter has underscored the fact that being authoritarian has different meanings and shows itself in different ways depending on culture. Have you ever seen a teacher or parent successfully be authoritarian? Have you ever seen a parent or teacher be authoritarian when it did not work well? What was different about the two ways of being authoritarian? Did the differences have something to do with culture?

2. Being culturally sensitive is no easy accomplishment. One can assume that virtually everyone has, on more than one occasion, been culturally insensitive. Can you remember such a time? And did this time reflect your not knowing enough about a culture? If it did, what do you now realize that you did not realize at the time you were insensitive?

3. How has this chapter changed your thinking about culture and educating students from different cultures? Put another way, how did you think about culture and schooling before reading this chapter, and how do you think about culture and school—particularly with respect to control/management issues—now that you have read this chapter?

---

1. Unless otherwise specified, the examples in this chapter come from observations and interviews made by Iris Ponte.

2. In this discussion and throughout the book, we prefer the term *African American* to *black* because its emphasis is more on ethnicity than race, and ethnicity is more the subject. However, there are respected scholars who use the term *black*, so in discussing what others have to say, we use this term also.

3. The term *Hispanic* is contested by those with roots in Spanish-speaking countries. However, so is every other term, including *Latino*. We use *Hispanic*, then, because there is no better term to refer to a large but diverse minority group.

4. Unless otherwise specified, the examples here come from Iris Ponte's work in Japan and China.

5. Teacher interviewed by Iris Ponte.

Chapter 10

THE MEDICAL MODEL AND ORGANIC APPROACHES TO BEHAVIOR MANAGEMENT

Johnny was out of control. One second he would be at his desk looking at a book, and the next he would be standing on the classroom radiator, shouting. His teacher knew something was wrong. Johnny was eventually diagnosed with ADHD. Reluctantly, his parents went along with the doctor's advice, and Johnny was given oral medication plus strategies for how to work in school. Over the next few months, Johnny's classroom behavior changed dramatically and for the better. He was able to sit and focus on his work as well as attend to class lessons. The teacher also noticed that he had an easier time making friends and working with other children.

We end our discussion by focusing on a group of approaches that are ordinarily adopted by physicians, not by educators. We do so because these approaches have had a significant impact on the behavior management of students with special needs. Here, too, we discuss the **medical model** that provides the context for developing and adopting these approaches. The main distinguishing feature of these approaches is their underlying assumption that problem behavior has its roots in biology. It is, then, the connection to biology that explains why they are called **organic approaches**.

Focusing on organic approaches will also help readers understand the purpose and meaning of diagnostic labels and how diagnostic labels help in defining problems and in guiding interventions for students with special needs. In Chapter 4, we

For material related to this concept, go to Video Clip 10.1 on the Student Resource CD bound into the back of your textbook.

221

CHAPTER OVERVIEW

Pathology, Diagnosis, and Syndromes

The Medical Model and Classification Systems
  The APA Classification System for Disorders
  Attention-Deficit/Hyperactivity Disorder
  Oppositional Defiant Disorder
  Conduct Disorder
  Learning Disabilities
  Autistic Disorder
  Mental Retardation

Limitations of the Medical Model and the *DSM* Diagnostic System

The Special Education System, the Medical Model, and Organic Approaches
  IDEIA Disability Categories

Organic Approaches and Medication for Managing Problem Behavior
  Medication for Managing Problem Behavior

discussed how today's special education system was originally intended as a more equitable and inclusive community approach for educating children with special needs. In Chapter 7, we discussed how special education is also an organizational approach because so much of its focus is on organizing assessment, planning, and implementation by teams of specialists. In this chapter, we discuss how the medical model and organic approaches differ from most educational approaches to managing the behavior of students with special needs.

Here, then, the main goal is to familiarize readers with the medical model and organic approaches so that readers can understand their strengths, limitations, and how they can complement the educational approaches discussed in previous chapters. We begin by examining the various meanings of key terms featured by clinicians adopting the medical model, in particular, the terms pathology, diagnosis, and syndrome.

PATHOLOGY, DIAGNOSIS, AND SYNDROMES

Pathology is a medical term referring to any abnormal condition requiring treatment. As a medical term, it refers mostly to biologically caused physical afflictions; however, when used to refer to mental disorders in childhood and adolescence, the term is essentially descriptive—that is, no single type of cause is implicated.

Different forms of pathology consist of constellations of symptoms called *syndromes*. Syndromes make up the diagnostic categories that we commonly associate with psychological disorders. If, for example, a child engages in repetitive behavior such as hand flapping, avoiding eye contact, using language to echo the language of others, and, in general, failing to interact with others, the various behaviors and absence thereof form a pattern captured by the diagnostic category of *autism*. We need know nothing about the causes of autism to make this diagnosis. Furthermore, the diagnosis of autism refers solely to the syndrome and not to the person. This goes along with the contemporary trend in the field of education to accept the uniqueness of each child and the idiosyncratic mixture of biological, psychological, and social factors that create problem behaviors and learning difficulties.

The distinction between the person and his or her pathology is crucial. For decades, researchers have documented the common tendency in all of us to reduce a person to his or her diagnostic label (Dembo, 1982). What this means is that all of us, leading professionals included, are prone to seeing those with a diagnostic label as if they *are* their diagnosis; for example, rather than saying a child has the condition **attention-deficit/hyperactivity disorder** (ADHD), we say that the child "is an ADHD child." It takes effort and practice to wean us of this bad habit.

However, if we keep clear the distinction between persons and their diagnoses, we have a better chance of keeping clear how we can supply the supports needed to help children and adolescents thrive in schools. Educators have no influence over biological causes of pathology and, most of the time, no influence over familial causes either. But educators do have considerable influence over whether problem behaviors associated with a diagnosis continue in school and whether children and adolescents with diagnoses get the supports they need to help them function effectively in the classroom.

This said, educators need to know something about the medical model and organic approaches, both to be able to partner with medical professionals and to be clear about the meaning of diagnosed students' problem behavior. Here, then, we provide a brief overview of the medical model, the most used classification system for defining pathology, and organic approaches to managing children's behavior.

THE MEDICAL MODEL AND CLASSIFICATION SYSTEMS

What is often referred to as the medical model is principally an approach to defining, explaining, and treating problems. The approach is rooted in the scientific tradition of relying on close observation and systematic classification as well as on careful measuring, testing, and research to determine both the etiology (origins) of and best practice for treating pathology. The approach allows a community of clinical researchers to speak the same language regardless of their theories and to pool observations and research findings so that progress can be made in understanding and treating disorders. In addition, the approach allows administrators to plan their budgets because it helps in determining how many students we can expect to be diagnosed and how many in each diagnostic category.

The APA Classification System for Disorders

According to Cantwell and Rutter (2001), "classification constitutes a means of ordering information, of grouping phenomena and of providing a language by which to communicate with other people" (p. 3). In the United States, the most common classification system for diagnosing mental disorders is the *Diagnostic and Statistical Manual of Mental Disorders*, otherwise known as the *DSM-IV-TR* (American Psychiatric Association [APA], 2000). The *DSM-IV-TR* is the latest in a series of revisions of the system. It contains a listing of broad diagnostic categories that number around 300 different mental illnesses. The description of each disorder provides information on symptomology; trends in areas such as age, culture, or gender; family patterns; prognosis; associated complications; prevalence; risk factors; and information on predisposition. When combined, these pieces of information provide a comprehensive description of each of the syndromes.

The *DSM-IV-TR* also employs a **multi-axial system** that forces clinicians to make different kinds of judgments to ensure that they see a complete clinical picture (APA, 2000). Before a person is diagnosed as having a specific disorder, a clinician must first assess him or her on five axes, each of which provides information on a different domain relevant to the treatment process (see Figure 10.1). Axis I lists disorders that cause significant impairment, such as anxiety disorders, mood disorders, schizophrenia, and autism. Axis II consists of chronic, maladaptive patterns of behavior and thought, specifically, mental retardation and personality disorders. Axis III lists any general medical conditions that could have contributed to the onset of the presenting symptoms. Axis IV describes the patient's current psychosocial and environmental stressors. Last, Axis V asks the clinician to score the patient on a global assessment of functioning (GAF).

Used properly, the *DSM-IV-TR* can help educators in several ways. First, it can help to define when problem behaviors warrant a diagnostic label. All

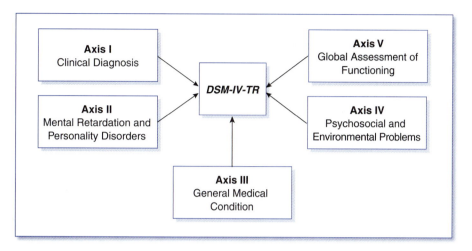

Figure 10.1 *DSM-IV-TR* Axes

children and adolescents act up at times and show symptoms. The *DSM-IV-TR* provides guidelines for determining when a pattern of acting up or a pattern of symptoms becomes clinically significant. It does so by defining how long symptoms must be present, how intense the symptoms need to be, and the setting(s) in which the symptoms must present themselves. For example, for a person to have dysthymia, a prolonged mood disorder, he or she must have a "chronically depressed mood that occurs for most of the day more days than not, and for at least 2 years" (APA, 2000). By setting an explicit time requirement for the presence of symptoms, the *DSM-IV-TR* helps increase the validity of diagnoses.

Second, the *DSM-IV-TR* can help educators set an appropriate level of tolerance. Once educators understand a diagnosis, they can alter their style of teaching to accommodate students' special needs. For example, if a child is diagnosed as having dyslexia—a learning disability that interferes with the child's ability to read—at the very least, a teacher can accommodate by giving the student extra time on book reviews and by providing support to any specialist working individually with the child. In sum, the medical model and the *DSM-IV-TR's* classification system for defining pathology can be helpful to educators in several ways.

That said, many educators choose to ignore the psychiatric labels altogether, believing that they are useless or that they get in the way of figuring out how best to teach. Others use them, but only to secure needed services and to keep perspective on what can be expected of a student in the short term. Regardless of use, educators need to keep diagnoses in mind when working with professionals

There are now so many disorders that some see an overuse of the term *disorder*.

who follow the medical model, especially when their students are being medicated. Below are brief descriptions of diagnostic categories that educators are likely to encounter. Please note that the descriptions of each of the diagnostic categories have filled hundreds of texts in their own right, so the interested reader should accept these descriptions as just summaries and purchase an ancillary text and/or take a course on developmental psychopathology or exceptional children.

Attention-Deficit/Hyperactivity Disorder

To be clinically diagnosed as having ADHD, one must exhibit characteristics of hyperactivity, impulsivity, and inattention—behaviors that can normally be observed in the classroom setting (APA, 2000). In accordance with the United States Department of Education's (2003) resource for identifying and treating ADHD, a diagnosis of ADHD requires that the child or adolescent meet several criteria:

1. *Severity.* The problem behavior must occur more frequently in the child or adolescent than in other children or adolescents at the same age.

2. *Early onset.* At least some of the symptoms must have been present prior to age 7.

3. *Duration.* The symptoms must have been present for at least 6 months prior to the evaluation.

4. *Impact.* The symptoms must have a negative impact on the child's academic or social life.

5. *Settings.* The symptoms must be present in multiple settings, not just at school.

Comprehensive studies have shown that the most common effective treatment for ADHD is stimulant medication (Group, 1999). Drugs such as Ritalin, Dexedrine, and Adderall are often used to reduce the symptoms of ADHD (Pelham et al., 1990, 1999).

ADHD in the Classroom

Signs of Hyperactivity and Impulsivity

- Fidgeting with hands or feet
- Inability to sit still in assigned seat
- Running or climbing in inappropriate situations
- Striking out at a peer
- Difficulty taking turns or waiting in line
- Interrupting peers

Signs of Inattention

- Forgetting to write down assignments
- Not turning in work on time
- Making careless mistakes

Oppositional Defiant Disorder

Oppositional defiant disorder (ODD) is a diagnosis given to children who consistently talk back to, argue with, disobey, or otherwise defy authority figures such as teachers and parents (APA, 2000). Occasional bouts of opposition are to be expected at any developmental stage, but when the frequency of oppositional behavior becomes abnormally high, ODD becomes a feasible diagnosis.

Oppositional Defiant Disorder in the Classroom

- Frequently throws temper tantrums
- Talks back to teachers and/or aides
- Refuses to comply with rules set by teachers or administrators
- Deliberately annoys peers or instructors
- Seeks revenge and is overly spiteful of peers or authority figures
- Blames others for his or her misbehavior

Conduct Disorder

Children and adolescents diagnosed with **conduct disorder** (CD) violate the basic rights of others and flout laws and societal norms (APA, 2000). Here is a short case study to illustrate the seriousness of CD:

> Sharon, a 15-year-old girl, was brought to the psychologist's office by her mother. Her mother explained that Sharon was suspended from school for assaulting a teacher and needed a "doctor's evaluation" before she could return to class. The history revealed that this was Sharon's 10th school suspension during the past three years. She had previously been suspended for fighting, carrying a knife to school, smoking marijuana, and stealing money from other students' lockers. When asked about her behavior at home, Sharon reported that her mother frequently "gets on my nerves" and, at those times, Sharon left the house for several days. The family history indicated that Sharon's father was incarcerated for auto theft and assault. (Searight, Rottnek, & Abby, 2001, p. 1581)

Seen as an early-onset version of antisocial personality disorder, CD manifests in remorseless hostile acts against humans, animals, and property (Blair, Mitchell, & Peschardt, 2005). Almost always, CD follows and then includes a diagnosis of ODD.

Conduct Disorder in the Classroom

Signs of Aggression

- Bullying
- Hitting peers or instructors
- Stealing from classmates

Signs of Destruction

- Destroys classroom materials without remorse
- Shows no real care for books or materials needed for homework
- Marks on walls and otherwise defaces public spaces

Signs of Deceit

- Lies to teachers, peers, and others to get his or her way
- Cheats in games
- Cheats on assignments or exams

Signs of Rule Violation

- Constant truancy or tardiness
- Violent reaction to discipline
- Extreme resistance to following set rules

Learning Disabilities

Learning disabilities, or learning disorders, as the *DSM-IV-TR* labels them, are defined by the U.S. Department of Education (1977) as follows:

"Specific learning disability" means a disorder in one or more of the basic psychological processes involved in understanding or in using language, spoken or written, which may manifest itself in an imperfect ability to listen, think, speak, read, write, spell, or do mathematical calculations. The term includes such conditions as perceptual handicaps, brain injury, minimal brain dysfunction, dyslexia, and developmental aphasia. The term does not include children who have learning problems which are primarily the result of visual, hearing, or motor handicaps; mental retardation; or emotional disturbance; or of environmental, cultural, or economic disadvantage. (p. 65083)

The *DSM-IV-TR* distinguishes between three major learning disorders: reading disorder, mathematics disorder, and disorder of written expression.

Reading Disorder (Dyslexia)

Often referred to as *dyslexia*, reading disorder manifests itself in the student's difficulty in recognizing and interpreting both letters and words, as well as difficulty in decoding the phonetic structure (sounds that make up a word) used in writing (Snowling, 2000). Children and adolescents with reading disorders score lower on intelligence subtests designed specifically to test reading comprehension (Shaywitz, 1998).

Reading Disorder in the Classroom

- Inability to recognize words and letters on a printed page
- A reading ability level well below expected
- Difficulty comprehending rapid instructions
- Difficulty remembering a sequence of instructions
- Failure to see similarities and differences in letters and words
- Inability to recognize that spacing organizes letters into separate words
- Inability to sound out the pronunciation of an unfamiliar word

Mathematics Disorder (Dyscalculia)

Mathematics disorder, or *dyscalculia,* as it is often called, is a syndrome characterized by poorer than expected skills in quantitative calculation and/or reasoning (APA, 2000). Students with dyscalculia have problems with recognizing numbers and with basic counting skills (Gross-Tsur, Manor, & Shalev, 1996). Impairment occurs not only in academic use of numbers, such as learning multiplication tables, but also in everyday use of numbers, such as at home, when counting the number of cups of flour to use in a cookie recipe (Hittmair-Delazer, Sailer, & Benke, 1995).

Disorder of Written Expression (Dysgraphia)

The disorder of written expression, often called *dysgraphia,* is characterized by problems in the child's writing skills (APA, 2000). Impairments in the student's spelling, grammar, syntax, punctuation, capitalization, use of correct letter size, the finishing of letters, and organization of ideas are common (Gregg, 1991).

Mathematics Disorder in the Classroom

- Difficulty in writing or printing numbers
- Difficulty counting
- Difficulty working with mathematical signs such as +, −, x, and /
- Difficulty learning names that include numbers
- Difficulty understanding and remembering number facts (e.g., multiplication tables)
- Inability to differentiate between letters and numbers

Disorder of Written Expression in the Classroom

- Poor spelling
- Errors in grammar
- Errors in punctuation
- Poor handwriting
- Pain while writing

Autistic Disorder

Often referred to as *classic autism,* autistic disorder (AD) is characterized by communicatory, social, and cognitive deficits that pervade all areas of the child's life (Frith, 2003). Besides major language deficits, the most striking symptom of autistic disorder is the child's extreme unresponsiveness to others (Dawson et al., 2004). In addition, children with AD often act in repetitive, self-stimulating ways and can become irritated or even violent at human contact (Smith, Press, Koenig, & Kinnealey, 2005).

Mental Retardation

The most recent revision of the Individuals With Disabilities Education Act (Individuals With Disabilities Education Improvement Act of 2004, Pub. L. 108-446, 118 Stat. 2647) defines mental retardation as "Significantly sub-average general intellectual functioning, existing concurrently with deficits in

Autistic Disorder in the Classroom

Communication Problems

- Lack of appropriate nonverbal behavior
- Verbal slurring and babbling (not age appropriate)

Social Interaction Problems

- Lack of interest in instructors and peers
- No engagement in imaginative play
- Dearth of empathy and sharing of emotions
- Prefers to play alone

Routines/Repetitive Behavior

- Jumping, flapping one's arms, making faces, or other self-stimulatory behavior
- Self-injurious behavior
- Repeating words or actions
- Obsessive following of a schedule or routine
- Very specific, inflexible ways of arranging toys and other items

adaptive behavior and manifested during the developmental period, that adversely affects a child's educational performance."

When a teacher feels that a student is falling behind academically for reasons not related to psychosocial factors, the teacher can recommend that the student see the school psychologist in order to be tested for mental retardation. Once consent has been given by the child's parents, the school psychologist will give the child a battery of tests in order to obtain the child's intelligence quotient (IQ), a measure of a person's learning potential. It is this number that clinicians use to help place a child into the appropriate category of mental retardation (see Table 10.1).

TABLE 10.1 Levels of Mental Retardation

Level	IQ Score
Mild	55–70
Moderate	40–54
Severe	25–39
Profound	Below 25

The majority of students with mental retardation have only mild retardation and will be only slightly slower than average in learning new skills and information. Students with severe to profound mental retardation can go far and lead satisfying lives if they have an active support system, a functional education, and early intervention.

LIMITATIONS OF THE MEDICAL MODEL AND THE *DSM* DIAGNOSTIC SYSTEM

The medical model has worked reasonably well for physical problems. However, the model has not worked as well for behavioral and psychological problems of children, despite the efforts and wisdom of able leaders in the field such as Michael Rutter (Rutter, Tuma, & Lann, 1988). Educators normally cannot, by reading the latest journals and research findings, determine what is best practice for helping a diagnosed child maximize his or her learning potential. Yes, there are guidelines, such as providing lots of structure and direction for children with autism. And yes, there are effective approaches, but as this book has made clear throughout, the goals and criteria for evaluating effectiveness change from one approach to another, making it difficult to say for sure what is "best."

Source: Michael Rutter.

Michael Rutter

Educators, then, have to remain reflective about their own approach and those of others and rely on their storehouse of methods as they remain flexible and sensitive to the individual differences among students with diagnoses. This really does not make the educator's task all that dissimilar to the task of the physician because, despite appearances, in medical practice there is a lot more ambiguity and need for judgment calls than might be expected from listening to medical talk about "evidence-based interventions" and "best practice" (Paauw, 1999).

Another limitation of the medical model and diagnostic categories is that diagnostic categories sometimes trivialize the seriousness and complexity of a particular situation. For example, William Garrison (1993) tells a poignant story of a child diagnosed with ODD. After years of neglectful parenting, the boy's adoptive parents abandoned him and left the child in the care of hospital staff, who had no means of providing him with the care he needed. Needless to say, his defiance was trivial compared to his problem of not having a family. Educators face similar situations to the one Garrison faced—situations in which students' diagnoses fail to describe the more serious problems in their life situations.

For material related to this concept, go to Video Clip 10.2 on the Student Resource CD bound into the back of your textbook.

Classification systems are also limited by the fact that children and adolescents with one diagnostic label often have another as well. This phenomenon, called comorbidity, seriously undermines our ability to identify main causes and best practices for pathology because it makes it almost impossible to sort out what is causing what.

Finally, the use of classification systems can lead to the harmful assumption that children and adolescents with diagnosed disabilities are subject to a different theory of human development and, therefore, require entirely different approaches to discipline and education than those used for students without disabilities (Sarason, 1982). On the contrary, students with disabilities often require the same kinds of supports as those without disabilities, only they require more of them. We need, then, to be clear about how to use classification systems in general and the *DSM-IV-TR* classification system in particular.

THE SPECIAL EDUCATION SYSTEM, THE MEDICAL MODEL, AND ORGANIC APPROACHES

The special education system is an educational approach to disabilities. Because it is not a medical approach, the term *pathology* is hardly ever used; instead of focusing on physical disease or mental disorders, the special education system focuses on how students *function in schools*.

By focusing on functioning, the special education system provides supports and services to students who have trouble functioning in schools. If a student has been diagnosed as having a disorder and that student is functioning fairly well in school, then no special education services will be provided. On the other hand, if a student without a diagnosis is functioning poorly in school, then that student might be provided with special education services.

IDEIA Disability Categories

To help determine when students need services, the special education system provides its own diagnostic categories described in the Individuals With Disabilities Education Improvement Act of 2004 (IDEIA). IDEIA lists a total of 13 different categories of disability that qualify students between the ages of 3 and 21 for services:

1. *Autism*: "A developmental disability significantly affecting verbal and nonverbal communication and social interaction, generally evident before age 3, that adversely affects a child's educational performance."

2. *Deafness:* "A hearing impairment that is so severe that the child is impaired in processing linguistic information through hearing, with or without amplification, that adversely affects a child's educational performance."

3. *Deaf-Blindness:* "Concomitant hearing and visual impairments, the combination of which causes such severe communication and other developmental and educational needs that they cannot be accommodated in special education programs solely for children with deafness or children with blindness."

4. *Emotional Disturbance:* "A condition exhibiting one or more of the following characteristics over a long period of time and to a marked degree that adversely affects a child's educational performance: (1) An inability to learn that cannot be explained by intellectual, sensory, or health factors; (2) An inability to build or maintain satisfactory interpersonal relationships with peers and teachers; (3) Inappropriate types of behavior or feelings under normal circumstances; (4) A general pervasive mood of unhappiness or depression; (5) A tendency to develop physical symptoms or fears associated with personal or school problems."

5. *Hearing Impairment:* "An impairment in hearing, whether permanent or fluctuating, that adversely affects a child's educational performance but that is not included under the definition of deafness."

6. *Specific Learning Disability:* "A disorder in one or more of the basic psychological processes involved in understanding or in using language, spoken or written, that may manifest itself in an imperfect ability to listen, think, speak, read, write, spell, or to do mathematical calculations, including conditions such as perceptual disabilities, brain injury, minimal brain dysfunction, dyslexia, and developmental aphasia. The term does not include problems that are primarily the result of visual, hearing, or motor disabilities, of mental retardation, or emotional disturbance, or of environmental, cultural, or economic disadvantage."

7. *Mental Retardation:* "Significant subaverage general intellectual functioning, existing concurrently with deficits in adaptive behavior and manifested during the developmental period, that adversely affects a child's educational performance."

8. *Multiple Disabilities:* "concomitant impairments (such as mental retardation-blindness, mental-retardation-orthopedic impairment, etc.), the combination of which causes such severe educational needs that they cannot be accommodated in special education programs solely for one of the impairments."

9. *Orthopedic Impairment:* "A severe orthopedic impairment that adversely affects a child's educational performance. The term includes impairments caused by congenital anomaly (e.g., clubfoot, absence of some member), impairments caused by disease (e.g., poliomyelitis, bone tuberculosis), and impairments from other causes (e.g., cerebral palsy, amputations, and fractures or burns that cause contractures)."

10. *Other Health Impairment:* "A condition that results in limited strength, vitality, or alertness, including a heightened alertness to environmental stimuli, that results in limited alertness with respect to the educational environment, that (1) is due to chronic or acute health problems such as asthma, attention deficit disorder or attention-deficit/hyperactivity disorder, diabetes, epilepsy, a heart condition, hemophilia, lead poisoning, leukemia, nephritis, rheumatic fever, and sickle cell anemia; and (2) adversely affects a child's educational performance."

11. *Speech or Language Impairment:* "A communication disorder, such as stuttering, impaired articulation, a language impairment, or a voice impairment, that adversely affects a child's educational performance."

12. *Traumatic Brain Injury:* A traumatic brain injury is defined as "acquired injury to the brain caused by an external physical force, resulting in total or partial functional disability or psychosocial impairment, or both, that adversely affects a child's educational performance."

13. *Visual Impairment Including Blindness:* "An impairment in vision that, even with correction, adversely affects a child's educational performance."

Under IDEIA, state and local educational agencies (LEAs) do not have to categorize children between the ages of 3 and 9 to receive government services. Children between these ages are eligible so long as they are experiencing delays in physical development, cognitive development, communication development, social or emotional development, or adaptive development such that these delays put them in need of special education or related services. The exact definition of what qualifies as a "developmental delay" is determined by each state and must be measured using appropriate assessments.

Children who qualify for government-sponsored services are eligible for the following:

Transportation, and such developmental, corrective, and other supportive services (including speech-language pathology and audiology services, interpreting services, psychological services, physical and occupational therapy, recreation, including therapeutic recreation, social work services, school nurse services designed to enable a child with a disability to receive a free appropriate public education as described in the individualized education program of the child, counseling services, including rehabilitation counseling, orientation and mobility services, and medical services, except that such medical services shall be for diagnostic and evaluation purposes only) as may be required to assist a child with a disability to benefit from special education, and includes the early identification and assessment of disabling conditions in children. (IDEIA § 602)

Note that identification and assessment of disabling conditions is essential to determining who receives services. This emphasis mirrors that of medical approaches in which the identification of pathology is needed to choose proper treatment.

Organic Approaches and Medication for Managing Problem Behavior

Medical professionals are most likely to adopt organic approaches to managing problem behavior. Nevertheless, educators need to understand what it means to take an organic approach, both to adopt a proper frame of mind toward its methodology and to be able to partner with professionals when medications are involved.

The first thing to note when adopting a proper frame of mind is that there is a widespread tendency to *reduce* problems to biological causes, especially when there is evidence that biology is a causal factor in the problem's onset. For a number of reasons already mentioned, educators need to resist this tendency. Stopping oneself from falling into this pitfall keeps educators alert to the many nonorganic causes of problem behaviors over which they have control. Put another way, medication is almost always but one of several "points of entry."

Reducing children's behavior problems to biological causes also makes little sense because causation is usually *circular,* not linear. That is, biological predispositions alone rarely lead to the development of psychopathology. Furthermore, environmental stressors, such as living in a poverty-stricken neighborhood with a high crime rate, can trigger biological problems, which, in turn, can lead to behavior problems (R. J. Comer, 2006).

In sum, there are good reasons for educators to adopt an antireductionist and circular view of mental disorders. Taking such a view helps educators to understand both the nature of students' problems and how to help them. That said, we can turn now to the subject of medications for managing the behavior of children and adolescents—the treatments that follow logically from adopting an organic approach.

Medication for Managing Problem Behavior

Most of the medications for managing children's and adolescents' problem behavior alter the supply of neurotransmitters, those chemicals that convey information from one brain cell to another. Some of these medications, called agonists, increase the supply of neurotransmitters in the brain. Examples of agonists include Ritalin and Dexedrine, the stimulant drugs most commonly used to treat ADHD. Other medications, called antagonists, decrease the supply of neurotransmitters. Examples include antipsychotic medications such as Clozapine and Risperdal.

Limitations of Medication

The following are some of the major limitations of relying on medication to manage problem behavior:

First, though students may experience relief of the major symptoms associated with their disorder, they may also experience serious side effects from medication. These side effects can cause academic and psychological impairment independent of the original pathology. For example, if a student diagnosed with ADHD takes Ritalin to reduce inattention and hyperactivity problems, he may experience the side effects of insomnia, stomachache, headache, and dizziness. These symptoms may, eventually, interfere with academic achievement even though the medication was supposed to be the solution for, not the cause of, problem behaviors.

A second limitation is that medication does not cure disorders or the causes of disorders; it only manages symptoms. For example, if a girl is depressed because she has a poor relationship with her father, giving her antidepressant medication will not automatically mend that relationship.

Third, medication only helps students use the skills that they already possess. It does not teach students new skills, nor does it create new potential or motivation to learn. That is, medication merely maximizes the skills, potential, and motivation already present by removing barriers imposed by a disorder.

Fourth, there are no longitudinal studies of the effect of medication on children and adolescents. Thus, we still do not know the long-term effects of medicating. This is important because if there are long-term problems, they are not being considered at the time medications are prescribed.

Last, there is a potential for overmedicating children and adolescents. With biological explanations for disability holding a privileged status in our society and with drug therapy receiving a great deal of media attention lately, we could

Taking medication for a disorder has become so common among students today that many now openly share the fact that they are on medication.

be overmedicating our youth. Consider the case of ADHD. The prevalence of ADHD has fluctuated between 2 percent and 18 percent over the past two decades (Rowland, Lesesne, & Abramowitz, 2002). ADHD's symptomology resembles that of disorders such as the learning disorders and ODD, allowing for the possibility of misdiagnosis. Also, no laboratory tests reliably predict ADHD. Nevertheless, we continue to prescribe stimulant medication to the majority of children and adolescents who receive the diagnosis of ADHD. In short, an overdiagnosis of mental disorders in children and adolescents could very well lead to a generation of overmedicated students.

From this discussion of medication, we can rightfully ask, "Is it appropriate to adopt an extreme view either for or against medicating students?" This discussion suggests it is not appropriate. On the one hand, innovations in medication and empirical trials by independent researchers and drug companies have led to educators being able to better support students with different disorders. Though drugs do not ordinarily eliminate a disorder's symptoms completely; they do ordinarily lessen their magnitude. On the other hand, and as just discussed, there are limitations to using medication to manage problem behavior, limitations inherent in the medical model and organic approaches. The limitations lead naturally to a discussion of special education, for special education is the education system's answer to these limitations and to meeting the educational needs of children with disabilities, including disabilities covered by *DSM-IV-TR's* list of mental disorders of childhood.

Educational Approaches That Are Also Organic Approaches

Not every organic approach to managing behavior features the method of medication. A few are true educational approaches that feature educational methods. They do so because they have a theory that connects the learning process to processes occurring in the brain. One example is **RAVE-O**, an approach for helping children with dyslexia (Wolf & O'Brien, 2001). Rooted in a well-developed theory linking dyslexia to deficits in brain functioning (Wolf, 2007), RAVE-O provides an enriched reading program with proven benefits for children with dyslexia. Organic educational approaches such as RAVE-O may well be the wave of the future.

Source: Kathleen Dooher.

Maryanne Wolf

Summary

In this chapter, we have seen how clinicians using a medical model have defined, understood, and treated serious psychological and behavioral problems. We have shown the logic behind *DSM-IV-TR*, the most used system of diagnostic categories. We have explained the purpose and reasoning behind using medications as methods for managing behavior. And we have pointed out that a few educational approaches are themselves organic approaches to helping students with disabilities. In doing so, we have tried to provide readers with an appreciation of the benefits of the medical model and organic approaches.

However, in this chapter we also have provided messages of caution, in particular, messages about educators needing to develop and use their own educational approaches and to not rely solely or mainly on organic approaches and medication. And we have given a clear message about the problem of reducing students to their diagnostic label.

In given these messages of caution, the overall message has been this: Organic approaches and medication have their place and value. However, they need to be complemented by distinct and powerful educational approaches, approaches that more centrally focus on helping students thrive in schools and learn.

Web-Based Student Study Site

The companion Web site for *Approaches to Behavior and Classroom Management* can be found at **www.sagepub.com/scarlettstudy**.

Visit the Web-based student study site to enhance your understanding of the chapter content. The study materials include practice tests, flashcards, suggested readings, and Web resources.

Key Concepts

Agonist

Antagonist

Attention-deficit/hyperactivity disorder

Autistic disorder

Comorbidity

Conduct disorder

Diagnosis

Diagnostic and Statistical Manual for Mental Disorders

Individuals With Disabilities Education Act

Learning disabilities

Medical model

Mental retardation

Multi-axial system

Neurotransmitters

Oppositional defiant disorder

Organic approaches

Pathology

RAVE-O

Syndrome

Discussion Questions

1. Think of a time when you and others were talking about a child or adolescent with a diagnosis (ADHD, autism, etc.). Did you speak of the child or adolescent as an "ADHD child," "autistic child," or whatever? If "yes," do you think doing so made it harder to relate to the child or adolescent as a child or adolescent?

2. Before reading this chapter, what did you think of using medication to help children with diagnoses such as ADHD? Now what do you think? If you have changed your opinion, what led to the change?

3. How does the special education system operate differently from the medical model and clinical-psychiatric way of defining problems? Do you see the differences as competing with or as complementing one another?

4. In what ways do you think differently now about children and adolescents with diagnostic labels than you did before reading the chapter? Are you now better able to think about what you can offer or what educators in general can offer?

Conclusion INTEGRATING DISCIPLINE AND CARE

The Chinese have a long-standing symbol for opposites, a symbol many in the West know about but do not fully appreciate. The symbol is the yin-yang circle (see Figure 11.1). It symbolizes the truth that so many of life's dualities complement rather than conflict with one another—at least in their ideal state.

FIGURE 11.1 Yin and Yang

Applying this symbol to behavior and classroom management, we find an enduring duality in the words *discipline* and *care*. Furthermore, we find that throughout the history of American education, these two have coexisted, not complementing but conflicting with one another. We found this in the debates over corporal punishment between Horace Mann and the Boston schoolteachers; we found it in the clash between progressive educators and the practice-to-habit educators at the beginning of the 20th century, and we find it today in debates between behaviorists and constructivists. That is, we have found that what Wilfred Cantwell Smith (1998) calls *conflict dualism* has played a greater role in debates over behavior and classroom management than has *complement dualism*.

The time is ripe for us to explore which of these two types of dualism better describes how the debates should be cast. This book makes a strong case for casting dualisms having to do with behavior and classroom management as complement dualisms. Let us see how this works by once again going through the book, this time using the yin-yang way of thinking to understand the various approaches and their treatment of dualities.

Consider first what was said in **Part II** about approaches that make relationship building the logical starting point and linchpin for behavior and classroom management. These approaches speak of several dualities. In the approaches emphasizing teacher-student relationships in Chapter 3, the main duality was between teachers showing care and teachers challenging students by having high expectations and exercising authority. In Chapter 4, Community Approaches, the main duality was between managing orderly, productive classrooms and managing classrooms that are moral.

Using a yin-yang way of thinking, the discussions of relationship approaches reveal that these dualities are complement dualities, or should be. In the discussions of teacher-student relationships in Chapter 3, we found that caring for students and challenging students go hand in hand. We saw this in students' view of what makes good teachers, and we saw this in the many examples provided, such as the example of Haitian teachers showing care in the way they challenge children to behave by remembering those who care for them.

Turning to Chapter 4 on community approaches, we found that managing classrooms so that they are orderly and productive need not—indeed, must not—conflict with managing classrooms so that they are just and caring. By emphasizing that we learn what we live, community approaches show that learning and living in a just and caring community go hand in hand, especially if the long-term aim is to create responsible citizens who use what they have learned to contribute to enhancing democratic society.

Part III pitted learning against development. Here, too, what at first appeared to be a conflict duality on closer inspection turned out to be a complement duality. Whenever we looked at actual examples of supporting learning or supporting development, we found the two to be inevitably intertwined. Take the example discussed in Chapter 5 of the fourth-grade teacher helping his students learn basic math skills by using a baseball game available on the Internet. Remember how the children would come to class having computed their players' statistics from the morning paper, then go on the Internet and calculate the players' rankings based on their statistics. Remember, too, how the entire class got into the act, and everybody seemed to have fun, boys as well as girls. Therefore, in being helped to learn math skills, the children were also being supported in developing as users of math and as members of a learning community.

Turning to **Part IV**, the main duality was between students and the classroom environment. Here, too, what appeared to be a clear distinction, one that pitted the individual against his or her physical and social environment, turned out to be not so distinct and clear. We saw this in Chapter 7, in the example of two boys racing down the middle of a classroom with a long open space; their "bad" behavior was not something individual or environmental but a combination of both. We saw this also in Chapter 8, in the example of the boy who walked across desks, thereby simultaneously showing himself to be a disruptive boy and someone who had been socialized in a dysfunctional interpersonal system or social environment. Student and environment are, then, inextricably bound up with one another, demanding that we think of them as yin to yang, and demanding, too, that we think of the purpose of behavior and classroom management as effecting a harmonious balance between both.

Part V, on accommodating diversity, presented us with a number of dualities, particularly those between authoritarian and nonauthoritarian and able (without a diagnosis) and disabled (with a diagnosis). However, once again, what at first appeared to be conflict dualities on closer inspection turned out to be complement dualities. For example, in Chapter 9, we found there was a nurturance we usually associate with being nonauthoritarian in the authoritarian ways that successful African American teachers use when teaching African American students from low-income families. Later, in Chapter 10, we saw that diagnostic labels, correctly used, describe syndromes, not people, making it clear that regardless of syndrome, students with and without disabilities are, first and foremost, students—thus echoing the psychiatrist Harry Stack Sullivan's (1953) famous phrase, "We are all more similar than otherwise" (p. xviii).

All this is to say that what we have been talking about all along is not "this versus that," nor even "this and that," but rather "this together with that"— and the prime examples have to do with discipline showing care. In other words, when all is right, discipline and care complement one another in precisely the ways predicted by the yin-yang symbol.

This yin-yang way of thinking about behavior and classroom management also suggests a new and better way to think about being eclectic. There is a common, and we would add, naïve, assumption that it is possible to weave together the variety of approaches to create one "super" approach that covers everything and everyone. However, and as our discussions clearly show, the minute we go from talking about behavior and classroom management to actually teaching students and managing classrooms, we find we need to make choices, and the choices we make inevitably feature one approach over others.

Furthermore, the minute we turn from talking about doing to actually doing, we find that our doing reflects who we are as persons. In other words, the minute we are engaged in actually managing behavior and classrooms, we find that our approach is, to a large extent, who we are. That is why it is so difficult to switch approaches.

However, if we keep in mind the main overarching duality between discipline and care, and if we see this duality as a complement duality, not as a conflict duality, then we gain a new and better meaning of "being eclectic." We do so because we understand that regardless of approach and regardless of who we are, there is the possibility for a meaningful eclecticism by doing what is essential in all approaches: integrating discipline and care.

Glossary

Accommodating diversity: One of the central components or tasks in behavior and classroom management, accommodating diversity refers either to accommodating cultural diversity or to accommodating diversity having to do with ability and learning differences.

Accommodating the nature of the child: One of the offshoots of the child study movement; for example, not forcing young children to go into a particular grade until they are "ready."

Active listening: Not just listening carefully, but by paraphrasing and repeating, showing that the speaker has been understood. Associated with the work of Thomas Gordon.

Adhocracy: Organizations in which specialists work closely together to come up with creative solutions to solve new problems.

Agonist: A medication that increases the number of neurotransmitters in the brain.

American individualisms: In families from higher socioeconomic classes, individualism is apt to mean "soft individualism" calling for sensitive caring on the part of caregivers. In families from lower socioeconomic classes, individualism is apt to mean "hard individualism" calling for parents to cultivate and support resilience and toughness in their children

Antagonist: A medication that decreases the number of neurotransmitters in the brain.

Approaches: Patterns of behavior and classroom management defined not simply by the methods emphasized but also by underlying value hierarchies, theories of change, and assumptions about development and what central tasks to attend to first and foremost.

Assertive discipline: A style of leadership that is neither hostile nor permissive and that states clearly what a teacher needs and requires from students. Associated with the work of Lee and Marlene Canter.

Attachment to teachers: Children using teachers in ways similar to the ways they use their parents, especially by "checking in," asking for help, and staying in physical proximity.

Attention-deficit/hyperactivity disorder: A disorder in childhood characterized by high rates of inattention and impulsive activity.

Autistic disorder: A serious disorder characterized by repetitive behavior, gaze aversion, ecolalia (echoing what others say), language delay, and otherwise failing to relate to others.

Behavioral-learning: Approaches that make use of the core concepts of stimulus, reinforcement, punishment (negative consequence), and schedules to systematically increase desired behavior and decrease undesirable behavior.

Being "withit": Being a teacher who can simultaneously monitor both individuals and the group. Associated with the work of Jacob Kounin.

Boss manager: William Glasser's term for obedience-oriented teachers.

Boundary: The concept systems theorists use to describe and evaluate the degree to which subsystems (such as the teacher and student subsystems) are differentiated and coordinated with one another.

Bullying: Ongoing harassment of one child or adolescent by a peer or group of peers.

Calvinist: The orthodoxy among a variety of American Protestant churches that emphasized the supreme power of God and the innate sinfulness of mankind, leading to a view of children as being prone to wickedness and needing to be taught to be obedient. From a Calvinist perspective, children were not to be trusted, hence the need for harsh forms of discipline such as corporal punishment.

Character education: A movement that began in the 19th century and continues today that explicitly makes schools responsible for educating children to improve their character and not just their minds.

Checking in: Children briefly telling a teacher what they are doing or accomplishing, a sign the child is attached to the teacher.

Child study movement: A movement that began at the very end of the 19th century among academics, designed to bring to the study of child development the methods of science so that research could improve policies and programs for children, including public schools.

Clear boundaries: In a systems approach, boundaries drawn in such a way that there is differentiation and communication/engagement between members of different subsystems.

Clear lines of sight: Setting up desks and the classroom physical space so that the teacher can see each and every student.

Closed plans: Architectural plans for early childhood centers distinguished by separate rooms for different activities.

Cognitive-constructivist: The theoretical tradition emphasizing the role of thinking in overall development and how we come to explain our world through actively exploring, interpreting, and problem solving. Often contrasted with traditions that treat the developing person as a passive recipient of knowledge transmitted by others.

Collectivist cultures: Those cultures that encourage group-mindedness and emphasize the importance of individuals identifying themselves in terms of their membership in groups.

Communicating high expectations: An essential component for establishing positive teacher-student relationships.

Community: A sense of oneness among members that (ideally, for some) can come from sharing moral values.

Comorbidity: When the same individual has more than one diagnosis (e.g., being diagnosed with both ADHD and dyslexia).

Conditions of worth: Statements made by adults that give the message "If you do such and such, you are O.K. as a person." Associated with the approach to counseling developed by Carl Rogers.

Conduct disorder: A disorder characterized by abusing others and/or not respecting others' rights.

Constructivist approaches: Constructivist approaches to educating children emphasize the need to help children engage in active exploring, interpreting, and problem solving.

Constructivist model: A model of teaching that emphasizes teachers supporting students actively puzzling and problem solving.

Control methods: Those methods whose main purpose is to get students to comply right now to ensure safety, order, and cooperation.

Controls from within: Those controls that come from the child or adolescent himself or herself, such as controls derived from a child's sense of right and wrong.

Conventional morality: Morality dependent on rules and procedures that have been internalized by the child, as evidenced by the child's seeing rules and procedures as applicable to everyone, regardless of status and authority.

Counseling approaches: Those approaches to discipline that derive from the psychoanalytic and related traditions that focused on attending to children's feelings and experience in an effort to help children gain insight and manage their emotions.

Critical constructivism: Involving students in puzzling and interpreting not just about what is good for them but also about what is good for all.

Culture: Refers to both surface behaviors such as language as well as to hidden value systems and images of what makes for good children, good adults, and good communities. A culture exists wherever a group takes a set of values, images, methods, and practices to be normative, that is, the "right way" to believe and act.

Deep structure: Refers to the unseen parts of culture, particularly the values, ideals, and images of what makes a mature individual and good community.

Defining operationally: Defining in a way that allows for direct observation and measurement.

Democratic: A way of living together defined especially by everyone having a voice in achieving a balance between respecting individual rights and the common good.

Democratic practice: Parenting or teaching that gives children a voice, that encourages children to negotiate conflicts by taking others' perspectives, and that engages children in reflecting on the common good.

Development: When distinguished from learning, development refers to changes in persons that usually occur over relatively long periods of time and that are qualitative changes judged using standards to assess approximations to some conception of maturity.

Developmental tasks: Those tasks that necessarily take years to master and must be mastered if an individual is to mature, such as thinking by reasoning, deciding right and wrong using universal principles, and forming a positive identity.

Diagnosis: The process and result of identifying the presence of one or more syndromes.

Diagnostic and Statistical Manual of Mental Disorders: The American Psychiatric Association's system of categories defining pathology and establishing the criteria for determining the presence of a disorder.

Diffuse boundaries: Boundaries drawn so ambiguously that there is too little differentiation between members of different subsystems.

Discovery model: A model of teaching that emphasizes teachers supporting students learning/discovering on their own.

Disorders of childhood: The term the American Psychiatric Association uses to define syndromes (patterns) of behavior that indicate serious dysfunction and that begin in childhood.

Domain-concordant: Teachers act in a domain concordant way when they respond to moral problems as moral problems (as when someone hits someone else) and to violations of convention as violations of convention (as when a student does not raise a hand when the rule is raise a hand before speaking).

Domain-discordant: Teachers act in a domain-discordant way when they respond to moral problems as violations of convention and to violations of convention as moral problems.

Ecological: Those approaches to behavior and classroom management that emphasize organization and keeping the class moving toward a main goal in any given activity period.

Effortless control: The not-so-effortless approach characteristic of Japanese teachers that leads to children controlling each other and themselves.

Ego development: Development of ability to not only assess inner and outer reality but also to act accordingly.

Ego supports: Supports given by others to help children and adolescents control their impulses and make good decisions on their own.

Enlightenment: A 17th- and 18th-century movement, largely in Europe, to make science and reasoning the major guide for understanding and acting in the world.

Exercising authority: An essential component for establishing positive teacher-student relationships.

Flow: The degree to which a class moves along smoothly and at a reasonable pace for the purpose of carrying out a program of action.

Group-mindedness: Concern for harmony and connection with the group rather than for individual advancement.

Guan: The Chinese concept linking being tough and authoritarian with being caring.

Guidance methods: Those methods whose main purpose is to help students act and think in more mature ways. Guidance methods try to educate and not simply control.

"I" messages: Messages conveyed by teachers to indicate that some behavior by a student or group of students is causing a problem for the teacher. Associated with the work of Thomas Gordon.

Ideal types (culture): The patterns of behavior that point to what a culture takes to be ideal. The patterns need not exist in reality; they function to establish the norms that guide a culture in raising and teaching children.

Identified problem student: The term that systems theorists use to refer to the student whom the teachers and others have (perhaps implicitly) labeled as the "bad" or "problem" student when a better way is to see the behavior of the student as reflecting a dysfunctional or problematic classroom system.

Inclusion model: The model of special education that integrates students with special needs into the life and work of regular classrooms.

Indirect directives: Rather than saying, for example, "Sit down," saying, "Do you think this is a good time to sit down?" when the question is really meant as a directive. Indirect directives are often unclear to students from minority cultures.

Individualized Education Programs (IEPs): Programs designed and implemented to give special support to children with special needs.

Individuals With Disabilities Education Act: The public law establishing the categories used in educational settings for helping to determine which students should receive special services.

In loco parentis: An older (pre-1970) view that teachers, principals, and all those running schools take the place of parents when students are in schools.

Inner processes: Those mental processes that are necessary if an individual is to develop and mature, processes such as perspective taking, symbolizing, reasoning, and developing ways to control impulses.

Interpersonal (family) systems: The theoretical tradition emphasizing the role that patterns of interactions within groups have on explaining problem behavior, so that the problem comes to be seen as in the system, defined by patterns of interactions, and not in any one individual.

Just and caring: The complementary components defining a moral community.

Lead managers: William Glasser's term for teachers who listen to students' ideas, develop students' trust that teachers have their needs at heart, and include students in evaluating both the work that is done and how to improve.

Learning: Changes in behavior or thinking that usually occur over relatively short periods of time and often as a result of direct instruction, modeling, or systematic reinforcement.

Learning approaches: Approaches that take teaching for learning to be the starting point and linchpin of successful behavior and classroom management.

Learning disabilities: Disabilities characterized by serious problems in reading, writing, or math.

Making learning relevant: A process linking curriculum to students' interests and to the world outside of school and making the learning process itself interesting.

Managing dilemmas: Ensuring that in achieving one goal (e.g., restoring order to the classroom), some other important goal (e.g., making school a positive place for children) is not undermined.

Matching methods: Choosing methods to match the nature of a particular student or group of students as well as to match the particular setting or circumstances.

Medical model: A model developed first to address physical problems and then later used with psychological problems. The model rests on assumptions about what is involved in being scientific (careful observation, systematic description using categories defined operationally, etc.).

Mental hygiene movement: A movement that began in the early part of the 20th century, largely among clinicians, that intended to prevent mental illness by attending to everyday problems and issues, such as the problem behaviors that occur in classrooms for "typical" children.

Mental retardation: Serious delays in thinking/cognition that are pervasive and affect functioning in virtually every domain.

Methods (for managing): Observable behaviors on the part of educators that perform some function having to do with behavior and classroom management.

Modified open plans: Architectural plans for early childhood centers with small and large activity spaces that are open enough to allow children to see the possibilities for play yet enclosed enough to give spaces specific identities (block corner, dramatic play corner, reading corner, etc.). Often, modified open plans also have meandering pathways between activity centers that allow children to see how to transition from one activity center to another—albeit circuitously.

Multi-axial system: A system for diagnosing that requires assessing different sets of facts, such as the *DSM-IV-TR* system, which requires assessing facts related to syndromes and facts related to psychosocial stressors in the environment.

Nature-nurture debate: The debate over whether our behavior and achievements derive mostly from our genes (nature) or from our upbringing (nurture).

Negative reinforcement: Any consequence experienced as positive, because something negative has been taken away, that makes it likely that a behavior will increase.

Negative reinforcement trap: Negative reinforcement that unwittingly leads to maintaining problems or that causes new problems. Negative reinforcement traps often play a central role in fostering and maintaining coercive behavior when a teacher and student negatively reinforce one another to act in coercive/overcontrolling ways.

Neurotransmitters: Those chemicals that convey information from one brain cell to another.

Open plans: Architectural plans for early childhood centers distinguished by the presence of open spaces without partitions.

Oppositional defiant disorder: A disorder characterized by refusal to cooperate with those in authority.

Organic approaches: Those approaches to behavior management that explain problem behavior in terms of deficits or problems in biology and that often treat problem behavior using drugs/medication.

Organization: One of the central components or tasks in behavior and classroom management, organization refers to the organization of time, space, materials, and groups of children and educators as well as to the interpersonal classroom systems that may require restructuring (reorganizing).

Organizing teaching teams: Organizing to ensure smooth coordination of schedules and collective problem solving.

Organizing the physical environment: Organizing classroom space and the built environment as well as being thoughtful about preparing and storing materials.

Organizing the social environment: Grouping students to maximize learning and other important values, providing appropriate and clear rules and routines, and monitoring both individuals and the class as a whole.

Organizing the temporal environment: Organizing time so that there are clear schedules, well-supported transitions, and sensible decisions made about time devoted to instruction.

Pathology: The medical term for serious problems that require intervention.

Perspective taking: The mental operation of taking another's point of view or a point of view other than that of the self—a prerequisite for social, emotional, and cognitive development.

Points of entry: A concept pointing out that there are always many causes of any given problem, making it possible to "attack" a problem in many different ways or at different points of entry.

Positive connotation of function: Reframing by finding a positive function in the behavior of a student or group of students.

Positive connotation of motive: Reframing by finding a positive intention on the part of the student or students.

Positive reinforcement: Any consequence experienced as positive, because something positive is added, that makes it likely that a behavior will increase.

Positive reinforcement trap: Positive reinforcement by teachers or other caregivers that unwittingly leads to maintaining problems or that causes new problems.

Postconventional morality: A moral system that relies on universal principles and judgments about extenuating circumstances.

Power: In systems theory, one of the main considerations for evaluating a classroom system in terms of whether the teacher has sufficient power over students.

Practice-to-habit theory: A theory popular in the 19th century, and still popular today, that says getting children to "behave" creates good habits, which, in turn, create good character.

Praise/encouragement: Abstract praise for achievements versus encouragement that is specific (concrete) and focused more on process.

Preconventional morality: The first stage of morality, in which children rely on what adults say is right and wrong or on the rules adults impose and that define right and wrong. That is, for children in a preconventional stage, morality is "on the outside."

Prevention methods: Methods designed to prevent problem behavior.

Professional bureaucracy: Organizations consisting of specialists who work alone using the special skills developed in their specialized training.

Programs of action: Those units of time calling for the class as a whole to move in a particular direction to achieve a particular goal.

Progressive education: A term covering a wide range of approaches designed to address problems in schools at the end of the 19th century, particularly the problems of teachers being too authoritarian and students being too passive and unmotivated to learn on their own; it is associated with the work of John Dewey and with constructivist approaches to educating children.

Proximity control: A method suggested by Redl and Wineman to help children control themselves, involving adults simply staying close by to make children feel secure.

Psychodynamic: Often used interchangeably with the word *psychoanalytic*, psychodynamic refers to the theoretical and clinical tradition begun by Sigmund Freud that emphasizes the importance of feelings; conflicts between feelings; the unconscious nature of the feeling life; and the need for parents, teachers, and other caregivers to help children to develop ways to understand, express, and manage their feelings.

Punishment (negative consequence): Any consequence that makes it likely that a behavior will decrease.

Punishment trap: Punishment by teachers or other caregivers that unwittingly leads to maintaining problems or that causes new problems.

Putting morality on the inside: Kohlberg's phrase for the process of going from pre- to conventional morality, signaled primarily by children coming to "own" rules rather than feel rules are imposed from the outside.

Pygmalion effect: The phenomenon of students getting better or worse as a function of others' expectations.

Qualitative changes: Changes, such as going from conventional to principled moral judgment or from thinking egocentrically to thinking by considering how others think, that represent transformations (new patterns) and not just quantitative increases such as increases in vocabulary.

Quality school: William Glasser's term for schools that create a positive school atmosphere, that meet individuals' needs, and that make it satisfying to produce good work.

RAVE-O: An educational approach to helping children with dyslexia that is rooted in a biological theory of dyslexia.

Reactive approach: An approach, such as the classroom systems approach, designed to react to (chronic) behavior problems rather than to prevent problems.

Reframing: A preferred method of the classroom systems approach that requires providing a positive interpretation of or "spin" on behavior initially framed as bad behavior.

Regroup for targeted learning: Having students in the same class learn together (regardless of ability) for most activities but regroup according to ability for specific activities (such as reading).

Relationship building: One of the central components or tasks in behavior and classroom management, divided generally between dyadic (e.g., teacher-student) relationships and relationships that form the larger classroom or school community.

Relationship-resistant: Children and adolescents who (often unconsciously) actively resist forming a relationship (positive or negative) with an adult.

Rigid boundaries: In systems theory, boundaries drawn so heavily that there is too little communication and too little engagement between members of different subsystems.

Schedules of reinforcement or punishment: Different ways that reinforcements and punishments are administered (e.g., continuously vs. randomly), with each schedule being appropriate for a different stage in the process of change.

Service learning: Learning that comes from field placements outside school and in the context of serving others.

Showing care: Expressed in a variety of ways and behaviors, including listening carefully, providing specific help, and expressing high expectations; essential for positive teacher-student relationships.

Showing interest: Essential component for establishing positive teacher-student relationships.

State interest rights: The rights established by law to protect the common good. State interest rights provide a rationale for limiting students' individual freedom in classrooms and schools, especially in matters having to do with curriculum and learning.

Stimulus: Any antecedent that makes it likely (probable) that a behavior will occur.

Stimulus trap: Stimulus provided by teachers or other caregivers that unwittingly leads to maintaining problems or that causes new problems.

Storming the back door: Reframing by finding positive behavior not associated with the misbehavior of a student, such as finding a disruptive student is a dancer outside school.

Styles of control: Most commonly distinguished using the categories of authoritarian, authoritative, and permissive styles of control.

Subsystems: The naturally occurring subgroups within the overall classroom and school community (teachers, students, administrators, etc.).

Supporting development: One of the central components or tasks in behavior and classroom management; the focus is on accommodating age and stage, supporting long-term development, supporting qualitative changes in persons, and supporting mastery of developmental tasks and inner processes.

Syndrome: Patterns of symptoms that are referred to when using diagnostic labels.

System: Generally, a concept referring to interrelated parts forming a functioning whole. In the context of the classroom systems approach, the term *system* refers to transactional patterns and how they maintain a system.

Systems approaches: Those approaches that view the problem behavior of individuals as reflecting the presence of dysfunctional systems; approaches that emphasize the need to change dysfunctional systems.

Systems theory: The theoretical tradition emphasizing the role that patterns of interaction within groups play in explaining problem behavior, so that the problem comes to be seen as in the system, defined by patterns of interactions, and not in any one individual.

Taking ownership of problems: What Thomas Gordon advocated when he suggested using "I" messages.

Target behaviors: In behavioral-learning approaches, those behaviors chosen or targeted for systematic modification, so they either increase or decrease in frequency, duration, and/or strength (intensity).

Teaching defensively: Always having to react to students' misbehavior rather than prevent misbehavior.

Teaching for learning: One of the central components or tasks in behavior and classroom management. Approaches featuring teaching for learning include those that treat behavioral-learning approaches as well as approaches using traditional models of teaching.

Theories of change: Largely derived from psychology, the major theories of how humans change and develop include psychoanalytic, cognitive constructivist, behavioral-learning, ecological, interpersonal systems, and organic theories.

Time engaged in learning: Time when students are actually engaged in the learning process, not necessarily or usually the same as time spent on instruction.

Tracking: The system of grouping students according to ability, not proven to be effective.

Transactional patterns: Patterns of interaction that arise from two or more individuals having to get particular jobs done or functions performed, such as the job of maintaining a degree of order needed if students are to learn.

Transdisciplinary team: Teams of educators with different specialties who teach one another something about their specialties in order to share responsibilities when teaching together.

Transmission model: A model of teaching that emphasizes teachers transmitting their knowledge.

Types of authority: Authoritarian, authoritative, permissive.

Unitarian: A liberal Protestant faith tradition that contributed to Horace Mann's (founder of the American public school system) belief that children are innocent and vulnerable to temptation, on the one hand, but responsive to moral persuasion and the modeling of virtue, on the other.

Value hierarchies: A system of values (e.g., orderliness, children being engaged in puzzling) that ranks some values higher (more important) than others. Value hierarchies partially define an approach to behavior and classroom management.

Values: As used to distinguish approaches, values are whatever is deemed worthy or morally "right."

References

Ainsworth, M., Blehar, M., Waters, E., & Wall, S. (1978). *Patterns of attachment.* Hillsdale, NJ: Lawrence Erlbaum Associates.

Alberto, P., & Troutman, A. (1999). *Applied behavior analysis for teachers* (5th ed.). Upper Saddle River, NJ: Merrill-Prentice Hall.

Althof, W., & Berkowitz, M. (2006). Moral education and character education: Their relationship and roles in citizenship education. *Journal of Moral Education, 35*(4), 495–518.

American Psychiatric Association. (2000). *Diagnostic and statistical manual of mental disorders* (Text rev.). Washington, DC: Author.

Astor, R. A., Benbenishty, R., Zeira, A., & Vinokur, A. (2002). School climate, observed risky behaviors, and victimization as predictors of high school students' fear and judgments of school violence as a problem. *Health Education and Behavior, 29*(6), 716–736.

Avildsen, J. (Director). (1989). *Lean on me* [Motion picture]. United States: Warner Bros.

Ballenger, C. (1998). Culture and behavior problems: The language of control. In W. G. Scarlett (Ed.), *Trouble in the classroom: Managing the behavior problems of young children* (pp. 143–159). San Francisco: Jossey-Bass.

Barber, B. (Ed.). (2002). *Intrusive parenting: How psychological control affects children and adolescents.* Washington, DC: American Psychological Association.

Baumrind, D. (1970). Socialization and instrumental competence in young children. *Young Children, 26*(2), 104–119.

Baumrind, D. (1971). Harmonious parents and their preschool children. *Developmental Psychology, 4*(1), 99–102.

Bear, G. (2004). *Developing self-discipline and preventing and correcting misbehavior.* Boston: Allyn & Bacon.

Beatty, B. (1995). *Preschool education in America.* New Haven, CT: Yale University Press.

Becker, W., Engelmann, S., & Thomas, D. (1975). *Teaching 1: Classroom management.* Champaign, IL: Research Press.

Biklen, D. (1989). Redefining schools. In D. Biklen, D. Ferguson, & A. Ford (Eds.), *Schooling and disability* (pp. 1–25). Chicago: University of Chicago Press.

Blair, J., Mitchell, D. R., & Peschardt, K. (2005). *The psychopath: Emotion and the brain.* Boston: Blackwell.

Blatz, W., & Bott, H. (1930). *The management of young children.* New York: W. Morrow & Company.

Blount, J. (1999). The visceral pleasures of the well-worn rut: Internal barriers to changing the social relations of American classrooms. In R. Butchart & B. McEwan (Eds.), *Classroom discipline in American schools: Problems and possibilities for democratic education* (pp. 85–109). Albany: State University of New York Press.

Bowen, H. C. (1893). *Froebel and education by self-activity.* New York: Scribner's Sons.

Bowen, M. (1978). *Family therapy in clinical practice.* New York: Jason Aronson.

Bredekamp, S. (Ed.). (1986). *Developmentally appropriate practice in early childhood programs serving children from birth through age 8.* Washington, DC: National Association for the Education of Young Children.

Brendtro, L. (1969). Establishing relationship beachheads. In A. Trieschman, J. Whitaker, & L. Brendtro (Eds.), *The other 23 hours* (pp. 51–99). Chicago: Aldine.

Bringuier, J. (1980). *Conversations with Jean Piaget* (B. M. Gulati, Trans.). Chicago: University of Chicago Press.

Bronfenbrenner, U. (1989). Ecological systems theory. In R. Vasta (Ed.), *Annals of Child Development* (Vol. 6, pp. 187–250). Greenwich, CT: JAI Press.

Brophy, J. (1999). Perspectives on classroom management: Yesterday, today, and tomorrow. In J. Freiberg (Ed.), *Beyond behaviorism: Changing the classroom management paradigm* (pp. 44–55). Boston: Allyn & Bacon.

Brophy, J. (2006). History of research on classroom management. In C. Evertson & C. Weinstein (Eds.), *Classroom management: Research, practice, and contemporary issues* (pp. 17–43). Mahwah, NJ: Lawrence Erlbaum Associates.

Brown, A. (1980). Cherokee culture and school achievement. *American Indian Culture and Research Journal, 4,* 55–74.

Bruner, J. (1984). Language, mind, and reading. In H. Goelman, A. Oberg, & F. Smith (Eds.), *Awakening to literacy: The University of Victoria symposium on children's response to a literate environment: Literacy before schooling* (pp. 193–200). Exeter, NH: Heinemann Educational Books.

Butchart, R. (1998a). Introduction. In R. Butchart & B. McEwan (Eds.), *Classroom discipline in American schools: Problems and possibilities for democratic education* (pp. 1–18). Albany: State University of New York Press.

Butchart, R. (1998b). Punishments, penalties, prizes, and procedures: A history of discipline in U.S. schools. In R. Butchart & B. McEwan (Eds.), *Classroom discipline in American schools: Problems and possibilities for democratic education* (pp. 19–50). Albany: State University of New York Press.

Butchart, R., & McEwan, B. (Eds.). (1998). *Classroom discipline in American schools: problems and possibilities for democratic education.* Albany: State University of New York Press.

Cambone, J. (1994). *Teaching troubled children: A case study in effective classroom practice*. New York: Teachers College Press.

Canter, L. (1996). Discipline alternatives. First the rapport—Then, the rules. *Learning, 24*(5), 12–14.

Canter, L., & Canter, M. (1976). *Assertive discipline: A take charge approach for today's educator*. Santa Monica, CA: Canter and Associates.

Canter, L., & Canter, M. (1997). *Assertive discipline: Positive behavior management for today's classrooms*. Santa Monica, CA: Lee Canter Associates.

Cantwell, D., & Rutter, M. (2001). Classification: Conceptual issues and substantive findings. In M. Rutter, E. Taylor, & L. Hersov (Eds.), *Child and adolescent psychiatry* (3rd ed., pp. 3–19). Cambridge, MA: Blackwell Science.

Carducci, R. (1976). A comparison of I-messages with commands in the control of disruptive classroom behavior. *Dissertation Abstracts International, 36*(11B), 573.

Cazden, C. (1988). *Classroom discourse: The language of teaching and learning*. Portsmouth, NH: Heinemann.

Chao, R. (1994). Beyond parental control and authoritarian parenting style: Understanding Chinese parenting through the cultural notion of training. *Child Development, 65*(4), 1111–1119.

Chao, R. (2001). Extending research on the consequences of parenting style for Chinese Americans and European Americans. *Child Development, 72*(6), 1832–1843.

Charles, C. M., & Senter, G. W. (2008). *Elementary classroom management* (5th ed.). Boston: Pearson.

Charney, R. (2002). *Teaching children to care: Management in the responsive classroom* (2nd ed.). Greenfield, MA: Northeast Foundation for Children.

Chomsky, N. (1957). *Syntactic structures*. The Hague: Mouton.

Clayton, J. B. (2003). *One classroom, many worlds: Teaching and learning in the cross-cultural classroom*. Portsmouth, NH: Heinemann.

Cohen, R. M. (1991). *A lifetime of teaching: Portraits of five veteran high school teachers*. New York: Teachers College Press.

Cohen, S. (1964). *Progressives and urban school reform*. New York: Columbia University Teachers College, Bureau of Publications.

Colvin, G. (2004). *Managing the cycle of serious acting-out behavior*. Eugene, OR: Behavior Associates.

Comer, J. (2003). Transforming the lives of children. In M. Elias, H. Arnold, & C. Hussey (Eds.), *EQ + IQ = Best leadership practices for caring and successful schools* (pp. 11–22). Thousand Oaks, CA: Corwin Press.

Comer, R. J. (2006). *Abnormal psychology* (6th ed.). New York: Worth Publishers.

Condorcet, J. A. (1976). *Entwurf einer historischen darstellung deer fortschritte des menschlic hen geistes*. Frankfurt, Germany: Suhrkamp. (Original work published 1789)

Cowley, S. (2001). *Getting the buggers to behave*. New York: Continuum.

Cremin, L. (1965). *The genius of American education*. New York: Vintage Books.

Cremin, L. (1976). *Traditions of American education*. New York: Basic Books.

Cutts, N., & Moseley, N. (1941). *Practical school discipline and mental hygiene.* New York: Houghton Mifflin.

Davis, M. I. (2005). The buck reward system. In R. Stone (Ed.), *Best classroom management practices for reaching all learners: What award-winning classroom teachers do* (pp. 1–6). Thousand Oaks, CA: Sage.

Dawson, G., Toth, K., Abbott, R., Osterling, J., Munson, J., Estes, A., et al. (2004). Early social attention impairments in autism: Social orienting, joint attention, and attention to distress. *Developmental Psychology, 40*(2), 271–283.

Dehyle, D. (1992). Constructing failure and maintaining cultural identity: Navajo and Ute. *Journal of American Indian Education, 31*(2), 24–47.

Delpit, L. (1995). *Other people's children: Cultural conflict in the classroom.* New York: The New Press.

Dembo, T. (1982). Some problems in rehabilitation as seen by a Lewinian. *Journal of Social Issues, 38*(1), 131–137.

DeVries, R., & Kohlberg, L. (1990). *Constructivist early education: Overview and comparison with other programs.* Washington, DC: National Association for the Education of Young Children.

Dewey, J. (1963). *Experience and education.* New York: Collier MacMillan.

Dodman, N. (1996). *The dog who loved too much: Tales, treatments, and the psychology of dogs.* New York: Bantam Books.

Donald, D. (1995). *Lincoln.* New York: Simon & Schuster.

Doyle, W. (2006). Ecological approaches to classroom management. In C. M. Evertson & C. S. Weinstein (Eds.), *Handbook of classroom management: Research, practice, and contemporary issues* (pp. 97–127). Mahwah, NJ: Lawrence Erlbaum Associates.

Dreikurs, R., & Grey, L. (1990). *The new approach to discipline: Logical consequences.* New York: Dutton.

Elkind, D. (1987). *Miseducation: Preschoolers at risk.* New York: W.W. Norton & Company.

Emmer, E., Evertson, C., & Anderson, L. (1980). Effective classroom management at the beginning of the school year. *Elementary School Journal, 80*(5), 219–231.

Emmer, E., Evertson, C., Sanford, J., Clements, B., & Worsham, M. (1989). *Classroom management for secondary teachers.* Englewood Cliffs, NJ: Prentice Hall.

Erikson, E. (1950). *Childhood and society.* New York: Norton.

Evertson, C. M., & Weinstein, C. S. (Eds.). (2006). *Handbook of classroom management: Research, practice, and contemporary issues.* Mahwah, NJ: Lawrence Erlbaum Associates.

Fairbank, J. K., & Goldman, M. (1992). *China: A new history* (2nd ed.). Cambridge, MA: Harvard University Press.

Foucault, M. (1980). *Power/knowledge.* New York: Pantheon Books.

Freiberg, J. (Ed.). (1999). *Beyond behaviorism: Changing the classroom management paradigm.* Boston: Allyn & Bacon.

Frith, U. (2003). *Autism: Explaining the enigma* (2nd ed.). Oxford: Blackwell.

Fung, H. (1999). Becoming a moral child: The socialization of shame among young Chinese children. *Ethos, 27*(2), 180–209.

Garcia, E. (1991). *The education of linguistically and culturally diverse students: Effective instructional practices.* Santa Cruz: University of California, Santa Cruz, National Center for Research on Cultural Diversity and Second Language Learning.

Garrison, W. (1993). *Small bargains, children in crisis and the meaning of parental love.* New York: Simon and Schuster.

Gathercoal, F. (1993). *Judicious discipline* (3rd ed.). San Francisco: Caddo Gap Press.

Gathercoal, F. (1998). Judicious discipline. In R. Butchart & B. McEwan (Eds.), *Classroom discipline in American schools: Problems and possibilities for democratic education* (pp. 197–216). Albany: State University of New York Press.

Gay, G. (2000). *Culturally responsive teaching: Theory, research, and practice.* New York: Teachers College Press.

Gesell, A., Halverson, H., Thompson, H., Ilg, F., Castner, B. Ames, L., et al. (1940). *The first five years of life.* New York: Harper & Row.

Glasser, W. (1969). *Schools without failure.* New York: Harper & Row.

Glasser, W. (1986). *Control theory in the classroom.* New York: Harper & Row.

Glasser, W. (1992). *The quality school: Managing students without coercion* (2nd ed.). New York: Harper & Row.

Glasser, W. (1998). *The quality school: Managing students without coercion* (Rev. ed.). New York: HarperCollins.

Glassman, M. (2001). Dewey and Vygotsky: Society, experience, and inquiry in educational practice. *Educational Researcher, 30*(4), 3–14.

Glickman, C., & Tamashiro, R. (1980). Clarifying teachers' beliefs about discipline. *Educational Leadership, 37,* 459–464.

Good, T., & Brophy, J. (1989). Teaching the lesson. In R. E. Slavin (Ed.), *School and classroom organization* (pp. 25–65). Hillsdale, NJ: Lawrence Erlbaum Associates.

Gordon, T. (1974). *Teacher effectiveness training.* New York: Peter H. Wyden.

Gordon, T. (2003). *Teacher effectiveness training* (2nd ed.). New York: Three Rivers Press.

Green, J. (1969). *The educational ideas of Pestalozzi.* New York: Greenwood Press.

Greenberg, M., & Speltz, M. (1988). Attachment and the ontogeny of conduct problems. In J. Belsky & T. Nezworsk (Eds.), *Clinical implications of attachment* (pp. 177–218). Hillside, NJ: Erlbaum.

Gregg, N. (1991). Disorders of written expression. In A. M. Bain, L. L. Bailet, & L. Cook-Moats (Eds.), *Written language disorders: Theory into practice* (pp. 65–97). Austin, TX: Pro-ED.

Gregory, A., & Weinstein, R. (2004). Connection and regulation at home and in school: Predicting growth in achievement for adolescents. *Journal of Adolescent Research, 19*(4), 405–427.

Gross-Tsur, V., Manor, O., & Shalev, R. S. (1996). Developmental dyscalculia: Prevalence and demographic features. *Developmental Medicine and Child Neurology, 38*(1), 25–33.

Group, M. C. (1999). A 14-month randomized clinical trial of treatment strategies for attention deficit/hyperactivity disorder. *Archives of General Psychiatry, 103*(4), 805–807.

Haley, J. (1987). *Problem-solving therapy* (2nd ed.). San Francisco: Jossey-Bass.

Hall, E. (1976). *Beyond culture.* New York: Doubleday.

Hanish, L., Kochenderfer-Ladd, B., Fabes, R., Martin, C., & Denning, D. (2004). Bullying among young children: The influence of peers and teachers. In S. Swearer & D. Espelage (Eds.), *Bullying in American schools: A social-ecological perspective on prevention and intervention* (pp. 141–160). Mahwah, NJ: Lawrence Erlbaum Associates.

Harris, P. (1928). *Changing conceptions of school discipline.* New York: MacMillan.

Heath, S. B. (1978). *Teacher talk: Language in the classroom.* Arlington, VA: Center for Applied Linguistics.

Heath, S. B. (1983). *Ways with words: Language, life, and work in communities and classrooms.* Cambridge: Cambridge University Press.

Henry, S. E., & Abowitz, K. K. (1998). Interpreting Glasser's control theory: Problems that emerge from innate needs and predetermined ends. In R. Butchart & B. McEwan (Eds.), *Classroom discipline in American schools: Problems and possibilities for democratic education* (pp. 157–196). Albany: State University of New York Press.

Hittmair-Delazer, M., Sailer, U., & Benke, T. (1995). Impaired arithmetic facts but intact conceptual knowledge: A single-case study of dyscalculia. *Cortex, 31*(1), 139–147.

Hitz, R., & Driscoll, A. (1988). Praise or encouragement? New insights into praise: Implications for early childhood teachers. *Young Children, 43,* 6–13.

Holt, M. K., & Keyes, M. A. (2004). Teachers' attitudes toward bullying. In D. L. Espelage & S. M. Sweare (Eds.), *Bullying in American schools: A social-ecological perspective on prevention and intervention* (pp. 121–140). Mahwah, NJ: Lawrence Erlbaum Associates.

Horne, A., Bartolomucci, C., & Newman-Carlson, D. (2003). *Bully busters: A teachers' manual for helping bullies, victims, and bystanders.* Champaign, IL: Research Press.

Hoy, A. W., & Weinstein, C. (2006). Student and teacher perspectives on classroom management. In C. Evertson & C. Weinstein (Eds.), *Classroom management: research, practice, and contemporary issues* (pp. 181–222). Mahwah, NJ: Lawrence Erlbaum Associates.

Hughes, J. N. (2002). Authoritative teaching: Tipping the balance in favor of school versus peer effects. *Journal of School Psychology, 40*(6), 485–492.

Irving, J. (1988). An analysis of the problems of disappearing black educators. *Elementary School Journal, 5,* 303–314.

Jackson, D. D. (1965). Family rules: Marital quid pro quo. *Archives of General Psychiatry, 12,* 589–594.

Jenkins, C. (2001). What is a good teacher? In R. Stone (Ed.), *Best practices for high school classrooms: What award-winning secondary teachers do* (pp. 4–10). Thousand Oaks, CA: Sage.

Johnson, E. W. (1981). *Teaching school.* New York: Walker.

Jones, F. H. (1987). *Positive classroom discipline.* New York: McGraw-Hill.

Jones, R., & Tanner, L. (1981, March). Classroom discipline: The unclaimed legacy. *Phi Delta Kappan,* 494–497.

Jones, V., & Jones, L. (2004). *Comprehensive classroom management* (7th ed.). Boston: Pearson Education.

Karweit, N. (1989). Time and learning: A review. In R. E. Slavin (Ed.), *School and classroom organization* (pp. 69–93). Hillsdale, NJ: Lawrence Erlbaum Associates.

Katz, L. (1989). Mothering and teaching—some significant distinctions. In L. Katz (Ed.), *Current topics in early childhood education* (pp. 47–63). Norwood, NJ: Ablex.

Katz, L. (1995). *Talks with teachers of young children: A collection.* Norwood, NJ: Ablex.

Kenny, M., Simon, L., Brabeck, K., & Lerner, R. (Eds.). (2001). *Learning to serve.* Boston: Kluwer Academic.

Knapp, M. S., Adelman, N. E., Marder, C., McCollum, H., & Needels, M. C. (1995). *Teaching for meaning in high-poverty classrooms.* New York: Teachers College Press.

Kohlberg, L. (1980). Stages of moral development as a basis for moral education. In B. Munsey (Ed.), *Moral development, moral education, and Kohlberg.* Birmingham, AL: Religious Education Press.

Kohlberg, L. (1984). *Essays on moral development* (Vol. 2). San Francisco: Harper & Row.

Kohlberg, L., & Lickona, T. (1990). Moral discussion and the class meeting. In R. DeVries & L. Kohlberg (Eds.), *Constructivist early education: Overview and comparison with other programs* (pp. 143–184). Washington, DC: National Association for the Education of Young Children.

Kohlberg, L., & Mayer, R. (1972). Development as the aim of education. *Harvard Education Review, 42,* 449–496.

Kohn, A. (1996). *Beyond discipline: From compliance to community.* Alexandria, VA: Association for Supervision and Curriculum Development.

Koshewa, A. (1999). *Discipline and democracy: Teachers on trial.* Portsmouth, NH: Heinemann.

Kounin, J. (1970). *Discipline and group management in classrooms.* New York: Holt, Rinehart & Winston.

Kounin, J., & Gump, P. (1958). The ripple effect in discipline. *Elementary School Journal, 59,* 158–162.

Kuhn, D. (Ed.). (1995). *Development and learning: Reconceptualizing the intersection* (Vol. 38). New York: S. Karger.

Kusserow, A. (2004). *American individualisms.* New York: Palgrave Macmillan.

Landrum, T. J., & Kauffman, J. M. (2006). Behavioral approaches to classroom management. In C. M. Evertson & C. S. Weinstein (Eds.), *Handbook of classroom management: Research, practice, and contemporary issues.* Mahwah, NJ: Lawrence Erlbaum Associates.

Lapsley, D., & Narvaez, D. (2006). Character education. In K. A. Renninger & I. Sigel (Eds.), *Handbook of child psychology: Child psychology in practice* (Vol. 4, pp. 248–296). Hoboken, NJ: John Wiley & Sons.

Lerner, R. (2007). *The good teen: Rescuing adolescence from the myths of the storm and stress years.* New York: Random House.

Lewis, C. (1995). *Educating hearts and minds.* New York: Cambridge University Press.

Lewis, C., Watson, M., & Schaps, E. (2003). Building community in school. In M. Elias, H. Arnold, & C. Hussey (Eds.), *EQ + IQ = Best leadership practices for caring and successful schools* (pp. 79–92). Thousand Oaks, CA: Corwin Press.

Little Soldiers, L. (1989). Cooperative learning and the Native American student. *Phi Delta Kappan, 71*(2), 161–163.

Lovaas, O. I. (1977). *The autistic child: Language development through behavior modification.* New York: Irvington.

Maag, J. (2004). *Behavior management: From theoretical implications to practical applications* (2nd ed.). Belmont, CA: Thomson Wadsworth.

Martin, N. K., Shoho, A., & Yin, Z. (2003). Attitudes and beliefs regarding classroom management styles: The impact of teacher preparation vs. experience. *Research in the Schools, 10*(2), 29–34.

Martin, N. K., & Yin, Z. (1997, February). *Attitudes and beliefs regarding classroom management styles: Differences between male and female teachers.* Paper presented at the Southwest Educational Research Association, Austin, TX.

Martin, N. K., & Yin, Z. (1999). Beliefs regarding classroom management style: Differences between urban and rural secondary level teachers. *Journal of Research in Rural Education, 15*(2), 1–5.

McCadden, B. (1998). Why is Michael always getting timed out? Race, class, and the disciplining of other people's children. In R. Butchart & B. McEwan (Eds.), *Classroom discipline in American schools: Problems and possibilities for democratic education* (pp. 109–134). Albany: State University of New York Press.

McCarthy, J., & Banally, J. (2003). Classroom management in a Navajo middle school. *Theory Into Practice, 42*(4), 296–305.

Meier, D. R. (1997). *Learning in small moments: Life in an urban classroom.* New York: Teachers College Press.

Menendez, R. (Writer/Director). (1988). *Stand and deliver* [Motion picture]. United States: Warner Bros.

Minuchin, S. (1974). *Families and family therapy.* Cambridge, MA: Harvard University Press.

Molnar, A., & Lindquist, B. (1989). *Changing problem behavior in schools.* San Francisco: Jossey-Bass.

Moore, G. T. (1987). The physical environment and cognitive development in child-care centers. In C. Weinstein & T. Davis (Eds.), *Spaces for children: The built environment and child development* (pp. 41–72). New York: Plenum.

Munsey, B. (Ed.). (1980). *Moral development, moral education, and Kohlberg.* Birmingham, AL: Religious Education Press.

Nansel, T. R., Overpeck, M., Pilla, R. S., Ruan, W. J., Simons-Morton, B., & Scheidt, P. (2001). Bullying behaviors among U.S. youth: Prevalence and association with psychosocial adjustment. *Journal of American Medical Association, 285*(16), 2084–2100.

Neill, A. S. (1960). *Summerhill: A radical approach to child rearing*. New York: Hart.

Noblit, G. W. (1993, Spring). Power and caring. *American Educational Research Journal, 30,* 23–38.

Noddings, N. (2002). *Educating moral people: A caring alternative to character education*. New York: Teachers College Press.

Nuby, J. F., Ehle, M. A., & Thrower, E. (2001). Culturally responsive teaching as related to the learning styles of Native American students. In J. Nyowe & S. Abadullah (Eds.), *Multicultural education: Diverse perspectives* (pp. 231–271). Victoria, BC: Trafford.

Nuby, J. F., & Oxford, R. L. (1997). Learning style preference of Native American and African American students as measured by the MBTI. *Journal of Psychological Type, 26,* 1–15.

Nucci, L. (2001). *Education in the moral domain*. Cambridge, UK: Cambridge University Press.

Nucci, L. (2006). Classroom management for moral and social development. In C. M. Evertson & C. S. Weinstein (Eds.), *Handbook of classroom management: Research, practice, and contemporary issues* (pp. 711–734). Mahwah, NJ: Lawrence Erlbaum Associates.

Olweus, D. (2001). Peer harassment: A critical analysis and some important issues. In J. Juvonen & S. Graham (Eds.), *Peer harassment in schools: The plight of the vulnerable and victimized* (pp. 3–20). New York: Guilford Press.

Olweus, D. (2004). *Bullying at school*. Malden, MA: Blackwell.

Paauw, D. (1999). Did we learn evidence-based medicine in medical school? Some common medical mythology. *Journal of the American Board of Family Practice, 12*(2), 143–149.

Pace, J., & Hemmings, A. (2006). Understanding classroom authority as a social construction. In J. Pace & A. Hemmings (Eds.), *Classroom authority: Theory, research, and practice* (pp. 1–32). Mahwah, NJ: Lawrence Erlbaum Associates.

Patterson, G. R. (1982). *Coercive family process* (Vol. 3). Eugene, OR: Castalia.

Pelham, W. E., Aronoff, H. R., Midlam, J. K., Shapiro, C. H., Gnagy, E. M., Chronis, A. M., et al. (1999). A comparison of Ritalin and Adderall: Efficacy and time-course in children with attention deficit-hyperactivity disorder. *Pediatrics, 103*(4), 805–807.

Pelham, W. E., Greenslade, K. E., Vodde-Hamilton, M., Murphy, D. A., Greenstein, J. J., Gnagy, E. M., et al. (1990). Relative efficacy of long-acting stimulants on children with attention deficit-hyperactivity disorder: A comparison of standard methylphenidate, sustained-release methylphenidate, sustained-release dextroamphetamine, and pemoline. *Pediatrics, 86*(2), 226–238.

Pellegrini, A. D. (1995). *School recess and playground behavior*. Albany: State University of New York Press.

Peterson, R., Loveless, S., Knapp, T., Basta, S., & Anderson, S. (1979). The effects of teacher use of I-messages on student disruptive and study behavior. *Psychological Record, 29,* 187–199.

Pewewardy, C. (2002). Learning styles of American Indian/Alaska Native students: A review of the literature and implications for practice. *Journal of American Indian Education, 41*(3), 22–56.

Philips, S. (1983). *The invisible culture.* New York: Longman Press.

Piaget, J. (1932). *The moral judgment of the child.* Glencoe, IL: Free Press.

Piaget, J. (1977). Development of teaching methods. In H. Gruber & J. Voneche (Eds.), *The essential Piaget* (pp. 710–719). New York: Basic Books.

Pianta, R. (2006). Classroom management and relationships between children and teachers: Implications for research and practice. In C. Evertson & C. Weinstein (Eds.), *Classroom management: Research, practice, and contemporary issues* (pp. 685–710). Mahwah, NJ: Lawrence Erlbaum Associates.

Power, C., Higgins, A., & Kohlberg, L. (Eds.). (1989). *Lawrence Kohlberg's approach to moral education.* New York: Columbia University Press.

Redl, F. (1966). *When we deal with children: Selected writings.* New York: Free Press.

Redl, F., & Wattenberg, W. (1959). *Mental hygiene in teaching* (2nd ed.). New York: Harcourt, Brace, & World.

Redl, F., & Wineman, D. (1965). *Controls from within.* New York: Free Press.

Reimer, J. (1989). A week in the life of cluster. In C. Power, A. Higgens, & L. Kohlberg (Eds.), *Lawrence Kohlberg's approach to moral education* (pp. 61–72). New York: Columbia University Press.

Rogers, C. (1951). *Client-centered therapy.* Boston: Houghton Mifflin.

Rogoff, B. (2003). *The cultural nature of human development.* New York: Oxford University Press.

Roller, P. (2005). Ideas to help students thrive in a stimulating and successful learning environment. In R. Stone (Ed.), *Best classroom management practices for all learners* (pp. 120–127). Thousand Oaks: Corwin Press.

Rosenthal, R. (1987). Pygmalion effects: Existence, magnitude, and social importance. *Educational Researcher, 16*(9), 37–41.

Rosenthal, R., & Jacobson, L. (1968). *Pygmalion in the classroom.* New York: Rinehart and Winston.

Rowland, A. S., Lesesne, C. A., & Abramowitz, A. J. (2002). The epidemiology of attention deficit/hyperactivity disorder (ADHD): A public health view. *Mental Retardation Developmental Disabilities Research Reviews, 8,* 162–167.

Rutter, M., Tuma, A. H., & Lann, I. (Eds.). (1988). *Assessment and diagnosis in child psychopathology.* New York: Guilford Press.

Sarason, S. (1982). *The culture of the school and the problem of change* (2nd ed.). Boston: Allyn & Bacon.

Scarlett, W. G. (1998). *Trouble in the classroom: Managing the behavior problems of young children.* San Francisco: Jossey-Bass.

Scarlett, W. G. (2003). Proactive parenting for behavior problems. In Faculty of Tufts University's Eliot-Pearson Department of Child Development (Eds.), *Proactive parenting: Guiding your child from two to six* (pp. 66–95). New York: Berkley Books.

Scarlett, W. G., Cox, E., & Matsudaira, M. (2001). Academic service learning: Development for synthesis and synergy. In L. Simon, M. Kenny, K. Brabeck, & R. Lerner (Eds.), *Learning to serve: Promoting civil society through service learning* (pp. 407–414). Santa Barbara, CA: ABC-CLIO.

Scarlett, W. G., Naudeau, S., Salonius-Pasternak, D., & Ponte, I. (2004). *Children's play*. Thousand Oaks, CA: Sage.

Searight, H. R., Rottnek, F., & Abby, S. L. (2001). Conduct disorder: Diagnosis and treatment in primary care. *American Family Physician, 63*(8), 1579–1588.

Seki, M. (2005). *Approaches to emotional and behavioral difficulties*. Medford, MA: Tufts University.

Selman, R., & Hickey-Shultz, L. (1990). *Making a friend in youth*. Chicago: University of Chicago Press.

Shaywitz, S. E. (1998). Dyslexia. *New England Journal of Medicine, 338,* 307–312.

Skrtic, T. (1991). The special education paradox: Equity as the way to excellence. *Harvard Educational Review, 61*(2), 148–206.

Slavin, R. E. (Ed.). (1989a). *School and classroom organization*. Hillsdale, NJ: Lawrence Erlbaum Associates.

Slavin, R. E. (1989b). Grouping for instruction in elementary schools. In R. E. Slavin (Ed.), *School and classroom organization* (pp. 159–172). Hillsdale, NJ: Lawrence Erlbaum Associates.

Smith, N. (1983). *Experience and art*. New York: Teachers College Press.

Smith, S. A., Press, B., Koenig, K. P., & Kinnealey, M. (2005). Effects of sensory integration intervention on self-stimulating and self-injurious behaviors. *American Journal of Occupational Therapy, 59*(4), 418–425.

Smith, W. C. (1998). *Patterns of faith around the world*. Boston: Oneworld.

Snowling, M. J. (2000). *Dyslexia*. Oxford: Blackwell.

Spock, B. (1946). *Baby and child care*. New York: Pocket Books.

Stockdale, M. S., Hangaduambo, S., Duys, D., Larson, K., & Sarvela, P. D. (2002). Rural elementary students', parents', and teachers' perceptions of bullying. *American Journal of Health Behavior, 26,* 266.

Strauss, M. (1994). *Beating the devil out of them: Corporal punishment in American families*. New York: Lexington Books.

Sullivan, H. S. (1953). *The interpersonal theory of psychiatry*. New York: Norton.

Swisher, K., & Dehyle, D. (1989, August). The styles of learning are different, but the teaching is just the same: Suggestions for teachers of American Indian youth. *Journal of American Indian Education,* 1–14.

Tauber, R. (1999). *Classroom management: Sound theory and effective practice*. Westport, CT: Bergin & Garvey.

Thornton, R. (2000). Tribal membership requirements and the demography of "old" and "new" Native Americans. In G. Sandefur & R. Rindfuss (Eds.), *Changing numbers, changing needs: American Indian demography and public health*. Washington, DC: National Academy Press.

Tobin, J. (1997). Playing doctor in two cultures: The United States and Ireland. In J. Tobin (Ed.), *Making a place for pleasure in early childhood education* (pp. 119–158). New Haven, CT: Yale University Press.

Trieschman, A., Whittaker, J., & Brendtro, L. (1969). *The other 23 hours*. Hawthorne, NY: De Gruyter.

Tyler, K., & Jones, B. (1998). Using the ecosystemic approach to change chronic problem behavior in primary schools. *Pastoral Care, 16*(4),11–20.

U.S. Department of Education. (1977). Assistance to states for education of handicapped children: Procedures for evaluating specific learning disabilities. *Federal Register, 42,* 65082–65085.

U.S. Department of Education. (2003). *Identifying and treating attention deficit hyperactivity disorder: A resource for school and home.* Retrieved from http://www.ed.gov/teachers/needs/speced/adhd/adhd-resource-pt1.pdf

Vygotsky, L. (1978a). Interaction between learning and development. In M. Cole, V. John-Steiner, S. Scribner, & E. Souberman (Eds.), *Mind in society* (pp. 79–91). Cambridge, MA: Harvard University Press.

Vygotsky, L. (1978b). *Mind in society: The development of higher psychological processes.* Cambridge, MA: Harvard University Press.

Walker, J., Shea, T., & Bauer, A. (2004). *Behavior management: A practical approach for educators* (8th ed.). Columbus, OH: Pearson-Merrill Prentice Hall.

Walsh, D. J. (1999). Good eyes and long eyes: Some good things about Japanese preschools. *Japanese Journal for the Education of Young Children, 8,* 103–114.

Watson, M., & Battistich, V. (2006). Building and sustaining caring communities. In C. M. Evertson & C. S. Weinstein (Eds.), *Handbook of classroom management: Research, practice, and contemporary issues* (pp. 253–280). Mahwah, NJ: Lawrence Erlbaum Associates.

Weber, M. (1964). *The theory of social and economic organization.* New York: Free Press. (Original work published 1925)

Weiner, L. (2006). *Urban teaching: The essentials.* New York: Teachers College Press.

Weinstein, C. (1987). Designing preschool classrooms to support development: Research and reflection. In C. Weinstein & T. David (Eds.), *Spaces for children: The built environment and child development* (pp. 159–186). New York: Plenum Press.

Weinstein, C. (1999). Reflections on best practices and promising programs: Beyond assertive discipline classrooms. In J. Freiberg (Ed.), *Beyond behaviorism: Changing the classroom management paradigm* (pp. 147–163). Boston: Allyn & Bacon.

Weinstein, C., & David, T. (Eds.). (1987). *Spaces for children: The built environment and child development.* New York: Plenum Press.

Werner, H. (1937). Process and achievement: A basic problem of education and developmental psychology. *Harvard Educational Review, 7,* 347–353.

White, E. (1893). *School management: A practical treatise for teachers and all other persons interested in the right training of the young.* New York: American Book Company.

Wiener, M., Devoe, S., Runinow, S., & Geller, J. (1972). Nonverbal behavior and nonverbal communication. *Psychological Review, 79,* 185–214.

Wilkins-Canter, E., Edwards, A., Young, H., Ramanathan, H., & McDougle, K. (2000). Preparing novice teachers to handle stress. *Kappa Delta Pi Record, 36*(3), 128–138.

Wiseman, F. (Director). (1994). *High school II* [Motion picture]. United States: Zipporah Films.

Wolf, M. (2007). *Proust and the squid: The story and science of the reading brain.* New York: HarperCollins.

Wolf, M., & O'Brien, B. (2001). On issues of time, fluency, and intervention. In A. Fawcett & R. Nicolson (Eds.), *Dyslexia: Theory and best practices* (pp. 124–140). London: Whur.

Wolfgang, C. (2001). *Solving discipline problems: Methods and models for today's teachers* (5th ed.). Boston: Simon & Schuster.

Yinger, R. J. (1980). A study of teacher planning. *Elementary School Journal, 80,* 107–127.

Zahn-Waxler, C. R. F., Cole, P., Mizuta, I., & Hiruma, N. (1996). Japanese and United States preschool children's responses to conflict and distress. *Child Development, 67,* 2462–2477.

Zins, J., Weissberg, R., Wang, M., & Walberg, H. (Eds.). (2004). *Building academic success on social and emotional learning.* New York: Teachers College Press.

Index

275

About the Authors

W. George Scarlett has authored, coauthored, and coedited books on managing behavior problems in classrooms, parenting, children's play, and religious and spiritual development. His past research and consulting work at Harvard Project Zero, the Language and Cognitive Development Center, Clark University's Psychoeducation Center, the Cambridge-Somerville Mental Health Center, and Community Teamwork Inc.'s Head Start programs include extensive work with teachers and diverse populations of children. For over three decades, he has taught courses on approaches to behavior and classroom management.

Iris Chin Ponte is a former Watson Fellow and Fulbright Scholar who has done extensive research in early childhood education in the United Kingdom, Taiwan, China, Japan, and Newfoundland. She has authored and coauthored works on children's play and cultural perspectives on early education.

Jay P. Singh is a former recipient of the SRCD Horowitz Millennium Scholarship, the SRA Emerging Scholars Award, a member of Tufts University's PACE and IPC research teams, and a clinical associate at Yale University's EGLab. His major work focuses on emotion recognition biases in psychopathic development and allegiance effects in risk assessment tools.

About the Contributors

Yibing Li is a doctoral candidate in the Eliot-Pearson Department of Child Development at Tufts University, doing research in the Institute for Applied Research in Youth Development. She has published and presented works on children's and adolescents' schooling and academic achievement. Her research areas include school dropout prevention, academic motivation and engagement, and children's academic and psychosocial well-being.

Laura Beals is a doctoral candidate in the Eliot-Pearson Department of Child Development at Tufts University. She is the project coordinator for the Virtual Communities of Learning and Care project in the Developmental Technologies Research Group (DevTech). Her research includes engineering education for elementary school children and new technologies for human development.

Dave Murray is an illustrator and multimedia artist working in the Boston area. After completing dual degrees in fine art and child development, he was an administrator at the School of the Museum of Fine Arts, where he remains today as the associate dean of admissions. Currently, he is developing a body of work that focuses on the retelling of morality tales through the use of inflatable toys and breakfast cereal.